ICT, Pedagogy and the Curriculum

Subject to change

Edited by
Avril Loveless and Viv Ellis

London and New York

First published 2001 by RoutledgeFalmer
2 Park Square, Milton Park, Abingdon, Oxon, OX14 4RN

Simultaneously published in the USA and Canada
by RoutledgeFalmer
270 Madison Ave, New York NY 10016

RoutledgeFalmer is an imprint of the Taylor & Francis Group

Transferred to Digital Printing 2005

Typeset in Bembo by
Florence Production Ltd, Stoodleigh, Devon

British Library Cataloguing in Publication Data
A catalogue record for this book is available from the British Library

Library of Congress Cataloging in Publication Data
    ICT, pedagogy and the curriculum: subject to change/edited by
    Avril Loveless and Viv Ellis.
       p. cm.
    Includes bibliographical references and index.
    1. Educational technology.   2. Information technology.
    3. Computer-assisted instruction.   4. Internet in education.
    5. Education–Effect of technological innovations on.
    I. Loveless, Avril.   II. Ellis, Viv, 1965–
    LB1028.3 .I32 2001
    371.33′4–dc21   00–062798

ISBN 0–415–23429–8 (hb)
       0–415–23430–1 (pb)

Printed and bound by Antony Rowe Ltd, Eastbourne

For Margarita

Contents

Figures

Tables

Contributors

Roy M. Bohlin is Professor of Educational Technology at California State University, Fresno, where he teaches educational technology classes and co-ordinates the efforts to infuse technology into the teacher preparation programme. His primary research interests include the motivation of learners and the interaction of instructional variables with computer anxiety, attitudes of self-efficacy, locus of control and confidence.

David Buckingham is Professor of Education at the Institute of Education, University of London, where he directs the Centre for the Study of Children, Youth and Media. He has conducted several major research projects on children's interactions with electronic media and on media education. His recent publications include: *The Making of Citizens: Young People, News and Politics* (Routledge) and *After the Death of Childhood: Growing Up in the Age of Electronic Media* (Polity Press).

Glenn L. DeVoogd serves as Assistant Professor in the School of Education and Human Development at California State University, Fresno, where he teaches courses in literacy development. He has experience as a bilingual teacher, as Director of Educational Services for children of migrant farmworkers, and as a technology staff developer.

Viv Ellis is Lecturer in English in the Research and Graduate School of Education at the University of Southampton. He has taught in schools and universities in the UK and the USA and has published in the areas of literacy and technology studies, English (secondary) teacher education, and education for social justice.

Roy Hawkey is Head of Education at the Natural History Museum, having previously been a teacher and a university lecturer in science education. His current role, developing educational policy and programmes, enables him to combine his research interests in informal learning environments, in scientific literacy and in ICT in science education.

Robert Mawuena Kwami is a Lecturer in Music Education at the University of London's Institute of Education, where, as Co-ordinator of Music CPD–INSET courses, he has developed programmes in music technology and non-Western musics. His teaching experience is extensive, and includes primary, secondary and tertiary levels in Ghana, England, Scotland and Wales.

Donna LeCourt is an Assistant Professor of English at Colorado State University, where she teaches courses in literacy instruction, writing, and cultural studies. She has published articles in *Computers and Composition, Journal of Advanced Composition, Strategies*, and contributed chapters to a variety of edited collections, such as *Feminist Cyberscapes*.

Steve Long is a Senior Lecturer in Art and Design Education at the University of Brighton. Having taught art in secondary schools, his current research interests are centred on the impact of digital technology on the art and design curriculum and on the relationship between visual education and the broader curriculum.

Avril Loveless is a Senior Lecturer in ICT in Education at the University of Brighton. She has published a number of books and papers relating to the use of ICT in learning and teaching. Her current research interests include pedagogy and ICT, and the creative use of digital technologies in the visual arts.

Katrina Miller is a Senior Lecturer in Science Education at the University of Brighton. With a background in sociology and primary education, she takes a critical view of current paradigms in education and uses every opportunity to shift student conceptions of science and science education.

Jack Sanger is currently a member of a European panel concerned with the protection of young persons from aspects of the media. He is also an author on computer games, video technology and schooling, as well as being the Head of the Centre for Educational Policy and Leadership at Anglia Polytechnic University. He has been running research projects concerning teaching and learning in all phases of education since 1983.

Margaret Scanlon is a Research Officer in the Centre for the Study of Children, Youth and Media at the Institute of Education, University of London. The project on which she is working looks at the production, characteristics and uses of broadly educational media designed for use in the home. Prior to joining the Institute, she worked as a researcher at the National Foundation for Educational Research and at the South Bank University.

Julian Sefton-Green is Media Education Development Officer at the Weekend Arts College in London and the author of many publications in the area of media education, literacy, digital technologies and cultural studies.

Michelle Selinger is Director of the Centre for New Technologies Research in Education (CeNTRE) at the Institute of Education, University of Warwick. She was until recently involved mainly in mathematics education, and she developed the mathematics materials for the primary and secondary PGCE courses at the Open University. Her current research is in the field of telematics, and in pedagogy and ICT.

Ilana Snyder is a Senior Lecturer in the Faculty of Education, Monash University, Australia. Her teaching and research focuses on changes that impact on literacy, and on pedagogical and curriculum practices associated with the use of new digital and communication technologies. Her books explore these changes. She participated in a major Australian national literacy and technology project that issued in the report entitled *Digital Rhetorics*.

Acknowledgements

The editors would like to acknowledge the following individuals and organisations who have contributed in some way to the development of this book: Brian Archer, Catherine Beavis, Alan Cooper, Cecilia Delatori, colleagues in the Association for IT in Teacher Education and the National Association for the Teaching of English, Geoff Simkins, the staff and pupils of Woodway Park School in Coventry, Pat Montgomery, and staff and students at the University of Brighton.

We would particularly like to thank Leigh Ward for his meticulous attention to the preparation of the manuscript.

Preface

Stephen Heppell

At the end of reading this provocative book one might happily pass a relaxed coffee break or two, in staffroom or senior commonroom, seeking to clarify a vision of the future. Technology in particular encourages us to do this, most probably because the speed of change means that anticipation is more than an idle conceit: it is a survival tactic. The contents of this book suggest that it may be a survival tactic for education too and an urgent task.

Depressingly, in education anticipating emerging trends has also been historically important so that we can confiscate the manifestations of those trends at the school door before they threaten to precipitate change: ballpoint pens, transistor radios, calculators, computer games, mobile phones . . . can you imagine the chaos that might have resulted if an entire generation was allowed to adopt ballpoint pens willy-nilly? Probably not, but many readers of this book, for some spurious reason or another, will have been banned from the classroom for using such pens. Education, rightly conservative with children's lives, is downright paranoid about technology, seeking to confiscate, assimilate or smother it before any damage can be done! It is clear, however, that, this time, the changes brought by the current wave of technology cannot be confiscated at the school gate, are embedded in our social and economic lives and will precipitate change in our learning institutions.

It does not help that our anticipation of the future has so often been wide of the mark – either the vector or speed of change are misjudged: my venerable 1959 schoolboy's copy of *The Story of Man* concludes with a final chapter 'What of tomorrow?' in which it is anticipated that by around the year 2000 'rockets will be rushing about space' (so far so good), 'atomic and solar energy will enable us to employ yet more machinery' (you can see where this is leading), so that 'we shall work less and thus have more time both to amuse and improve ourselves' (we wish) and concludes that 'today there are still places where people go hungry and are insufficiently clothed, but the day will come when there will be enough of the good things of life for everyone' – a vision which clearly erred on the sunny side. My 1955 edition of *The History of the World* (which ran to a rather encouraging 155 pages only) saw a darker side too:

> When your Daddy was a boy there was no television. What will your children have tomorrow, that you have never dreamed of today? That depends on you. Every discovery has a good use and bad. Aeroplanes can whisk us away on trips and holidays or they can drop bombs to blow up homes and factories and towns.

Will our technologically induced learning futures show that we made a good use or a bad of the opportunities presented? Future economic prosperity will tell us tomorrow, but today it is hard to know where to look for the right answer; when fiction attempts to anticipate our learning futures the differences between visions cannot be simply explained by misjudged vectors of prognostication or errors about the speed of change; there is simply an extraordinary variety of anticipated learning scenarios embedded in novels: the Skinnerian baby programming from Huxley's *Brave New World*, the implanted silicon wisdoms of Gibson's *Johnny Mnemonic*, the chanted acquiescence of Orwell's *1984*, the escalating schoolboy violence of Golding's *Lord of the Flies* – the common factor is a uniformly bleak view that new and emerging forms of education and learning will be downright awful. It is no coincidence that what we might characterise as 'jolly' books painting their own lighter view of the future miss out learning altogether: the word 'school' appears only once in the whole of Adams' *Hitchhikers' Guide to the Galaxy*, and that is only to flesh out a bit of historical context. This uniformly bleak suite of anticipations of the impact of technology on our learning futures goes some way to explain why we continually make the error of subjugating technology to our present practice rather than allowing it to free us from the tyranny of past mistakes. The paradox here is that education is so terrified of the dark side of change that, by closing down on the more creative, but inevitably uncertain, directions, it probably vouchsafes the bleakest of futures.

And there are so very many mistakes: for administrative convenience we seat thirty-five children in a single classroom where the only thing they have in common is to have been born between two Septembers; newly emerging computers offered us the ability to build better learning communities that transcend age, culture, geographical proximity and curriculum but instead we find those computers being sold into the classroom as a productivity tool to manage the registration and monitoring of these uni-aged classroom prisoners. Our examination and assessment system is a creaking edifice built on failed and antiquated technology; for example, the inability of past technology to moderate spoken contributions pushed oracy out of an examination process where performance was distilled down to be simply mastery of notational representation, but when computers appeared they were seized immediately by the examination system, not to repair the damage from a fatal over-reliance on pen technology but to produce a further distillation of learning into the execrable OCR sheets of multiple-choice questions. Other than that, by and large, the possession of a computer in the examination room is still regarded as cheating. Twenty years after we introduced the skills of authoring by word processor into schools our children are still frisked at the door of the examination room to ensure that they do not enter with a computer and, heaven forbid, actually evidence those skills. Examinations are currently skewed to avoid the possibility that children might demonstrate a capability that could not be criterion-referenced against previous generations', or other countries'. At the time of writing the UK 'A' level (18+) mathematics syllabus is being revised to intentionally reduce the opportunity for candidates to demonstrate capability with a calculator. One justification offered is the comparison with students in Germany where there is very low technology penetration and classroom computers remain relatively scarce. It is hard to see where this nonsense might end; Brazilian footballers play better than ours do and their schools have far higher levels of illiteracy. Should we cut back on years of progress with books to improve our football scores? Would this be progress or cultural vandalism? The problem with genuine steps forward is that it is so hard to reference them against criteria from the past, thus providing evidence that a step forward has really been made. It is certainly hard to weight footballing skills against reading, decade on decade.

This fear of the unknown, of the dark side of ICT, is indeed a powerful force, yet giving way to the fear results in the kind of criminally wasteful nonsense illustrated above. But while fiction writers, and too often policy makers, struggle to illustrate a delightful or seductive vision of future learning there are two other indicative straws in the wind that we do well to note.

First, of course, children themselves have shown no such fear of the uncertainties that lie ahead largely because they can see how the present system, with all its strengths, is failing in many places. They can see, starkly, the many faults in our present organisation of learning because they are actively engaged in the system. They see talented friends who fall by the wayside because their adept creativity or oracy does not quickly enough translate into notational form and is discounted; they see bright minds dulled by the numbing blandness of what they call 'worksheet teachers' offering all too little progression or challenge; they see peers who are wonderfully adept within a subject area woefully misrepresented by their attempts to summarise that capability in a brief 'closed' examination; they see how well older and younger students work in their orchestras, sports clubs, theatre groups, families and, indeed, online, but they marvel that such mentoring is largely precluded in the tested curriculum. Most of all they see the catastrophic lack of ambition that is posted for them in their ICT activity, as a bland homogeneity is imposed to ensure a common skillset that ignores the diverse and electrifying talents that so many children exhibit with computers outside the formal curriculum. Computers open multifaceted doors to unexpectedly creative delights, yet increasingly those delights are sampled outside of the formal curriculum and offered little progression or continuity within it. Reports by young students expressing their dissatisfaction at secondary level are legion, as their skills in Logo, in control technology, or in art, are sacrificed at the altar of uniformity ('I'm sure you can do that, but first let's work through this cutting and pasting exercise, not everyone is as lucky as you, you know . . .').

Perhaps worst of all they see the criminal waste of using a wonderful learning and creative tool to deliver multiple-choice drill and practice questions that ensure a compliance with yesterday's curriculum; there is something genuinely surreal about a computer being used to teach mental arithmetic, yet it happens at more than one in ten schools in the UK. This generation of wired children is busy embracing the new creative freedoms that technology offers them in the way that maybe their parents embraced the musical freedoms that rock, and electronic instruments, brought them. It is therefore highly illuminating to focus on their creative use of these new information and communication technologies. We find the asynchronous replacing the synchronous (as for example in the heavy use of SMS text messaging on phones – how many adults over 30 know where to find the '!' key on their mobile phone?), we find a hunger for process above product: a child beating the top-level game boss rushes across to friends not with 'Look at my score' but with 'Let me show you how I did it'. Children attend today's movies already well steeped in the details – out-takes, casting, creative disagreements – that surrounded the process of movie making, and they enjoy their viewing all the more for having acquired this meta-knowledge from the Web, from discussion forums, from fanzines and from friends. We know that children, faced with a new suite of software tools, constantly push out the envelope – acutely aware of what the 'previous lot' did and anxious to exceed their efforts. They have a tight, innate, ipsative referencing of their own progress which they regard as reliable and which carries their esteem more robustly than the multiple tests they are exposed to elsewhere. We do not need to be a cyber-geek or a futurologist to see that when these wired young people find themselves in the working world and discover that the things they valued, but within the curriculum ignored, are actually of considerable economic, social and creative value, then they will ask serious questions about the schooling that they will accept in the future for their own children and – as it was in music – youth moving to parenthood will be an unstoppably powerful engine for change.

The second substantial straw in the wind is offered to us by the economic imperative that underpins education. The ICT resources that were once found in school classrooms were initially cutting edge: people broke into schools to steal computers. Now, of course, they regard schools as a place to dump outdated ones and we must look elsewhere for indicators of the impact that new technology might have on an organisation or institution. Looking to the most 'wired' companies we can observe clear trends – each enabled by technology – that we might reasonably anticipate will be observable shortly in learning organisations and institutions too: physical scale is reduced as economies of scale are achieved in new ways; tiers of middle management vanish as communication is better handled; hierarchies flatten as individuals are empowered; teamwork is not merely encouraged, its absence is seen as a sacking offence; processes are awarded above products; global organisations become not merely viable but, through the richness of experience that they offer, desirable. And, finally, the conditions of work will be seen as an essential tool in the crafting of creativity and imagination. It is unthinkable that education will develop in a way much different from this; if it were to plough a different furrow the relationship between the needs and values of the economy and the outputs of education would be fractured with a resultant collapse in educational funding.

We are literally then able to see the future – not in the literature of science fiction, but in the combination of the overt ambition of a new generation of wired learners with the certainty of new forms of organisation. It is an exhilarating vision. The tough question for alert readers, though, is whether the inevitable results of this vision will reside in schools or elsewhere. In a worst-case scenario, education's paranoid fear of change – of the dark side that innovation might bring – together with an inability to articulate a coherent vision of the future could lead to an uninspired and uninspiring education system desperately trying to bar the door of creativity and innovation as increasing numbers of our most able students simply walk away from it to look for their learning elsewhere. This book is full of clear warning lights on the instrument panel of our learning lives. Like all warning lights, we ignore them at our peril as they herald first breakdown and then collapse. Having read the book you will need to do better than engage in debate during a relaxed coffee break or two: you need to heed the warnings and act.

Editors' introduction

> When Cat had been very young – too small, really, to remember much
> about it – her dad had been a teacher of history, but as the Web
> became more and more advanced, a single person could teach hundreds
> of kids. Then Websuits were invented, and the old-fashioned lessons
> vanished for ever. Kids learned by experiencing whatever they were
> being taught – learning had become an adventure, and a game. It must
> be tremendous fun, Cat thought wistfully, but the Web had put her
> dad on the scrap-heap, and he refused to have anything to do with it.
> He had grown more and more bitter and angry, and after her mum
> had left he taught Cat and her brothers and sister himself and didn't
> seem to know, or care, what they were missing.
>
> (Furey 1998: 29)

This is a common, for some dystopian, view of the future of schooling, set
in the year 2027. Read by a teacher, it may reflect anxieties about the future
of teaching and schools; read by a child, it may present some attractive possibilities. This dystopian view is not shared by the editors of and contributors to this book, who believe that the history of technology indicates that
we often shape the future of schooling through the powerful metaphors of
the past. The mere presence of technology will not be a catalyst for radical
change in our education systems. It is more likely that it will be used in
unexpected ways after a period of trying to make it fit into the old systems.
What is important, however, is that this period of accommodation is characterised by participants who are well informed, reflective, imaginative, collaborative, creative, democratic and critically aware of issues of access, equity
and social justice. Participants, that is, who have been actively involved in
an education system which fosters this approach to change in society – a
society which can be described as the 'Information Society'.

The idea of editing a book such as this arose from a series of conversations with teachers and teacher educators about the profile of information
and communications technologies (ICT) in education in the UK, the USA
and Australia. We felt that the introduction of these technologies into

classrooms and schools is having an impact on teaching and learning that does not necessarily reflect the ways in which children and young people experience and appropriate the technology in their lives outside school. Neither are the prophetic claims being made about the role of ICT in learning being realised in classroom practice as a whole. There was a shared concern that the nature of teacher training in new technologies has focused more on skills and techniques. Radical change requires a deeper understanding of the challenges ICT makes to ways of knowing curriculum subjects and of the changes it might bring to the practice of the profession in terms of time, place and authority.

We also felt that the term ICT is itself problematic. The words 'information and communications technology' describe a set of technologies with particular applications which vary enormously in purpose and scope within and between subject contexts. The term 'ICT' is also accompanied by a set of conceptual understandings that relate to a notion of capability, literacy or 'how to deal' with information using technology. The contributors to this book come from a variety of discourse traditions and from a range of anglophone countries and use the terms 'ICT', 'IT', 'digital technologies' and 'technology' to express this range of understandings.

This book has been written at a time of proliferating political pronouncements on the importance of ICT in the preparation of an adaptable workforce for the 'Information Society' and training curricula, expected outcomes, skills tests, etc., for serving and pre-service teachers. In the UK there is a focus on training for all practising teachers in classroom practice with ICT and an exponential growth in books, handbooks and online materials for sharing and exchanging ideas, case studies and curriculum materials. The purpose of this volume is to complement the already available materials and experiences with contributions from authors who raise questions and concerns about the relationship between ICT and formal education. Each contributor is involved in the use and development of ICT within his or her own subject or field, yet each is concerned to highlight the complexity of the influence of ICT within his or her area of work and experience.

The book addresses the relationship between digital technologies and formal education – highlighting three particular themes:

- the broader cultural context;
- approaches to and performances in pedagogy;
- representations of 'subject knowledge' within a compartmentalised curriculum and the ways in which these can be challenged and developed.

One of the aims of the book is to draw attention to the range of ongoing discussion and reflect the progress of the 'collective thinking' in this fast-developing area. There are common themes that run through a number of the contributions. There are also ideas and positions that contradict and challenge each other. Some authors describe ways in which subject knowledge, as represented in traditional school curricula, is changed by the visual, dynamic and provisional nature of ICT and discuss ways in which boundaries can be blurred between subject domains when technology is involved. There is also a discussion of the ways in which the use of ICT can mask the nature of pupils' learning and misconceptions, or provoke a different way of looking at the learning processes within a subject.

These debates underline the need for a thorough subject knowledge in teachers who are able to identify conceptual understandings, intervene, interact and represent this knowledge in order to scaffold learners' experiences. Throughout the book, the contributors emphasise the need to adopt a critical approach to the utopian visions that 'all will be well with ICT'. They highlight the difficulties of specifying the content of the thorough subject knowledge teachers need.

PART I: THE CULTURAL CONTEXT

Initiatives for ICT in education are proposed and implemented in a cultural and political context that reflects a number of tensions and contradictions. Indeed, Jack Sanger describes the 'cultural airlock' through which children and young people move in their experiences of digital technologies in and out of schools and formal education. The chapters in Part I present three contentious views of the challenges that face the purposes of schooling and the roles that teachers and parents might play in educating young people.

Sanger speculates on possible scenarios for the future of schooling in the UK, based on e-learning models and current debates in higher education. He presents a vivid picture of the extent to which learning experiences might be mediated and controlled by educational structures and the extent to which citizens might be able to become critical participants in the process. Buckingham, Scanlon and Sefton-Green describe the ways in which the 'digital dream' is sold to 'good' teachers and parents. Their chapter analyses the marketing discourse of ICT through a consideration of an educational technology trade show and promotional material for parents. It examines the relationship between education, entertainment, commercial interests and teacher and parent responsibilities. Snyder focuses on the cultural change engendered by new technologies, particularly around the 'turn to the visual', the complex interaction between old and new media and the nature of the literacies that these changes require.

PART II: PEDAGOGY AND ICT

ICT challenges current descriptions and practices of pedagogy in terms of the perceptions of time, place, authority and purpose of teaching. Learning and teaching are often assumed to 'take place' in particular slots of a timetable in particular classrooms associated with particular curriculum subjects. Information and communications technology can afford opportunities to extend the connections between learners, teachers, and information beyond the formal 'school day' and the agreed sources of information. The chapters in Part II present a discussion of the perceptions and beliefs that underpin teaching and how they can be supported or changed by the use of ICT. These ideas are developed to explore the ways in which the authors' own beliefs are embodied in their practice with new technologies.

Loveless, DeVoogd and Bohlin address the ways in which ICT can act as a catalyst to examine the factors which affect pedagogy – from beliefs and behaviours to resources and routines. They argue that it is possible to look at the influence of ICT on these different factors and illustrate how one aspect, an understanding of the nature of information and knowledge, might affect classroom teaching strategies. LeCourt outlines how ICT can allow teachers to perform radical critical pedagogies that can support learners' new understandings of their positions and possibilities within a culture. She presents a theoretical framework for critical pedagogy and, using particular examples of synchronous conferencing and chat, illustrates the argument by discussing her own teaching in higher education. Hawkey describes the development of the QUEST website at the Natural History Museum in London. This site reflects his beliefs about knowledge, pedagogy and power in science education and demonstrates ways in which ICT can be used to express one's pedagogy in an engaging and thought-provoking manner.

PART III: ICT AND THE CURRICULUM

Part III examines the role that ICT plays in challenging the construction of subjects and the boundaries between them. Three of the subjects discussed – English, mathematics and science – represent the 'holy trinity' or core curriculum of current UK policy. The two subjects in the Expressive Arts domain – art and music – represent an area both liable to being 'squeezed' by the core and one in which important and interesting developments related to ICT are taking place. Each chapter highlights debates that are provoked by the use of ICT, practically and potentially. Some common themes, such as new media literacies, can be identified and discussed in different subject areas. The representations and understandings of 'ways of knowing' within and between subject areas might shift as a result of the use of ICT by learners and teachers. There are, however, interesting differences in the approach of the authors, each of whom also identifies the unique contribution that his or her subject domains might make to the development of an educated person.

Ellis uses the metaphor of 'analogue clock' and 'digital display' to consider the challenges and opportunities presented to a language and literature curriculum by digital technologies and emphasises the need for continuity with traditions of expressive development and critical literacy. Selinger describes the ways in which ICT plays a role in modelling and representing mathematical knowledge and processes – visually, dynamically and collaboratively – from graphical representations to dynamic notebooks on the Web. Although welcoming the range of opportunities that ICT provides, she recognises the need for further work in 'synthesising the visual and symbolic aspects of mathematical cognition'. Miller presents an argument for reconfiguring the identity of primary science teachers, drawing on the image of the 'cyborg'. She outlines possibilities for a future science curriculum which collapses boundaries between school science and the public understanding of science, complementing Hawkey's approach by highlighting a curriculum construction in relation to gender. Long responds to a view of ICT as a new medium for visual literacy by highlighting the challenges that digital technology raises for the processes of the art curriculum. He acknowledges the potential of digital culture in the curriculum and the role of the visual in a critical approach to media. He argues, however, that art makes a distinct and unique contribution to processes of expression and creativity and should play a substantial and relevant role in the formal curriculum. Kwami considers the role of technology in music composition and notation in the curriculum over the last forty years. He speculates on a redefinition of musical literacy that involves different interfaces and input–output devices, promoting a curriculum that acknowledges the role of community and culture in contemporary musical experience and expression.

The penetration of ICT in culture, pedagogy and the curriculum will provoke a variety of images of teachers, learners and knowledge. The different chapters in this book contribute to the discussion of the question – 'In the Information Society, what does it mean to be educated and what are teachers for?' Like Cuban, we share the view that the

> challenge to those deeply committed to school improvement, including researchers, teachers, administrators, and parents, is to acknowledge that both continuity and change are interwoven in the schooling

process. To disentangle one from the other and attach positive or negative connotations is to misconstrue the very nature of schooling and classroom instruction.

(Cuban 1986: 109)

We believe that the interactions between learners, teachers and knowledge will be far more complex, engaging and unpredictable than the image presented at the beginning of this Introduction.

Avril Loveless and Viv Ellis

REFERENCES

Cuban, L. (1986) *Teachers and Machines: The Classroom Use of Technology Since 1920*, New York: Teachers' College Press.
Furey, M. (1998) *The Web: Sorceress*, London: Orion Children's Books.

Part I

The cultural context

Chapter 1

ICT, the demise of UK schooling and the rise of the individual learner

Jack Sanger

It is a capital mistake to theorise before one has data.
(Sherlock Holmes, *A Scandal in Bohemia*,
by Arthur Conan Doyle)

INTRODUCTION

This is a chapter that deals with United Kingdom educational *futures*, and as such it would be dubiously regarded by Sherlock Holmes. On the other hand it may be regarded as a useful exploration of vital current educational issues, and as contributing to the debate concerning the rethinking of teaching and learning over the oncoming years. Essentially, it begins with a critical view of what education has achieved in the British experiment in mass schooling over the last 100 or so years. Against this backdrop, the rise and rise of ICT, together with a view of education as a consumer market for corporate provision, is seen to pose a threat to stagnating educational systems. The chapter then explores briefly examples from what is happening in the higher education sector, with threats emerging from corporate and virtual provision, as evidence of changes that are already under way at the higher end of the educational spectrum. This is followed by the application of a scenario-building technique to infer four visions of what might happen to the schooling process in the early part of the twenty-first century, based on present evidence. It ends with the author's own view of which of these, currently, is the most likely to occur.

We are coming to the end of the great experiment in mass schooling. The Government's continuation of the regressive crusade of its predecessors to control the teaching and learning processes through an outdated National Curriculum will soon seem like some stubborn but ill-conceived effort to hold back the tide. In Canute's case it was a deliberate attempt on his part to demonstrate the inexorable force of nature over the powerlessness of the human individual. In the Government's it is a demonstration to the people of its faith in a system of mass education: a system which, on a daily lived basis, has seen far more failure than success, has produced generations of spectacularly unskilled workers, with absurdly high rates of illiteracy and innumeracy and which extinguishes the desire to continue to learn in so many, young and old. The beginning of the new millennium will see the need to re-think the cost of schooling, the plant, the teachers, the support systems, as ICT becomes cheap and more easily accessible to the everyday user. How long will we support a Victorian system that tends to produce a meritocratic elite and a mass of barely educated, disenfranchised and uninterested also-rans?

We belong to an emerging society in which schools increasingly attune their activities to the pursuit of 'objectives' or 'outcomes', dislocated from the everyday lived world of their charges. The prescriptive focus of the National Curriculum on redundant content, skills and competences is not a dream for the future, or a survival kit for the present but, rather, a fundamentalist nostalgia for a time when every worker had his or her place, followed a single occupational future and when morality was constructed by an establishment of Church and State. The exception is the concentration on literacy and numeracy as being 'process-oriented' essentials in any citizen's armoury.

Meanwhile, our students live in a world of pluralist morality, constantly evidenced in TV talk shows, designer clothes, soaps, sex, unplanned births, sexually transmitted disease, recreational drugs, music, computer games and videos. They are the consumers of expensive ads and the objects they advertise belong to the world of entertainment and edutainment. Every minute of any day they can enter high-gloss mediated worlds that cost astronomically more to construct than any of their experiences in the classroom. For them a PC is a leisure window. But a cultural airlock separates the two worlds. In schools the PC is a work tool. Schools provide no routes for young students to understand, navigate and deconstruct media-induced experience, unless they are taking media studies or sociology. Nor are they allowed to be creative with it. In the main, teachers disown popular media as shallow entertainment, likely to cause more ill than good, the source of children's illiteracy, lack of concentration, violence or premature sexual drive (Sanger et al. 1997).

In the world outside the classroom the young consumer is gradually being educated in ways a school does not begin to recognise. Using entertainment technology, the young user can develop hand–eye co-ordination, spatial relations, graphical awareness, parallel reading from non-linear scripts, multi-line plots and problem solving. They can browse the internet to satisfy the quixotic desires of anarchism, fetishism or consumerism. Edutainment opens immediate access to gender politics, the bizarre and the dysfunctional, the disillusionment with work and the new profiles of family life, the cross-cultural, the interracial, the nature of war and suffering, abuse, poverty, famine, disease, the hypocrisy of politicians and the lies of adults. In other words, a child has an entrée, through the vast array of available technology, into the same Pandora's box with which adults have to grapple. Edutainment knows no national borders. It is a dynamic Escher lithograph of surfaces and depths, hiding, revealing, distorting and making constantly ambiguous.

In schools, rules and conventions constrain you in what you say and do and think. They determine what is knowledge, what is useful, what is moral, what is right for the child at this time, at that age. But the child moves through an airlock into the unregulated world beyond, feeling the sudden withdrawal of the steadying hand on the shoulder, to be left to stumble upon, to discover, to explore the unrestricted. Young people inhabit, more and more, media-rich bedrooms (Livingstone and Bovill 1999) with video recorders, cable TV, games machines and PCs. The domestic market for technology has outstripped any possibility of schools keeping up. The marketing of domestic merchandise is now so accurate that consumers can buy goods whose 'lean manufacture' is designed to individual requirement, whereas, in schools, the basic unit of consumerism is 'the class'. Just as teachers do not, in their classrooms, venture into popular culture, except in the specialist areas of sociology or media studies, in the main, parents don't interfere that much in their children's lives, since all of this is 'since their time' and the technology is bemusing and/or intimidating.

UNIVERSITY FUTURES IN THE USA

Given this brief scenario of the present state of technology and education, what futures are likely to stem from it? How can we make predictions from it? A University of Michigan website provides a possible methodological route forward.

This University of Michigan site uses a brainstorming approach to delineate four possible future scenarios for higher education in the USA. It describes the rationale of creating a structured matrix from the brainstorm:

> The four scenarios that grew out of this structuring matrix can be seen as explorations of the four corners of the possible. They are meant to provoke thought and discussion about the future of higher education and scholarly communication.
>
> (http://www.si.umich.edu/V2010/matrix.html)

Their original brainstorm produced the following list:

- cost containment
- productivity of the faculty (staff members)
- faculty work rules and practices

- teaching–research balance
- competitors, present and potential
- new collaborations, public and private
- the nature of knowledge work
- digital literacy/kinds of knowing
- educational technology
- digital copyright
- physical v. digital space
- certification
- student testing–quality control
- worldwide student demography
- public accountability.

The brainstorm suggests to those involved that higher education will undoubtedly be under very significant threat from external pressures and internal complacency:

> As a result, we believe education represents the most fertile new market for investors in many years. It has a combination of large size (approximately the same size as health care), disgruntled users, low utilisation of technology, and the highest strategic importance of any activity in which this country (USA) engages. . . . Finally, existing managements are sleepy after years of monopoly.
>
> (http://www.si.umich.edu/V2010/matrix.html)

Resulting from this immersion in debate about the key forces that may affect higher education in the early part of this new century, they produce quadrants whose axes are *competition* and *digital literacy*. At the high end of the competition axis, education is a market open to all-comers, public and private. At the low end, it remains a market competed for by present university interests.

And so they move to the development of the four scenarios. On the website, these scenarios are written in four different formats to maximise drama, from the anecdotal first-person ruminations on the demise of a tradition to the third-person *post hoc* analysis of market change. For example, one begins:

> You are all aware of my deep regret, my personal sense of loss on this occasion. I've been with this institution for 22 years, and it's a small enough place that I know all of you personally. So enough of the official talk of falling enrolments and bad investments and infrastructure debt overload. . . . But we underestimated both the drop in the life span of a college degree and the price students would pay to have that degree renewed again and again.

Another states:

> Multimedia pushed Chavez and Pinsky into the new realm of faculty stars. A select few of these digerati pulled in multimedia dollar incomes from their digital packagings, whether CD-ROMs or online courses. Many universities positioned themselves well in this area by taking on the role of 'studio' to their stars – acting as production company and distributor. The star system increased competition among faculty and began to make the AAU look in some respects like the NFL – a few superstars demanding and getting outrageous salaries and bonuses.

The narrative augmentation is stripped away, edited and summarised here, in order to give a sense of some of the issues that underpin each scenario.

Low competition – low digital literacy in HE

Universities stand still. Shrinking student numbers result in higher fees. Academic productivity contracts introduced. Some turn into academies for foreign students. Some develop contracts with corporations to provide accredited training. 'Life-long learning contracts introduced.' Some technology introduced on campus but it is peripheral to the old flesh-and-blood pedagogies. Big Ten get bigger and sell their information and resources to others – knowledge retail outlets. Mergers take place. Corporate providers leave the education market alone. Parents begin to look for alternatives to the high cost provision.

High competition – low digital literacy in HE

Fall in parental support for universities. New multimedia providers move in with government support. Leaner, more responsive, faster changing, edutainment-based training and education. Specialised providers develop virtual courses for professional markets. Assessment and certification online. Tied to a continuing professional development on subscription version of life-long learning. Students stay home to study using technology. Big Ten survive. Others quickly die.

High competition – high digital literacy in HE

Most universities can't compete because of increasing professional specialisation. A high proportion go to the wall. Corporate providers do it better: onsite, at work. Universities too expensive for most of the workforce. Digital resources introduce real-time problem solving, modelling and complexity far more graphically than can staff in classes. The best universities survive, offering an education for the whole person – expensively.

Low competition – high digital literacy in HE

The paperless age has dawned, as universities become virtual. They have beaten off the competition from corporate providers. Professors become 'stars' as multimedia rights are protected and their work is sold globally. They leave tenure and become educational consultants. Tenure becomes the coinage of second-class lecturers. Borderless provision means huge markets, particularly for United States' super universities. Actual residency becomes minimal or unimportant for all foreign students. Introduction of team certification and other forms of co-operative certification to meet industries' needs for certification.

Looking at the four scenarios provokes, perhaps, an uncomfortable feeling of recognition. None of them seems too extreme to be ruled out, at least by this reader. There are many examples of private industry–university collaboration. For example, Deakin University in Australia has a collaborative project with the Coles Myer retail outlet to provide training and qualifications for all staff. Ford has a 'private' university in Valencia, Spain, that also involves collaboration with Anglia Polytechnic University in the delivery of Masters' courses for middle managers. The largest development in Britain involves the siting of the Microsoft research facility next to Cambridge University in order to secure 'the best brains'. However, these developments follow a traditional pattern that is about to be ruptured by the desire of industry to move beyond collaboration and into the market of education itself. A current collaborative project, involving the Centre for Educational Policy and Leadership at Anglia Polytechnic University and commissioned by the CVCP and HEFCE, is exploring the impact of virtual and corporate universities in Europe and the USA on UK higher education. A parallel study is being undertaken in Australia. The UK study will provide advice to policy makers on how higher education institutions should respond to the new global markets, considering both the opportunities and challenges which are being created and the potential for UK universities to compete in the new environment. The recommendations from the work cover both national policy and the implications for individual institutions in terms of

• the regulatory framework in which the higher education sector operates;
• the changing demands from higher education consumers both in domestic and international markets;
• accreditation and quality assurance issues;
• the organisation and governance of institutions;
• teaching and learning strategies;
• staffing, infrastructure and overall costs.

This enquiry into the threat of virtual and corporate competition is already touching on many of the elements included above. It suggests that most British universities still do not realise that ICT is not just a bolt-on tool to traditional delivery. Nor is it just a convenient distance-learning instrument. Eventually it will provide completely individualised learning opportunities for every world citizen, a true multimedia learning environment in the home and at the touch of a button.

SCHOOLING FUTURES IN THE UK

Following the same analytical approach, what are the main issues facing schools, as a result of technological change, in the UK during the early part of this century? Here are some suggestions:

- The National Curriculum
- children's rights
- multi-ethnicity and religious diversity
- cost containment
- productivity of the teachers
- national conditions of service
- teaching–professional development balance
- competitors, present and potential
- new collaborations, public and private
- the nature of knowledge for working futures
- global economy and national needs
- digital literacy/kinds of knowing
- educational technology
- digital copyright
- physical v. digital space
- qualifications
- student testing/quality control
- worldwide student demography
- public accountability
- parental involvement.

Utilising the same scenario-building techniques as were used for Michigan's website, let us construct four possible schooling futures for around the year 2020. We will use the same axes – *competition* and *digital literacy*. They are not mutually exclusive but embrace a wide range of possibility. The point of the exercise, it is reiterated, is not to predict with certainty but to embrace a wide range of possible eventuality and afford ourselves time to think proactively about what actions we might take, before events over-take us.

Steady-state

Governments continue to act regressively, concentrating on the 3Rs plus bolt-on computer literacy. Class size increases to around 40–50 pupils per teacher owing to teacher shortages. Annual teaching hours are increased. Extra-curricular activities suspended indefinitely. Buildings and resources deteriorate. Bigger percentage of pupils suspended and expelled. Closed-circuit television and guards introduced into schools, thus reducing the curriculum and staff budgets. Boys' underachievement levels break all records. Male proportion of the working population continues to decrease. Proportion of male teachers in secondary schools drops below 30 per cent. Private-sector and religion-funded schooling grow again for those of the middle classes who want safe schooling and inside track.

Globalisation

Schools become too expensive to be run by the State. The end of national boundaries as multi-nationals enter education industry. Curricular focus on the 'Global Worker'. Governments collaborate with Disney, Nickelodeon and other private providers for edutainment channels, multimedia convergence education in the home, individualised curricula with electronic continuous assessment and certification and video-link help-lines. Pupils attend community centres for two days per week to learn citizenship, parenting, personal care, multicultural heritage, political awareness, media studies, finance and leisure studies. Children's rights result in their being respected as customers.

Monopolies

Successful schools get larger and larger, like mini-industrial estates, while unsuccessful schools close and are sold off to finance and merge with these expansions. Schools' sole aims are to meet league table and National Curriculum requirements. Professional development becomes highly instrumentalised. More pupils suspended and expelled to maintain success rates. More pupils forced to 'leave' rather than take exams that would have negative effect on league tables. Highly resourced intranet with multi-user interface run by school conglomerates. School-refuser centres spring up, run by Group4 and other private companies but without real resources, thus perpetuating and enlarging an illiterate, innumerate and computer-illiterate underclass.

The rise of the individual learner 17

Free-market differentiation

Government gradually moves out of schooling, except for the no-profit bottom 40 per cent and special education. Schools become privatised and specialised. National resources poured into health and the ageing population. Private industry endows and controls its own schools to 'grow' workers with industry-standard multi-functional skills. Specialised science schools, arts schools and language schools develop, supported by their own dedicated technologies. Universities set up school contracts to take sixth-formers and provide continuous intranet-based assessment. Bottom 40 per cent attend new 'survival schools'.

Some early signs of the above scenarios are already emerging. Current education policy in England seeks to establish a national 'core' curriculum and a diffusion of learning into the workplace. Another example, this one from the USA: the Cisco Networking Academy Program (CISCO Systems Inc. 1999) is a partnership between business, governments and communities. It provides a model for e-learning. Cisco already has 2,532 academies in 50 American states and 39 countries. At the time of writing, the British Government is announcing the arrival of new kinds of secondary school, outside the remit of local authorities, schools that will be wholly or partially funded by private enterprise, religious bodies or charities. While there are hopes that these schools will develop in what are currently underprivileged areas, bringing much-needed resources to these areas, the die is cast for some of the scenarios outlined above coming to be realised. The model has already been developed in the USA, where Ford Motors funds schools, partially to develop its staff of the future and partially to nurture its consuming clients of the future.

A TALE OF FUTURE PAST

The seeds of the future are more often than not perfectly visible in the present − but irritatingly indistinguishable from the rest of the data with which we are confronted. Only historians are capable of 20–20 vision. The work of the author, mentioned at the beginning of this text, involved case studies in both domestic and school settings. In it the chasm between home and school was inescapable. The later study by Livingstone and Bovill (1999) tends to confirm at least the domestic side of the equation. As commercial interests look to open up domestic markets even further and accelerate the progress of convergence, the arrival of dedicated multi-media cable channels will find education too lucrative a market to ignore. In a sense recent governments have increased the likelihood of this happening by establishing the National Curriculum. They have created a market entity that can be manipulated *en masse*. There is implicit acceptance of this by the British Government. In his recent address 'Modernising comprehensive education', the Minister for Education David Blunkett (2000) announced that by 2003 one in every four UK schools will have strong support from business.

And what of the future? Which is the most likely scenario? Certainly education will have to compete for state funds in an increasingly competitive climate of social provision. An ageing population with increased life spans and insecure or non-existent pension provision will create untold havoc with national fiscal policy in the areas of health and social services. Governments will need to raise taxes *and* push the cost of education increasingly on to the private citizen. Reducing this cost will see the demise of schools in the post-primary sector and the rise of individualised provision through convergent technologies using multimedia programming. Whoever may be providers managing the transition to individualised online learning and assessment, so that they are sensitive to learning styles and maintain motivation, will become very wealthy indeed. They will employ a new breed of highly paid professional educators who will be at ease with distance education and will number their students in the hundreds. The model has begun in higher education. The Higher Education Funding Council for England is already establishing an e-university. This e-university will deliver online courses. It involves a select group of institutions with overseas partners and commercial associates.

There will still be compulsory attendance for one or two days per week at centres that manage socialisation and citizenship as the Government tries to keep society cohesive, but the citizenry will grow increasingly anarchic and less compliant as they access and choose the information, beliefs and attitudes that interest them. Education will no longer be a tool of social control but a marketplace of competing religious and secular ideologies, each with an imperative to create a consumerism that pays. It will become harder for individuals to develop a critical understanding of the bias and media manipulation of commercial interests. No sooner will we have thrown off the shackles of one form of mass schooling and education than the vacuum will be filled by another – more pernicious, equally constraining and equally unlikely to enable citizens to become critical consumers of the social forces which enmesh them.

In order that *none* of the various doomsday scenarios is realised will require the British Government (along with other governments) to rethink the notion of what constitutes a curriculum (national or otherwise) and make the consumption of media and media technology central issues in education. It will result in a citizenry which is even less gullible in the face of government spin doctoring than is currently the case but one which might withstand and influence, for the good, the curricula of corporate interests.

REFERENCES

Blunkett, D. (2000) 'Modernising comprehensive education'; online (available: http://www.dfee.gov.uk/speech1/mce.shtml).
CISCO Systems Inc. (1999) *CISCO E-Learning*; online (available: http://www.cisco.com).
Livingstone, S. and Bovill, M. (1999) *Young People, New Media*, London: London School of Economics and Political Science.
Sanger, J. with Willson, J., Davies, B. and Whittaker, R. (1997) *Young Children, Videos and Computer Games: Issues for Parents and Teachers*, London: Falmer.

Chapter 2

Selling the digital dream
Marketing educational technology to teachers and parents

David Buckingham, Margaret Scanlon and Julian Sefton-Green

New media and communications technologies have always been surrounded by expansive claims about their educational value. If we look back to the early days of television, and even before that to the advent of the cinema, it is easy to find examples of such utopian views. These new media would, it was argued, quickly supersede traditional styles of teaching and learning. They would give children access to new worlds of discovery, re-awaken their thirst for learning and release their natural spirit of enquiry. It was even suggested by some that these new technologies would make schools and teachers redundant.

Perhaps, inevitably, history permits a degree of scepticism about these claims. We all know schools in which technology has remained unused in cupboards or been employed in limited ways which fall absurdly short of the promise it is seen to offer. Larry Cuban's book *Teachers and Machines* (Cuban 1986) provides ample evidence of the failure of such experiments in the history of educational technology. The basic 'grammar' of education has, he argues, remained largely unchanged for much of the twentieth century; and educational reforms often fail to have much lasting impact because they do little to change the basic institutional character of the school.

In the light of such arguments, it is hard not to feel a similar degree of scepticism about the advent of digital information and communications technologies (ICTs). One might be tempted to conclude that these new media are just another illusory, magical solution to some imagined educational problem; and that they will almost certainly fail to fulfil the enormous claims that are made on their behalf. There is undoubtedly some truth in this position; and one of our primary aims in this chapter is to question – indeed, to puncture – some of the rhetorical claims that are typically made in this regard. Nevertheless, this is more than just another case of history repeating itself.

Looking a little more closely at the history of educational technology – and particularly at educational television – there are three points that relate in an interesting way to our present situation. First, these utopian claims about the educational potential of new media sit awkwardly alongside simultaneous arguments about their negative impact on children. During the 1950s and 1960s, television was being strongly promoted to parents and teachers as an educational medium; and yet there was already growing concern about the effects of screen violence on children's behaviour – and, more broadly, about the detrimental influence of television entertainment on child development (Himmelweit, *et al.* 1958). 'Education' and 'entertainment' seem, in this situation, to be regarded as mutually exclusive categories: education is necessarily good for children, while entertainment is automatically bad.

Second, these early claims about the educational value of the medium are – at least to some degree – inseparable from commercial interests. This is most obviously the case in the USA, where the promotion of television as an educational medium was a key part of the attempt to encourage parents to invest in television sets, and hence to build up the audience for advertisers (Melody 1973). The history in the UK, given its much stronger emphasis on public service objectives, is rather different; but here, too, the provision of educational programming has helped to secure the legitimacy of what is in part an enormously profitable commercial industry.

Third, it is important to note the reasons why earlier experiments in educational technology failed to deliver on their promises. Not the least important of these was indifference – or, indeed, active resistance – on the part of teachers. This was, it should be emphasised, not simply a form of conservatism, or merely a failure to keep up with the times. It was partly a result of the technological emphasis of the reformers, and their failure to provide training and support that would help to embed these new media more centrally in the curriculum and in teachers' practice. But it was also a result of teachers' awkward insistence on their own professionalism, and an accompanying reluctance to allow the curriculum to be dictated from outside, by television companies or by the publishers of these new educational media.

As we shall indicate, these issues are still very much at stake in the enthusiastic promotion of ICTs for education, both in schools and in the home. The relationship between 'education' and 'entertainment', the role of commercial companies and the resistance to change are all important factors in the contemporary situation. Yet in several respects the balance of forces has now changed; and in this sense, we are witnessing more than just another recurrence of a familiar pattern of educational change. Before proceeding to our empirical analysis, then, we need to sketch in the bigger picture.

EDUCATION, EDUCATION, EDUCATION

Tony Blair's now-familiar response to an interviewer's question in 1997 about his three main priorities in the coming general election can be taken as an index of what has become a growing preoccupation within contemporary British culture. The quality of education is not just a recurrent theme in political debate, but also a focus of intense anxiety for many parents.

There are several reasons for this new emphasis on education. In an era in which state welfare provision is increasingly seen to be problematic, education remains one of the more obviously legitimate areas for government intervention. Educational initiatives may be affordable and visible in a way that attempts to address longer-term issues such as poverty and social exclusion are not. Education has also been one of the key areas in which central government has sought to control the autonomy of local government, and thereby to centralise power.

More broadly – and despite the evidence of decades of sociological research – education is still seen in meritocratic terms. It offers the promise of upward mobility in a time during which inequalities of income have in fact continued to grow. In the international arena, education is charged with producing a well-trained workforce, and thereby with advancing our competitive position as a nation. And in much more local terms, it is increasingly seen to be responsible for the moral regulation of children – for keeping idle hands busy, and thereby preventing the possibility of delinquency and crime. Both pragmatically and philosophically, therefore, education appears to provide solutions to many of the problems of contemporary society.

The current preoccupation with education is most obviously manifested in the emphasis on 'standards' that New Labour has inherited from the Conservatives. National testing and the publication of league tables of schools' examination results have generated a culture of competition and anxiety, both among children and among parents. The Government's renewed emphasis on homework – for example, in the form of homework clubs – reflects an educational 'work ethic' that is not expected to let up once children walk out of the classroom door. At the time of writing (early in 2000), the Government is proposing to lengthen the school day by 1.5 hours: children are to work an 8-hour day, as compared with the average 5.5 hours of their European peers.

In this context, learning and leisure have become increasingly difficult to separate. For adults, 'lifelong learning' and the growing emphasis on qualifications and educational credentials are turning both the workplace and the home into new sites for education (Edwards 1997). Meanwhile, leisure providers – sports centres, museums, youth clubs, community arts projects – are also increasingly charged with educational responsibilities, and required to justify themselves in these terms. The Government's controversial Millennium Dome in London is perhaps the most emblematic example of this penetration by education into the sphere of leisure. In the process, the boundaries between education and entertainment – between 'learning' and 'fun' – have become increasingly problematic.

MONEY, MONEY, MONEY

Many of the developments identified above are driven by – or at least inextricably connected with – the work of commercial corporations. Private companies have increasingly taken over areas of leisure and cultural provision that were previously the responsibility of national or local government; and many public organisations have reorganised themselves on commercial principles. In the process, the boundaries between the public and the private have become ever more blurred – a tendency that is now actively promoted by a government whose solution to most social problems lies in the development of 'public–private partnerships'.

This growing colonisation of the public sphere by commercial forces is a function of the global expansion of capitalism in the post-war era, particularly following the demise of the USSR. Right across the developed world, 'the State' has effectively retreated, leaving the provision and management of many key services to the market. Deregulation, both nationally and in terms of international trade, has been seen as essential to economic growth and prosperity; and nation-states themselves are increasingly unable, or unwilling, to control the activities of global corporations.

As public services have fallen into decline, government involvement no longer possesses the legitimacy it held in earlier decades. State-provided welfare is increasingly regarded not as an entitlement for all but merely as a 'safety net' for those most at risk; while many cultural institutions such as museums and public libraries have either been forced into decline or required to levy charges which themselves result in falling attendance, and of course, one of New Labour's earliest demonstrations of its commitment to education was its introduction of tuition fees for university students.

These developments impact on schools in several ways. Most obviously, we are now seeing a gradual privatisation of schooling – a trend that is much further advanced in the USA (Bridges and McLaughlin 1994; Buckingham 1997; Kenway and Fitzclarence 2000). This is most spectacularly the case in the growing number of schools and local authorities whose management has been handed over to commercial companies; yet it is also apparent in other government initiatives such as Education Action Zones and specialist schools, which are required to attract commercial sponsorship. Meanwhile, the devolution of school funding from local authorities to individual schools – the so-called Local Management of Schools – means that schools are now much more independent consumers of commercial goods and services than in the past.

In this situation, private corporations large and small have become increasingly interested in the education market. As we will show, this development is most apparent in the area of ICTs, where Microsoft, Apple, ICL and others compete to be seen as sponsors of the latest educational initiatives. Yet even in more traditional areas, such as book publishing, there is intense competition to corner the market: the publisher Heinemann, for example, enjoys a monopoly on providing resources for one of the main English syllabuses, while other publishers are competing to make textbook deals with examination boards (which are, of course, profitable private companies in their own right).

Meanwhile, companies with interests in very different areas, such as supermarkets, are increasingly keen to promote themselves as sponsors of education. Tesco's highly successful 'Computers in Schools' scheme, for example, is a key aspect of its promotional strategy in what has become a highly competitive sector of retailing; while Rupert Murdoch's News International has a parallel 'Books in Schools' scheme in association with Walkers, makers of potato crisps. These initiatives reflect the general ascendancy of 'promotional culture' (Wernick 1991); and, in this context, education has a strong 'feel-good factor' that renders it particularly valuable as a means of defining and promoting a given brand. Here, again, resources from the private sphere – in this case, the parents who actually shop at Tesco and buy their Walkers' crisps – are increasingly being used to supplement shortfalls in public provision.

PLUGGING IN TO EDUCATION

As we have implied, information and communication technologies play a particularly important role in this situation. Technology, we are often told, is reconfiguring social institutions and relationships. It is blurring the boundaries between homes, schools and workplaces, and between parents, teachers and students. It is reconfiguring social spaces, altering our sense of time and place, and redefining what counts as knowledge and learning. Yet, given such developments, it is clearly simplistic to account for them in terms of technology alone. New information and communication technologies have emerged from an ongoing process of scientific development that possesses its own dynamic; and yet, like earlier technologies, they cannot be seen in isolation from broader social and economic forces (Webster 1995; Dutton 1996).

The increasing penetration by ICTs into all areas of social life – not least education – is driven largely by capitalism's relentless search for new markets. The internet is now largely a commercial medium that is used for commercial purposes. Although the market is still far from saturated, planned obsolescence has become a key factor in the accelerating introduction of new products and services; while the rise of 'e-commerce' suggests that these technologies are themselves becoming crucial to the operation of contemporary markets in general. Meanwhile, there is a growing economic convergence between technologies, in which 'old' and 'new' media, as well as production and distribution, have become more and more integrated. In the age of AOL Time Warner, cultural production is increasingly characterised by what the critic Marsha Kinder (1991) called 'transmedia intertextuality', and driven by the logic of merchandising and commodification.

However, the effects of technology cannot be isolated from the ways in which it is used, and the wants and needs that it claims to satisfy. Different social groups have different degrees of access to technology, and use it in different ways; and while some inequalities may be disappearing here, others are becoming ever more powerfully inscribed. Thus, research suggests that there is a growing polarisation between the technology rich and the technology poor; and that girls still have less access to computers in the home than do boys. At the same time, access to technology is not a matter just of disposable income, but also of cultural values. Children from middle-class families with relatively traditional attitudes are less likely to use computers than are those from working-class families who are more 'modern' in their outlook; while, in general, girls may be more inclined than boys to use computers for communication (via e-mail, for example) than for playing games or using other software (Livingstone and Bovill 1999).

More broadly, one can argue that the meaning of technology is subject to an ongoing process of social negotiation. Computers are not merely 'consumables' like many other products. They are also symbolic goods that serve as markers of social distinction (Cawson et al. 1995). Among other things, they are seen to represent modernity, intellectual superiority and freedom from constraint. From being the preserve of geeks and nerds, they are now increasingly represented as the epitome of cool sophistication. Here, again, education plays a crucial symbolic role. Investing in computers is, so parents are told, a way of investing in your children's future. Computers give children access to worlds of knowledge that would otherwise be denied to them; and, so it is argued, they put children themselves in control of their own learning. Education and parenting without technology thereby become at least conservative, if not downright reactionary. It is the fundamental responsibility of good parents and teachers to 'catch up' with the children who are in their charge – although there is considerable room for debate about whether the promises here are actually fulfilled (Giacquinta et al. 1993; Sefton-Green and Buckingham 1996).

MARKETING DISCOURSE

The three areas we have briefly outlined here are in some respects mutually reinforcing. To some extent, each of them is characterised by a blurring of boundaries – between teachers and parents, schools and homes, education and entertainment, learning and leisure, public and private. As we have indicated, the implementation of digital technologies in education is driven largely by powerful economic and political forces; though that is not to say that the consequences of this development, and the ways in which technology is actually used, can necessarily be predicted or guaranteed.

In the following sections of this chapter, we analyse some of the discourses that are currently used to promote and legitimate these developments. Rather than looking at policy documents or handbooks for teachers, we consider some particular instances of marketing discourse aimed both at teachers and at parents. We believe this is an important focus of study, not least because it is this material that plays such a vital role in purchasing decisions. The role of commercial interests in this field is such that, in our view, there are few truly independent critical sources of information and advice for potential purchasers.

We look first at an event known as the BETT Show, an exhibition of educational resources for schools held annually in London, and then at some more diverse instances of marketing material aimed at parents. We do not claim as yet to have undertaken an exhaustive analysis of such material. We are merely offering a few symptomatic instances that might inform the more extensive and comprehensive analysis that, in our view, urgently needs to be undertaken.[1]

We would contend that the examples we have chosen represent part of a broader educational–technological complex. While not quite as conspiratorial as the military–industrial one, this complex represents an alliance between groups of quite different kinds – academics, journalists, educationalists, advertisers and commercial corporations. It is a complex that, in the UK, would include a number of high-profile university departments and research centres, weekly publications like the *Times Educational Supplement* and *Guardian Online*, and groups of teacher advisers and teacher trainers, as well as companies like Microsoft, Apple, ICL, the BBC, Dorling Kindersley, TAG, British Telecom and others. This is, by definition, a group of individuals and organisations that combines public and private interests. Yet while the discourses we analyse here are those of advertisers and marketers, we contend that they may not, in the end, be vastly different from those of the other groups we have mentioned here.

Selling technology to teachers: the BETT Show

The BETT (British Education, Training and Technology) Show is a large educational trade fair held annually in London. It provides a symptomatic example of the ways in which teachers are now targeted as consumers of technology within the education marketplace. In many ways, BETT is a prime example of the educational–technological complex in action, and of its distinctive combination of public and private interests. It is organised by EMAP Education (part of EMAP Business Communications, a publishing group) and sponsored by BESA (the British Educational Suppliers' Association) and the magazine *Educational Computing and Technology*, in association with the *Times Educational Supplement*, the Department for Education and Employment and Educational Exhibitions Limited.

BESA is the trade association for the educational supply industry and has a membership of over 220 manufacturers and distributors. These companies produce a range of products, including ICT hardware and software, teaching aids, furniture and other materials designed for use in educational settings ranging from pre-school to university level. The combined annual turnover in this sector is estimated at over £600 million (http://www. besanet.org.uk).

When it was founded in 1933, BESA's primary function was the organisation of regional exhibitions designed to keep teachers up-to-date with new developments in classroom resources. Its remit has broadened over time, with changes in government policy during the 1980s and 1990s playing an important role in its development. Of particular significance here was the introduction of Local Management of Schools (LMS) as part of the Education Reform Act of 1988. Prior to this, most purchasing decisions in education were taken by local education authorities (LEAs). By virtue of their large budgets, the LEAs wielded a significant degree of power in negotiating with potential providers of products and services, although from the point of view of many schools they were often unnecessarily bureaucratic. LMS passed much of the control over purchasing decisions to individual schools; and, in the process, teachers became a significant new consumer market.

Seeing this opportunity, BESA responded by introducing the Education Show (a forerunner of BETT) and a code of practice designed 'to give confidence to schools that they would be satisfied with any product or service bought from a BESA member'. Enthusiasm for ICT and the resulting increase in funding has massively expanded the market for hardware and software. This in turn has boosted BESA's role as the industry's representative and mediator between public and private sectors. This business-led 'partnership' between industry and education is something that BESA emphasises in its literature and press releases. As the chief executive explained:

The interdependency which is occurring between schools, commercial suppliers and their local support structure is the way forward for ICT in education and the consortium approach is to be welcomed where individual contributions are on the basis of specialist knowledge in a particular area. Whether to provide training for teachers or curriculum content, opportunities for partnerships exist and BESA is here to help.

(Press release 18 November 1998: BESA website)

The BETT Show is seen as a key element of this new relationship between public and private interests. According to the Official Show Guide, it 'demonstrates the partnership between the educational ICT industry and education itself'.

The BETT Show exhibits ICT resources, as well as running a series of seminars, awards events and training for teachers. According to the BETT Newsletter, almost one-third of UK schools sends teachers to the show each year. The organisers promote the show through information sent to schools and through more practical means, such as arranging transport. One example of how big this event has become is that in January 2000 BESA and Birmingham LEA chartered a train (dubbed the 'Education Express') with the dual objective of providing transport to the show and ICT training on board.

Sales pitches

The advertising and promotional material, displays and sales presentations at BETT can be analysed as *texts* – that is, as particular configurations of verbal and visual language. These texts invoke and employ broader *discourses*, which represent the meanings of technology and of education in quite particular ways.

Of course, the BETT Show is primarily a marketing event; and the background literature (letters of invitation, a printed official guide and a newsletter) sets the tone by 'selling' both the event itself and the products which it helps to showcase. These texts reassure teachers about the potential of ICT, while at the same time giving them cause for concern about their own role in this technological age. New technology is presented as exciting, innovative and a 'solution' for schools. At the same time, these texts focus on the responsibility of teachers to keep up-to-date and to use their ICT funding wisely.

The printed texts produced for the BETT Show present ICT as challenging enough for teachers to need some guidance, but not so challenging that they should be discouraged. Just as 'good parents' invest in technology in order that their child does not fall behind, so does the professional teacher. Providing children with a 'good' education means implementing government policy on ICT and using school funding wisely. The BETT Show claims to help teachers fulfil this role by providing them with the necessary information, thereby 'meeting all the ICT needs of [their] educational establishment' (from a circular to participants).

BETT 2000 displayed the products of more than 400 education suppliers, including some of the biggest names in computer hardware (such as IBM, Compaq, Dell, Time and Tiny) and software publishing (such as Dorling Kindersley, TAG, the BBC, the Learning Company and Two Can). Many of the exhibits used glossy pictures and images taken from the companies' CD-ROMs, web pages or books. These exhibits tended to be bright and colourful, in a manner characteristic of children's media: Two Can Publishing, for example, used multi-coloured pictures of space travel, the Earth and letters from the alphabet. Other companies (usually those with the largest exhibits) were minimalists: they tended to have the company name and a limited selection of key phrases, bullet points and images. The focus here seemed to be more on the company name and perhaps one particular initiative, rather than on a variety of different products, suggesting that the central aim was to do with branding rather than direct selling of products.

Some companies combined the minimalist and the product-centred approaches. For example, the software publisher Dorling Kindersley had two exhibits. One was a presentation area with seating and a large screen. The second exhibit had rows of posters showing different Dorling Kindersley products under various headings, including history, science and the various key stages of the curriculum. By contrast, the BBC had a grey bus with 'The Learning Journey Starts Here' written on the side. Various characters from children's television (for example, a Teletubbie) were shown at the windows on the upper deck of the bus, while the names of particular product ranges like *Key Stage 3 BITESIZE Revision* and *Revise WISE* were written on the lower deck windows. All the exhibits had computer terminals at which participants could try out the products on offer; and there were numerous company representatives on hand to offer advice and demonstrate how to use the technology.

Some companies also ran short presentations describing their products, providing timetables so those participants could plan ahead. Despite the high level of noise in the hall, the presentations ran very smoothly. Other exhibitors offered incentives to encourage people to attend the presentations. They made it clear at the beginning of the presentation that you would get a free gift (e.g. key rings, soft toys) or be entered for a prize draw (T-shirts, vouchers for a particular product) if you stayed until the end. After Microsoft's presentation, T-shirts were thrown to the winners in the crowd.

Some of the presenters sounded like market traders or hawkers addressing a group of potential customers. These presentations were fast moving, loud, 'punchy' and upbeat. The presenters spoke rapidly and the sales pitch was far from subtle. For example, one Microsoft representative demonstrated 'brand spanking new technology over from Seattle', contriving to mention Seattle as frequently as possible. Like market traders, these presenters used devices like repetition to emphasise what a bargain they were offering. One speaker, for example, repeated the phrase 'absolutely free' several times in succession, while another asked a cumulative series of rhetorical questions – 'Does this cost £2,000? No! Does it cost £1,000? No!' – before finally revealing the cost of his product.

Some presenters attempted to personalise their sales pitch by assuring the audience of their personal belief in the product and its relevance: 'If I didn't think you'd be interested in this I wouldn't be telling you' (TAG). One of the Microsoft representatives claimed that both he and his son used an E-Book (a hand-held device for reading) on a regular basis, and went on to tell a few anecdotes about doing so while they were on holiday.

Meanwhile, a person dressed as a furry animal wandered about the hall, while Oscar, the 'DELL Talking Robot', posed for photographers. The Digital Workshop exhibit consisted of a striped circus tent with balloons tied to the entrance. Inside, a video was being shown; and as people walked in they were promised a free gift. When the video ended, a juggler (dressed in black-and-white with striped socks) started juggling outside the tent, presumably to attract an audience for the next screening.

Other companies used more direct sales pitches. The Skills Factory selected key words and phrases from the reviews of its CD-ROM and presented these on a pink poster in much the same way that an advertisement for a film or show might do: '"Groundbreaking" – *The Teacher*. "A Joy To Use" – *Times Educational Supplement*. "Absolutely Brilliant" – Numeracy Co-ordinator, Manchester.' Several exhibits had large television screens showing advertisements or short promotional videos, often featuring fast-moving excerpts from their productions set to music. Both in the videos and in the presentations, attention-grabbing sales talk was occasionally balanced by the calmer, less upbeat voice of 'expert opinion' from academics or educationalists.

Learning without frontiers

As we have argued, there is growing recognition of the fact that education can take place in a range of sites and contexts. Several exhibitors at BETT were clearly marketing their products to both the domestic and school markets. As one of the lead articles in the Official Show Guide, written by the editor of the *Times Educational Supplement*, suggested,

> some of the most innovative educational developments are not happening in classrooms, but on the Internet – as young people trawl

the Web for facts and figures, advice, and even direct tutoring. Sites offering homework help are growing apace. Could we be witnessing the beginning of a world wide education service that, for the first time, takes place outside school?

For several BETT Show exhibitors, this clearly represented a broadening of their potential market. This was reflected in some of their slogans: 'Extending the classroom into the home: Knowledge through your television' (NTL); 'Non stop learning – non stop managed services' (Compaq); 'Portable learning' (ACER). Likewise, the Microsoft presentations used phrases like 'anytime anywhere learning' and 'learners without limits', and claimed that their products were 'bridging the gap between learning in and beyond the classroom'.

In other instances, the distinction between education and entertainment was blurred. Thus, some exhibits explicitly focused on the 'fun' element of learning. Sherston claimed that its *Grammar Show* was 'guaranteed to make learning grammar fun'; while *Sionics* claimed to 'Make serious science exciting'. For some, learning was a world of enchantment and excitement. Knowsley MBC and John Moores University described their product as 'an engaging educational CD-ROM . . . set in the eerie fictional world of Knowsley Wood', while the Lego stand emphasised inventing, investigating and exploring.

More ambitiously, however, technology was frequently promoted as empowering and emancipating: 'What ever you want to do, you can!' (Microsoft); 'Release your time – release your potential' (Capita). Teachers, it is implied, have been held back in some unspecified way, but can now be freed by technology. In this utopian vein, the BT advertisement even promised to take consumers to 'educational ICT heaven': '[Through technology], we are able to develop best-of-breed solutions that empower teachers, delight learners and enable everyone to realise their full potential.'

According to this kind of futuristic rhetoric, 'the digital age' is a 'new era': it offers 'new horizons in education' and an opportunity to 'build your future'. Such assertions are typically accompanied by images of outer space, the Earth, the Sun and the solar system. However hackneyed it may be, this uplifting rhetoric sits rather awkwardly with the more mundane claims that were also being made here. Compared with the promise of technological utopia, concerns about meeting the requirements of key stages and SATs – let alone about things like bargains and special offers – appear strangely mundane.

One of the recurrent themes that emerges from the discourse of BETT is the idea that new technology represents a 'solution' – although it is never quite clear what problems it solves. In keeping with the optimistic ethos, there are no problems at BETT, only *solutions*. This term was used in a variety of contexts. There were 'solutions for education', 'solutions for schools', 'solutions that delight you', 'portable, hand-held solutions', 'schools' computer solutions', 'integrated education ICT solutions', 'end-to-end solutions' and many more. Some companies emphasised that they can cater for all of our ICT requirements and seemingly provide the solution for everything. Thus, the Dan advertisement promised 'total solutions for schools . . . everything for a "one-stop" NGfL solution in schools'. Similarly, Clifton Reed described itself as 'a "one-stop" shop for ICT solutions' which offers 'cost-effective total solutions'. In some cases, the word 'solutions' was used in place of the product on sale: instead of providing hardware or software, these companies claimed to provide solutions. In this formulation, the technology seems to move beyond a mere consumer product, and to assume an almost metaphysical dimension; and, in the process, it is endowed with a magical ability to facilitate and expand teaching and learning.

The BETT Show obviously represents a particularly concentrated and intensive instance of the marketing of educational technology. Yet the sales pitches that we have described, and the discourses they invoke, are routinely recycled in the advertising pages and 'online supplements' of the educational press, and in the publicity material that pours into schools on a daily basis. This material addresses and positions teachers simultaneously as consumers in a marketplace and as professionals who will be judged by professional standards. It attempts to persuade them that technology is an indispensable 'solution' to their problems; and in doing so, it combines well-worn marketing techniques with endorsements from governmental and other educational authorities that may prove harder to resist.

Of course, we are not suggesting that the market has no place in education; or indeed that a non-commercial Eden-like world of teaching and learning pre-existed the serpent of ICT. In a mixed economy, state and public institutions are inevitably a kind of market. However, the traditional pattern of market regulation in education has changed; and there has been an alignment between the education market and the wider consumer market. In the new dispensation, teachers have become individual consumers, and can no longer rely on the bargaining power – and, to some extent, the expertise – of local education authorities, which have become significantly weaker players. The promotion of ICT in education represents one kind of 'public–private partnership', but it is arguably one in which the private is significantly more powerful than the public. In this situation, educational change cannot be explained simply by an appeal to notions of progress and effectiveness. We must also necessarily examine the expanding role of business interests in the hitherto relatively closed world of education.

Selling to parents

Parents are obviously another primary market for computer hardware, and for particular kinds of 'educational' software. Households with children are significantly more likely to possess a PC than those without. These days, 'good parenting' – like 'good teaching' – is widely seen to require this form of technological investment. Yet as potential consumers, parents are less easy to target than teachers. Promotional material is accordingly more dispersed: it appears in newspaper advertisements, catalogues and direct mail shots; in television commercials and specialist magazines; and, of course, on the World Wide Web. As with the schools' market, the distinction between promotion and consumer advice is often somewhat blurred. Consumer magazines and 'online' supplements in newspapers, for example, depend for their existence on advertising revenue, however hard-hitting their reviews may appear; and it is not always easy to tell the difference between the advertorials and the editorials.

In her research on the marketing of computer hardware and software in Australia in the mid-1990s, Helen Nixon (1998) points to the emergence of a new range of specialist magazines aimed specifically at the family market, with titles like *Computer Living, Family PC* and *Parents and Computers*. As Nixon shows, these magazines and the advertising they carried featured prominent images of 'happy techno-families'; and they played particularly on parental anxieties about their children's education. Parents were routinely exhorted to make good the deficits in their own knowledge, and thereby 'catch up' with their children. Computers were represented as an indispensable tool in the drive for educational success: 'they would give children an "educational edge" on the competition and help them "move to the front of the class"' (cf. Seiter 1993).

As we shall see, these discourses are still apparent in a good deal of marketing and consumer advice material aimed at parents. Catalogues and other promotional material produced by companies like Tiny (one of Britain's biggest retailers) continue to feature images of happy smiling families and children's enraptured faces bathed in the light of the screen – and they are still almost invariably white.

Nevertheless, in post-millennium Britain, there are strong signs that the promotional era is already over. Within the mainstream press, most advertising now focuses very directly on price, as major retail outlets like Time and PC World compete to offer the most enticing limited-period 'special offers'. As the restrictive local-rate telephone charges for internet access finally begins to disappear in Britain, there is a similar price war between internet service providers. Computer advertising on television is also increasingly characterised by the 'hard sell': the happy techno-families who used to gather at the PC World store a couple of years ago are now subjected to harangues about how many gigabytes they can buy for their money.

At the same time, the promotion is reaching out to new markets. A new magazine called *Click It!*, which comes from the same stable as the long-running *Family Circle*, provides some indication of how things are changing here. While claiming to be 'the family-friendly Internet magazine', *Click It!* is targeted almost exclusively at women: men barely feature here, and the space given over to children is also very limited. In many respects, it is hard to distinguish this magazine from any other leisure-oriented title for women, with its 'departments' on fashion, food, home, travel and entertainment. It contains advice about clothes shopping online, websites about dieting, finding romance via lonely-hearts sites and 'virtual beauty'. Like many family-oriented computer publications, the magazine proclaims its avoidance of 'techno speak'; and its traditional feminine appeal illustrates how the internet is now becoming a much more universal leisure medium.

In general, therefore, the family no longer seems to carry quite the ideological charge – and the marketing appeal – which it did a few years ago. Interestingly, consumer magazines like *Parents and Computing* are no longer published; and while titles like *PC Home* and *Internet Advisor* can be found, these publications are explicitly directed at the 'whole family', rather than dealing primarily with parenting.

There may be several explanations for this shift. On one level, one could conclude that the ideological battle has already been won. Parents no longer need to be persuaded that they should buy a computer in the first place, merely that they need to buy *this* particular computer because it will give them better value for their money. On another level, however, it may reflect a recognition of the complexity of purchasing behaviour. Particularly for parents on limited incomes, the need to work or study at home, or the wish to pursue a particular hobby, is often as important a consideration as the desire to educate or entertain one's children. The purchasing – and, of course, the subsequent use – of computers in the home reflects a balance between these different priorities (Silverstone and Hirsch 1992). In this respect, addressing consumers simply or primarily as 'parents' may not be sufficiently persuasive.

Dealing with danger

Nevertheless, within the range of material we have surveyed, there are a couple of key marketing discourses that are directed primarily at parents. In a sense, they are two sides of the same coin. On the one hand, parents need to be reassured that home computers – and, in particular, the internet – will not harm their children; while, on the other, they need to be persuaded that they will offer benefits that are suitably 'educational'.

Research in the UK suggests that one of the primary reasons for parents' reluctance to purchase computers or to subscribe to the internet relates to fears about online pornography. A recent series of 'citizen's juries' conducted in cities around Britain found that an astonishingly high proportion of parents (over 90 per cent) were concerned about this issue, and felt that their children should be protected. These anxieties are to some extent fanned by rival media – particularly the press – although newspapers themselves increasingly have commercial interests in new media (Britain's leading downmarket tabloid, the *Sun*, even owns its own internet service provider).

By contrast, the main task for the advertising and the consumer magazines is to assuage this anxiety, particularly by giving prominence to the various forms of blocking and filtering software available on the market. Anthropomorphically named packages such as *Net Nanny* and *Cyber Sitter* overtly claim to function as surrogate parents, although there is considerable debate about their effectiveness. Other utilities such as *KidDesk Internet Safe* create an entirely separate desktop for children, as well as offering the possibility of imposing time limits on internet use.

Articles on these themes are a staple of consumer magazines. Thus, *Internet Advisor* (April 2000) contains a consumer's guide to filtering programs that purport to 'stop your kids from surfing around those unsavoury Web sites'. Meanwhile, *Click It!* (Spring 2000) contains a more extensive piece about 'keeping your kids safe online', with recommendations for Cyberangels' list of 'cybermoms' approved links for safe kids sites' and 'Doug's Guide to Safe Surfing', featuring the popular Disney character. The best way to keep your children 'out of trouble', it advises, is to sit with them and 'take control of what they see': surfing the web 'ought, after all, to be a family activity rather than an escape for the child'. Strict surveillance, with the helpful assistance of global corporations like Disney and Microsoft, is clearly the recipe for good parenting.

A current series of television advertisements for AOL provides a somewhat more ambiguous example of this approach. The main focus here is on a boy (aged approximately 11–12) who has internet access in his bedroom: he is frequently seen working or playing on the computer, while his mother lingers anxiously in his bedroom doorway. However, his mother's concerns (primarily about the telephone bill, but implicitly also about unsuitable content) are assuaged by the appearance of Connie, the hologram from AOL, who exerts a watchful eye over his computer use. In her somewhat glitzy appearance, Connie is not exactly parental – in fact, the basic scenario is strikingly similar to the masturbatory teenage movie (and now TV series) *Weird Science*, in which two Bill and Ted clones use a computer to summon up and control their fantasy 'babe'. In this respect, AOL's Connie may represent a compromise between the technology fears of parents and the technological fantasies of male adolescents.

Learning and fun

Despite these concerns, the primary discourse addressed to parents in this kind of material is concerned with education. Magazines like *PC Home* and *Computer Active*, which claim to be directed at 'the whole family', provide extensive space for reviews and features on educational software. *PC Home* is currently running an offer which entitles new subscribers to a selection of 'free' educational and reference software produced by the British company Dorling Kindersley – a strategy which also, of course, provides advertising for DK's 'award winning' products. As in the magazines analysed by Nixon (1998), much of the advertising and editorial copy focuses on the educational benefits of children's software, and its ability to 'help your child stay one step ahead' – although there is an interesting contrast between this and the reviews of games, where moral and pedagogical concerns are evacuated in favour of a familiar celebration of 'addiction' and fantasy violence.

Nevertheless, 'education' is subject to a variety of definitions; and here, too, there may be tensions between the aspirations of parents and the perspectives of their children. Some of these are writ large in our key text in this section: a catalogue for a software distribution company called Brainworks (www.brainworks.co.uk), dated spring 2000 and distributed via broadsheet newspapers. Brainworks markets heavily discounted CD-ROMs produced by a range of software publishers, and offers a 'Home Learning Plan' that entitles subscribers to further discounts. The catalogue features illustrated descriptions of the software packages, complete with endorsements from parents, teachers and 'experts'. These 'review teams' will, it is argued, 'show you what is best and what is just a glossy waste of time and money' (although, of course, none of the software is negatively reviewed).

The cover of the catalogue features a child dressed as an archetypal 'swot', complete with large spectacles, slicked-down preppy hairstyle, formal shirt and bow tie. The catalogue purports to contain no fewer than '287 ways to boost your child's schoolwork'. Two representative quotations can also be found on the front cover: 'I used to think homework was boring – but with my new maths CD-ROM, it's much more interesting and fun!' (David Oliver, aged 8); 'My children have really leapt ahead with their classwork since we joined Brainworks. They are excited by learning because its [sic] fun' (James Derwent, parent).

These quotations signal two key themes that recur throughout the catalogue: the notion of gaining competitive advantage for your children and the relationship between learning and 'fun'. The claim that using such software will give your child a 'head start' in the educational race is quite unashamed. A message from Anne Civardi, editorial director, emphasises that the primary aim of Brainworks is to 'help your children do better at school and in their exams'.

The catalogue effectively contains a parallel curriculum that will take a child from reception class right through to GCSE, in many cases with 'printable workbooks' attached. In place of a real teacher, we have 'the best French teacher you can give your child'; while from Year 3 through to Year 10, your child can be in the company of 'Adi, the friendly alien ... the ideal teacher – always kind, funny, helpful and patient. Unlike many teachers facing large class sizes, he follows your children's progress at every level and makes sure that they fully understand all the core subjects in a fun and entertaining way.'

In thus capitalising on parental anxieties about testing and the inadequacies of state education, the catalogue clearly positions its ideal reader as a 'concerned parent'. The good parent will be the one who completes the application form for the Home Learning Plan: 'Yes, I am interested in giving my child a better education. Please enrol me in the Brainworks Home Learning Plan.'

The relationship between 'learning' and 'fun' is the other major theme in the catalogue as a whole. These terms frequently occur together. Thus, *Talking Tables* is a 'fun learning program that takes away some of the drudgery of learning those dreaded tables'; Freddi Fish will 'keep your children immersed in learning fun'; while Carmen Sandiego 'really does teach world history the fun way'.

Despite the persistent coupling of these terms, different values are associated with each. Thus, learning is a matter of acquiring 'essential skills', 'mastering games based on reading fundamentals' and 'following respected teaching methods'. The software is 'terrific for reinforcing language and phonic activities', 'a fantastic way to introduce the vital building blocks of reading skills' or a way of gaining practice in 'solving intriguing maths assignments'. This conception of education is also very strongly tied to current government policy. Many of the packs are described in terms of their relationship to key stages and SAT tests. *Starting to Read*, for example, 'fully supports the Government's literacy campaign' and will 'get anyone reading in as little as four hours'; while *Get Ready for School* will prepare your child for Baseline Assessment tests of their 'intellectual and social skills' shortly after they begin school at age 4.

Through its use of these terms, the catalogue represents education as a highly instructional process, a matter of acquiring and practising disembodied 'skills', albeit in a palatable and entertaining manner. At the same time, the quasi-technical terminology is likely to exclude the majority of parents, and thereby provoke further anxiety about their children's performance.

Meanwhile, *fun* is associated with quite different terms: it is about 'excitement', 'adventure', 'magic' and 'enchantment'. *Star Wars Yoda's Challenge* invites you to 'explore a galaxy of fun and learning'; while *Jump Ahead* will 'make learning to read a great adventure' and offers 'fundamental maths – made fun'. And yet, as these examples imply, where there is fun, learning is never far behind. With *Planet Shape* you can 'learn about shapes – and save the world!'; *Jump Ahead* enables you to 'learn basic reading skills – at the circus!'; while *Mighty Maths Number Heroes* teaches you to 'become a Maths superhero'. While the catalogue contains some TV-related packages that are clearly intended to be 'merely' entertaining (*Sabrina the Teenage Witch*, for example), many are extolled in educational terms: *Teletubbies*, for example, offers 'learning activities' and 'learning all the way', while *Pingu* contains 'barrels of learning fun'.

Most significantly, given its importance in theories of learning, 'play' is also aligned with 'fun'. Thus, on an inside page, Brainworks offers '287 ways to boost your child's schoolwork (and still let them play on the computer)'. As this implies, there is in fact a fundamental opposition here between *work* and *play*. Learning is work, while play is something parents might (perhaps reluctantly) allow their children to do. Learning is what responsible parents want to encourage; but in order to do so they have to present it in the context of pleasure and play. They have to add some sugar to the pill. Despite the rhetoric of 'fun learning' and 'learning fun', this approach thus effectively re-inscribes oppositions between education and entertainment – and, indeed, sustains a hierarchy in which educational 'work' is seen as the only truly worthwhile pursuit for children.

Our initial research on the market in educational software suggests that the titles which sell are those which make the strongest educational claims, particularly if they relate to testing and other government policies, such as the literacy strategy. Titles that make more 'progressive' claims – representing learning as a matter of 'discovery' – are less likely to succeed. In some instances, changing the packaging in order to emphasise such traditional educational claims – 'covers the whole Key Stage 1 maths curriculum' – has resulted in significant increases in sales. Here again, there is an interesting coincidence between market strategies and educational policies which contrives to sustain a highly reductive conception of what *counts* as 'education'.

Interestingly, some companies, such as Granada, are now offering special deals to schools and colleges to promote their educational CD-ROMs to parents. In a digital version of the Tupperware party, institutions 'keen to encourage the use of quality software in the home' are offered a 'Home Version Sales Kit' and free software vouchers as an incentive for multiple sales. In this approach, teachers are not merely a market: they have, in effect, become marketers themselves.

SOLUTIONS AND PROBLEMS

As we have shown, technology is frequently presented both to teachers and to parents as the solution to a whole range of social and educational problems; and yet it is a solution that, under present circumstances, is provided largely by the commercial market. In the process, both the problem and the solution are inevitably being defined in particular ways. What counts as a valid educational use of technology is, it would seem, inextricable from what sells.

The crucial absence here is of any critical discourse that might take us beyond a merely Luddite position. In particular, there is a need for impartial advice that comes from outside of what we have termed the 'educational–technological complex'. This need is particularly acute for parents, who in some respects represent the most vulnerable and isolated consumers here. Groups like PIN (Parents Information Network) and Childnet International, which offer such advice, are few and far between; and the struggle for funding makes it hard for such organisations to resist the temptations of commercial sponsorship. TEEM (Teachers Evaluating Educational Multimedia – available: http://www.teem.org.uk) is an organisation which attempts to produce tried, tested and thorough evaluations for teachers. It provides a free website from which teachers can find out about multimedia software that they want to use in the classroom. It claims to provide clear evaluations and case studies written by trained fellow professionals. Academics in this field – to whom one might look for a critical perspective, if not always for accessible advice – may themselves be too compromised by the pressing quest for research funding and sponsorship. Perhaps this book will itself represent the starting-point for a more informed and critical debate.

NOTE

1   The research described here was undertaken as part of a project funded by the Economic and Social Research Council UK: 'Changing sites of education: educational media and the domestic market' (1999–2001).

REFERENCES

Bridges, D. and McLaughlin, T. (1994) *Education and the Market Place*, London: Falmer.

Buckingham, D. (1997) 'Schooling goes to market: some lessons from the Channel One controversy', *International Journal of Media and Communication Studies*, 1; online (available: http://www.aber.ac.uk/~jmcwww/1997/channel1.html).

Cawson, A., Haddon, L. and Miles, I. (1995) *The Shape of Things to Consume: Delivering Information Technology into the Home*, Aldershot: Avebury.

Cuban, L. (1986) *Teachers and Machines: The Classroom Use of Technology Since 1920*, New York: Teachers' College Press.

Dutton, W. H. (1996) *Information and Communication Technologies: Visions and Realities*, Oxford: Oxford University Press.

Edwards, R. (1997) *Changing Places: Flexibility, Lifelong Learning and a Learning Society*, London: Routledge.

Giacquinta, J., Bauer, J. and Levin, J. (1993) *Beyond Technology's Promise*, Cambridge: Cambridge University Press.

Himmelweit, H. T., Oppenheim, A.N. and Vince, P. (1958) *Television and the Child*, Oxford: Oxford University Press.

Kenway, J. and Fitzclarence, L. (2000) *Selling Education: Consumer Kids, Consuming Cultures*, Milton Keynes: Open University Press.

Kinder, M. (1991) *Playing With Power*, Berkeley: University of California Press.

Livingstone, S. and Bovill, M. (1999) *Young People, New Media*, London: London School of Economics and Political Science.

Melody, W. (1973) *Children's Television: The Economics of Exploitation*, New Haven, CT: Yale University Press

Nixon, H. (1998) 'Fun and games are serious business', in J. Sefton-Green (ed.) *Digital Diversions: Youth Culture in the Age of Multimedia*, London: UCL Press.

Sefton-Green, J. and Buckingham, D. (1996) 'Digital visions: children's "creative" uses of multimedia technologies', *Convergence* 2(2).

Seiter, E. (1993) *Sold Separately: Parents and Children in Consumer Culture*, New Brunswick: Rutgers University Press.

Silverstone, R. and Hirsch, E. (eds) (1992) *Consuming Technologies*, London: Routledge.

Webster, F. (1995) *Theories of the Information Society*, London: Routledge.

Wernick, A. (1991) *Promotional Culture: Advertising, Ideology and Personal Expression*, London: Sage.

Chapter 3

'Hybrid vigour'

Reconciling the verbal and the visual in electronic communication

Ilana Snyder

In these times of immense change, much of which is directly associated with the technological advances of the last three decades, teachers are beginning to think about the implications of the use of new electronic media and information technologies for communication and representation. A cultural phenomenon of great significance integral to the use of the new technologies is the shift from the verbal to the visual in textual production and its subsequent impact on communication practices. Exploring some key elements of the shift provides the focus of this chapter.

The ideas of a number of key writers on how the shift impacts on education in general and on curricular and pedagogical practices in particular are examined. Attention is given to Gunther Kress (1995, 1997a, 1997b) and Jay Bolter (1996), both of whom have considered the turn to the visual in communication practices. Each argues that important changes to the semiotic landscape are taking place. According to Kress, we are witnessing a renewed emphasis on the visual that directly affects the ways in which meanings are made. Bolter contends that we are facing the possible displacement of the verbal by the visual. In a more recent publication, Bolter and Grusin (1999) expand Bolter's earlier thesis about the contested relationship between the verbal and the visual. Their theory of 'remediation' attempts to explain the complex interaction between old and new media. It proposes that new media 'refashion' or 'reshape' older media rather than create a radically new medium. 'Remediation' provides a useful framework within which teachers can begin to consider the cultural significance of the new multimodal media.

The ideas considered in this chapter are important for teachers as they suggest a theoretical context in which to work towards a greater understanding of the emergent multimodal textual formations that increasingly dominate the communication landscape. These new formations, together with the communication practices associated with their creation and use, are characterised by cyberfiction writer William Gibson's epithet 'hybrid vigour'. These textual formations have important implications for curriculum and pedagogical practices.

THE CHALLENGE

We live in times of immense and significant change – to industry, transport, the economy and social structures – and many of these changes are directly associated with the technological advances of the last three decades. In this context of rapid and far-reaching change, teachers are asking substantive questions about curricular and pedagogical practices. In particular, they are beginning to take account of the implications of the use of the new technologies for communication and representation. Many recognise the need to identify, describe, categorise and critique emerging communication practices and genres. Some are starting to build the theoretical frameworks required to understand the new textual formations and how meanings are made with them.

But this is no easy task, if for no other reason than the insistence on and speed of change in the evolution of electronic technologies. Efforts to understand the new textual formations and associated communication practices are 'keyed to the pace and rhythms of the information industries' (Moulthrop 1997: 668). Especially since the take-off of the World Wide Web, technological advances have been relentless. Radical new design tools are released 'at dizzyingly short intervals' (*ibid.*). Although the tyranny of what Michael Joyce calls 'an anticipatory state of constant nextness' (1999: 399) makes it difficult to perceive the emerging communication practices as a coherent development or a unified field, it is still important to work towards greater understanding of the hybrid multimodal textual formations and practices that increasingly dominate the communication landscape. At the very least, teachers need to find the language to talk about the changes, both among themselves and with their students. Teachers may even find it useful to invent new words – Ulmer (1999: xii), for example, suggests 'electracy' – because they help to emphasise that what is at stake is not only different hardware and software, but different social and cultural practices.

Society as a whole and education in particular are committed to what Ulmer (1999: xi) calls a 'new apparatus'. Ulmer uses the notion of apparatus to refer to the 'social machine organising language use in a civilisation'. He argues that the pressure to act comes from the society, and those in the business of education ignore it at their peril. There are choices: one is 'business as usual' – the computer can be used as an extremely efficient way to do the work of alphabetic literacy. Alternatively, teachers can come to accept that a language apparatus includes more than just the technology – such as the alphabet to represent speech and the camera to record visual images. It also includes the development of new practices for using the technologies. The challenge is not to continue the practices created in the context of alphabetic literacy but to discover the practices specific to the use of the new technologies.

Education is at a critical crossroads. Teachers have within their power the opportunity to shift their own and their students' beliefs and understandings about the new technologies – about their place in education as well as their wider cultural importance. Traditionally, many teachers, especially those in the humanities and social sciences, have seen technology as 'antithetical to their primary concerns' (Selfe 1999: 412). Although all humanities and social science teachers do not share this attitude, a general distrust of machines and a preference for the non-technological have prevailed. At the beginning of the twenty-first century, to ignore the cultural and educational significance of the technologies is shortsighted. As the new communication and information technologies are used more and more widely, teachers need to think critically about their use and provide their students with the skills to do likewise. If large numbers of teachers continue to dismiss new technologies simply as tools, using them to do what earlier technologies did, only faster and more efficiently, then they perpetuate acceptance of a limited notion of their cultural significance: they overlook the technologies' material bases and the expanding global economic dependence on them. Alternatively, if they present new technologies as both an important part of the cultural and communication landscape, and as a potentially valuable resource, they engender a different conception of the technologies' significance, and of their own and their students' place in an information- and knowledge-based society.

At the same time, however, teachers should not integrate new technologies into their classroom practice unquestioningly. Teachers everywhere are under enormous pressure to 'technologise' learning, and 'it is vital that educational purposes and standards are not sacrificed to the technological dance' (Lankshear and Snyder 2000: 1). I am not a technology 'booster' (Bigum and Kenway 1998), dedicated to pushing technologies into the education sector. That job is being done very effectively by governments and administrators, often in direct collaboration with corporate interests. Such powerful forces do not need any assistance. In contrast, I believe that teachers need to approach the technologising of education with caution, understanding and scepticism. Effective education should always be the priority, and technologies must remain in the service of that priority. Teachers need to guard against the possibility of technology driving curricular and pedagogical practices, rather than serving them for the enhancement of educational goals.

CHANGES TO THE COMMUNICATION LANDSCAPE

The use of new technologies is closely associated with fundamental changes to communication practices. Castells (1996) argues that because culture – defined as our historically produced systems of beliefs and codes – is mediated and enacted through communication, cultures themselves become fundamentally transformed: 'The emergence of a new electronic communication system characterised by its global reach, its integration of all communication media, and its potential interactivity is changing and will change forever our culture' (Castells 1996: 329). In this chapter, I concentrate on one significant dimension of this cultural metamorphosis – the increasing presence of visual images in the ways in which meanings are made.

From the time when the alphabet was invented, 2,700 years ago, until the twentieth century, written communication was more or less separated from the visual system of symbols and perception. A social hierarchy was created between written and visual communication: written discourse became the principal means by which human practices were recorded and interpreted. The ascendancy of writing was further entrenched by the invention of the printing press in the fifteenth century. But in the twentieth century, visual culture took 'an historical revenge' (Castells 1996: 328), first with photography, then with film and television, and now with the internet. The result is that in many spheres of communication images are becoming more and more dominant.

That there exists a connection between the expanding use of new technologies and the growing significance of visual images is indisputable. It is more difficult, however, to determine the nuanced nature of that connection. In Kress's view (1997a), the turn to the visual is closely associated with the construction and production of electronically mediated texts. He points out, however, that the shift from verbal to visual language cannot be attributed only to the increased use of the new technologies – the shift has profound social and political causes such as changes to the global economy and the growth of multiculturalism–multilingualism. Indeed, 'the globalisation of mass media makes the visual a seemingly more accessible medium, certainly more accessible than any particular language' (Kress 1995: 48). Under this new regime, the verbal is rendered subordinate – many readers will have chosen a meal in a restaurant in a country the language of which they do not speak from a pictorial menu. What was for hundreds of years the main means of giving information – the written word – is being increasingly marginalised. As Kress suggests, part of the explanation may be that visual language can move across cultural and linguistic divides with greater ease than verbal language. This is not to argue, of course, that images are devoid of cultural specificity. The point is that in many situations visual communication is more likely to be effective than is verbal.

Kress also proposes that electronic media make images into a much more available, accessible and usable mode of communication than they have been. He argues that because the technologies are better adapted to the visual than to the verbal mode, 'in a very real sense they promise an era in which the visual may *again* become dominant over the verbal' (Kress 1995: 25; my emphasis). Here Kress is reminding readers that before the invention of the printing press, which heralded the age of print and the reign of the printed word for the next 500 years, visual images proliferated and were integral to meaning making. Today, in the information age, a shift is again taking place. Whether it is called a new emphasis or a renewed emphasis on the visual is not as important as acknowledging that a shift from the verbal to the visual in communication is occurring, and that it is being made possible largely by certain changes in technology – electronic text, data processing and reproduction, image and colour reproduction, and layout practices. Written texts are becoming more visual than ever before. Moreover, for the first time in history, written, oral and visual modes of human communication can be integrated into the same system, as in multimedia (Castells 1996).

The shift from the linguistic to the visual in many areas of public communication is also associated with a change in the envisaged reader. The reader is decreasingly someone prepared to devote detailed, analytical, sustained attention to written language and increasingly someone who expects to find information more immediately, more rapidly, perhaps more impressionistically through visual modes – images, bold headlines, minimal text (Kress 1995).

THE RELATIONSHIP BETWEEN THE VERBAL AND THE VISUAL

Writers have characterised the relationship between the verbal and the visual in the context of electronic communication and representation in subtly contrasting ways. Kress (1997a: 58) describes the changes to semiotic practices that involve a greater use of visual forms of representation in many domains of communication as 'a tectonic shift'. Kress (1997a: 77) also depicts the relationship between the verbal and the visual as a competition. He believes that while the rapidly increasing use of visual modes of communication has a complex set of causes, 'the simultaneous development and the exponential expansion of the potentials of electronic technologies will entrench visual modes of communication as a rival to language in many domains of public life' (*ibid*. 55). Bolter (1996: 258) portrays the relationship between the two modes of representation in the context of the computer as 'the breakout of the visual'. Although the metaphor differs from Kress's 'tectonic shift', Bolter's notion of 'breakout' also conveys the sense of sudden and significant change. To both writers, the effects of the new technologies on communication are at least as far reaching as the shift from orality to literacy.

The computer, explains Bolter (1996), was designed about fifty years ago to solve numerical problems for scientists and engineers. The early designers soon realised that the machine could operate on other sets of arbitrary symbols. Led by artificial-intelligence specialists, computer scientists came to regard the computer as a 'symbol manipulator'. In the area of symbol manipulation, electronic technologies of communication and representation include writing systems such as word processing and hypertext – fully electronic writing made up of chunks of 'text' (verbal, visual, audio, animated, graphic, video) linked electronically (Snyder 1996). At least at this point in time, applications in symbol manipulation remain the economically and culturally dominant uses of the machine (Bolter 1996).

However, the computer is being used increasingly for perceptual presentation and manipulation. Computer graphics began in the 1960s, but it was not until recently that graphic techniques have become available to large numbers of users, through inexpensive machines and software, and to a large audience of viewers, through high-quality animation in television and film.

> Enhanced by synthesised or digitised sound, electronic graphics can deliver compelling perceptual experiences. As a symbol manipulator, the computer is a writing technology in the tradition of the papyrus roll, the codex, and the printed book. As a perceptual manipulator, the computer extends the tradition of television, film, photography, and even representational painting.
>
> (Bolter 1996: 257)

In the area of perceptual manipulation, electronic technologies of communication and representation also include digital graphics, animation and virtual reality.

How is this relevant to teachers? Bolter argues that digital graphics are becoming so widely used and influential that those involved in education need to think carefully about what he calls 'the growing tension' between verbal representation and graphic representation – the tension between the word and the image. 'The issue is not so much a conflict between ink on paper and pixels on a computer screen; it is rather a conflict between contrasting modes of representation' (Bolter 1996: 256–7). Bolter proposes that if 'hypertext calls into question the future of the printed book, digital graphics call into question the future of alphabetic writing itself' (1996: 256).

In developing his case that the verbal is under threat in the context of the computer, Bolter describes the principal ways in which digital graphics can be used. Graphics can be integrated into electronic documents, where they function more or less like graphics on a printed page. Graphics also can serve as elements of a hypertext. Further, graphics can function as icons, as they do in the conventional desktop metaphor: the trash can, the hand, the open folder are ubiquitous images familiar to all who use computers. Today, the computer can offer users a multimedia space that combines words, numbers, static images, animation and video. Many CD-ROMs, in particular games such as *Myst* (Strand 1993), achieve this multimodal experience in enthralling and artistic ways.

But, in current multimedia, the trend is not to integrate the verbal and the perceptual: 'Instead, perceptual presentation is being used to displace or replace verbal text' (Bolter 1996: 257). Video and animation dominate the screen, while verbal language is marginalised. Further, the displacement of the verbal is not limited to multimedia; something similar is happening in print. In fact, interesting parallels can be observed between print and electronic technologies.

Throughout history there have been genres that combine words, icons and pictures. Children today still enjoy rebus books, popular in the Renaissance, in which some of the nouns are replaced by drawings. A child can follow the story before being able to decipher the letters. Another example that captures the 'struggle' between verbal and visual modes of representation is the newspaper headline that draws out latent metaphors in its subject: 'Turbulent times ahead for United Airlines'; 'Mercedes slips earning gears' (Bolter 1996: 259). In such headlines, there are usually visual or tactile images. A further example is common in glossy computer magazines such as *PC Magazine*, particularly in advertisements. The headline claims that a certain software product will give a company 'a bigger piece of the pie'. The picture shows an apple pie with a large slice being removed. The image both reaffirms and dominates the verbal text. 'Words no longer seem to carry conviction without the reappearance as pictures of imagery that was latent in the words' (Bolter 1996: 260).

Bolter (1996: 257) uses two quite distinct terms to depict the relationship: computer graphics can enter into a variety of either 'competitive' or 'co-operative' relationships with electronic writing. Each term suggests a different position on the nature of the relationship: the first evokes the idea of a cultural struggle between two vying forces; the second, a collaborative, harmonious, cultural enterprise. The first suggests that the printed word may be subsumed by the graphical image; the second anticipates a future in which the word and the image co-exist peacefully. It seems that Bolter is somewhat ambivalent about how the relationship will continue to evolve, reluctant, perhaps wisely, to engage in the game of prediction.

The renegotiation of arbitrary signs and perceptual elements in communication is also apparent in the layout and content of newspapers. In some Australian newspapers, pictures dominate and organise the reports and articles. In certain cases, a picture and its caption replace a verbal story altogether. This phenomenon is captured evocatively in Ian McEwan's 1998 novel *Amsterdam*, in which Vernon Halliday, editor of the quality broadsheet *The Judge*, makes the decision to destroy Foreign Secretary Julian Garmony, a notorious right-winger, tipped to be the next prime minister. A double-sized blow-up of a photograph of Garmony dressed provocatively in women's clothes, staring directly at the camera, is to occupy the front page of *The Judge*.

> The photograph filled the entire width of eight columns, and ran from under the masthead to three-quarters of the way down the page. The silent room took in the simply cut dress, the cat-walk fantasy, the sassy pose that playfully, enticingly, pretended to repel the camera's gaze, the tiny breasts and artfully revealed bra strap, the faint blush of make-up on the cheekbones, the lipstick's caress that moulded the swell and semi-pout of the mouth, the intimate yearning look of an altered but easily recognisable public face. Centred below, in thirty-two-point lower-case bold, was a single line: 'Julian Garmony, Foreign Secretary'. There was nothing else on the page.
> [. . .]
> As a front page it would surely become a classic which one day would be taught in journalism school. The visual impact was unforgettable, as was the simplicity, the starkness, the power. McDonald was right, Vernon's instinct was unerring. He was thinking only of the jugular when he pushed all the copy on to page two, and resisted the temptation of a screaming headline or a wordy caption. He knew the strength of what he had. He let the picture tell the story.
>
> (McEwan 1998: 115–16)

At this powerful moment in the book, words are rendered redundant by the potency of the image.

The situation is different in Europe, where 'serious' newspapers often contain fewer pictures and more prose and where the pictures are subordinate to the printed word. Kress (1997a: 60–1) illustrates this contrast when he compares the front pages of two contemporary newspapers: Britain's tabloid, the *Sun*, and Germany's *Frankfurter Allgemeine*. On the front page of the *Sun*, writing is 'pushed to the margin' (*ibid.*: 62) which,

Kress suggests, is characteristic of many forms of public communication – publicity materials, brochures, advertising texts and so on. In the *Frankfurter Allgemeine*, the printed word remains dominant.

In the eighteenth and nineteenth centuries, writers controlled the visual by subsuming it to their prose. Visual images, either in the form of illustrations or as something more intrinsic to the meaning, were rare. Today, the visual element takes its place as a picture on the printed page. And this phenomenon is occurring not only in newspapers and magazines but in new media formations such as the World Wide Web.

Whereas Kress argues that multiculturalism–multilingualism is part of the explanation for the growing importance of the visual, Bolter (1996) contends that, today, the cultural importance of film and television is certainly part of the explanation. Indeed, media critics such as Postman (1985) argue that television presents an alternative to print literacy by offering a competing paradigm of communication. Yet despite the ubiquity of television and its immense cultural significance, the fact is that the newspaper is coming to resemble a computer screen, not a television screen. The mixture of text, images and icons turns the newspaper page into a static shot of a multimedia presentation.

Take the Melbourne daily, *The Age*. The front page is laid out in rectangles that resemble the windows of a multimedia screen. The left-hand column is divided into windows, each containing a short grab of information, which is elaborated inside the paper. Some of the grabs have pictures that to anyone familiar with multimedia are like iconic buttons. Even though they cannot perform the interactive functions of hypertext, these images resemble multimedia buttons that connect the reader hypertextually to another page, another section. *The Age* makes use of *ersatz* hypertextual links back and forth throughout its pages and these links are cued by small graphical images.

Despite this apparent convergence of modes of representation in different media, Bolter (1996) argues that the breakout of the visual has more potential in multimedia than in print, perhaps because computer applications do not feel the weight of the tradition of print. In many examples of multimedia, graphics dominate the written text. Further, multimedia includes video and sound which 'are particularly effective at displacing verbal text' (Bolter 1996: 262).

Compare, for example, a print edition of *Macbeth* and the BBC Shakespeare (1995) CD-ROM of the play. Although many contemporary print editions of *Macbeth* contain attractive and elaborate illustrations, clearly the text is the more important component. By contrast, the CD-ROM of the play is designed to help students' understanding by providing historical background, video of performances, interviews with directors and actors, literary commentaries and so on. The CD 'begins' with the text of the play, or at least the full text is available. But users are encouraged to move away from the text to enjoy video and audio segments. Although audio and video are supposedly included to explain the text, 'these media soon reverse that relationship' (Bolter 1996: 262). The text of Shakespeare's play becomes secondary to stories told in sound and pictures. Bolter speculates that through such translations, 'computer-controlled video may come to play as important a role as television in realising for our culture the breakout of the visual' (*ibid.*).

Multimedia environments contain both verbal and graphical components, but the ultimate graphical environment is virtual reality (VR). In a typical VR system, the user wears a head-mounted display, a helmet with eyepieces covering each eye. The computer controls the user's entire field of view. Virtual environments offer an 'apparently unmediated perception of another world' (Bolter 1996: 268). It is as if the user is located in a graphical world, inhabiting the point of view of any person, animal or object.

VR 'can be understood as a paradigm of the whole realm of computer graphics' (Bolter 1996: 268). And, he argues, computer graphics are gaining more and more cultural importance. Computer graphics and animation have already reached a wider audience than hypertext or even word processing: for example, hundreds of millions of people have seen *Aladdin* and *The Lion King*. Computer graphic environments are reinforcing our culture's desire for a kind of representation without words, in which the user inhabits and experiences the world through immediate perception. It gratifies the desire for pure visual experiences – for a seemingly unmediated form of perception.

However, despite the path that VR seems to be taking us down, electronic technologies do not promote a single mode of representation. All sorts of relationships between word and image are defined in the world of electronic networks – from VR to non-graphical. Verbal representation can never be totally eliminated – it is used in the writing of the programs, for a start. At most, the written word could be devalued in comparison with perceptual representation.

Even if VR is not the future, it does seem that electronic technologies are moving us towards an increasing dependence on, and interest in, the visual. The World Wide Web epitomises this progression. Although web documents can be purely verbal, usually graphics and video are included along with the words. The Web is eclectic and inclusive and continues to borrow from a full range of visual and verbal media. Web documents represent experiments in the integration of verbal and visual communication.

Prior to the Web, the internet used principally alphabetic media (the book, the letter, the report). Although it was possible to transmit graphics, most users were limited to ASCII (American Standard Code for Information Interchange) text. Its only advantage was speed – realised particularly in the context of e-mail. In its beginnings, the Web too used only textual data. Berners-Lee proposed the World Wide Web hypertext service so that scientists could more readily share their papers and numerical data. But in 1993, Andreesen and colleagues at the University of Illinois created the first graphical browser, the forerunner of Netscape, which permitted static pictures along with the text on the page. The result was that the Web began to engage a much larger audience of users – not just more academics and researchers, who were already using e-mail, but others throughout the industrialised world who were attracted to the possibilities of a new communication medium. Further, the Web could now incorporate a whole range of earlier media: in addition to the letter and the scientific report, it could include the magazine, the newspaper and graphical advertising. Web designers looked to graphic designers for inspiration and the principles of web page design became similar to those for laying out magazine articles, advertisements and title pages (Bolter and Grusin 1999).

The Web has incorporated all sorts of printed information, but it has also begun to deliver animation, fuller interactivity, and digital video and audio. The Web still incorporates the personal letter, the book and the magazine, but now also multimedia, radio, film and television. 'It rivals all these forms by promising greater immediacy and by recontextualising them in the encompassing electronic environment of cyberspace' (Bolter and Grusin 1999: 200). It seems that the ultimate ambition of the web designer is to integrate and absorb all other media.

'HYBRID VIGOUR': MULTIMODAL COMMUNICATION AND REPRESENTATION

Ultimately, whether or not teachers are persuaded by Bolter's characterisation of the relationship between the verbal and the visual as verbal text struggling 'to assert its legitimacy in a space increasingly dominated by visual modes of representation' (Bolter 1996: 271) is less important than the need to raise awareness of cultural shifts and renegotiating. Teachers are witnesses to a professionally pertinent cultural debate that requires exposure, discussion and comment.

As computing power increases, the potential of multimodal communication is accelerating. The challenge for teachers is to come to understand the hybrid forms that are emerging in which verbal and visual modes of representation are combined in new ways. On the whole, this kind of multimodality has been overlooked. The new texts are often approached through ways of seeing conceived in an older mode of communication. Images are thought of as illustrations – even when they fill the entire page or screen and constitute the major mode of communication.

Bolter argues that 'trained as we are, formed as subjects as we are in a culture in which the written was central, the move to the visual fills us with nostalgia and foreboding' (1996: 28). However, it is possible to adopt a more sanguine approach: both to avoid romanticising a print-based past and to stop demonising a future that is likely to be increasingly dominated by electronic multimodality. The responsibility lies with teachers: they need to take these new forms of multimodality into account in their classrooms. Otherwise, at least as far as school education is concerned, future generations are condemned to learn anachronistic ways of seeing and making meaning.

Theoretical work that begins to elucidate facets of multimodality provides a useful framework within which teachers may consider the cultural significance of the new visual media. In their book *Remediation: Understanding New Media* (1999), Bolter and Grusin take further Bolter's earlier thesis about the contested relationship between the verbal and the visual. Their theory of 'remediation' offers an explanation of the complex ways in which old and new media interact.

Bolter and Grusin (1999) contend that new visual media achieve their cultural significance by paying homage to, rivalling and refashioning earlier media such as perspective painting, photography, film and television. They call this process of refashioning 'remediation' and note that earlier media have also refashioned one another: photography remediated painting, film remediated stage production and photography, and television remediated film, vaudeville and radio.

Bolter and Grusin explain the two principal strategies of remediation: 'transparent immediacy' and 'hypermediacy'. Each of these strategies has a long and complicated history. A photograph, a perspective painting and a computer system for virtual reality are attempts to achieve transparent immediacy by ignoring or denying the presence of the medium:

> All of them seek to put the viewer in the same space as the objects viewed. The illusionist painter employs linear perspective and 'realistic' lighting while the computer graphics specialist mathematicises linear perspective and creates 'models' of shading and illumination. Furthermore, the goal of the computer graphics specialists is to do as well as, and eventually better then, the painter or even the photographer.
>
> (Bolter and Grusin 1999: 9–10)

A medieval illuminated manuscript, an early twentieth-century photomontage and today's buttoned and windowed multimedia applications are instances of hypermediacy – a fascination with the medium itself. In medieval manuscripts, the large initial capital letters might be elaborately decorated, but they still constitute part of the text itself and readers are challenged to appreciate the integration of text and image. Designers of hypermediated forms ask readers–viewers to take pleasure in the act of mediation. Although these two strategies may appear to be contradictory, they are what Bolter and Grusin (1999) describe as the two halves of remediation.

Both new and old media invoke the twin logic of immediacy and hypermediacy in their efforts to remake themselves and each other. To fulfil people's desire for immediacy, 'live' point-of-view TV programmes show viewers what it is like to accompany a police officer on a dangerous raid. Film makers spend millions of dollars to film on location or to recreate period costumes and places to make viewers feel as if they are really there. 'In all these cases, the logic of immediacy dictates that the medium itself should disappear and leave us in the presence of the thing represented: sitting in the race car or standing on a mountain top' (Bolter and Grusin 1999: 5–6).

At the same time, there is also the impetus to create hypermediacy – many websites are 'riots of diverse media forms: graphics, digitised photos, animation and video' (Bolter and Grusin 1999: 6). Televised news programmes feature multiple video streams, split-screen displays, composites of graphics and text. Immediacy depends on hypermediacy. For example, the CNN site is hypermediated – arranging text, graphics and video in multiple panes and windows and joining them with numerous hyperlinks; yet the website borrows its sense of immediacy from the televised CNN newscasts – remediation in process.

Bolter and Grusin (1999) use the term 'immediacy' in at least two senses: epistemological and psychological. In the epistemological sense, immediacy is transparency: the absence of mediation. It is the notion that the medium can erase itself and leave the viewer in the presence of the objects represented. In its psychological sense, immediacy names the viewer's feeling that the medium has disappeared and the objects are present to her, a feeling that her experience is therefore 'authentic'. Hypermediacy also has two corresponding senses. In its epistemological sense, hypermediacy is opacity – the fact that knowledge of the world comes to individuals through media. The viewer acknowledges that she is in the presence of a medium and learns through acts of mediation, or indeed learns about mediation itself. The psychological sense of hypermediacy is the experience of the medium – an experience of the real. The appeal to the 'authenticity' of experience is what brings the logics of immediacy and hypermediacy together.

There are interesting connections between Bolter and Grusin's 1999 theory of remediation and Lanham's 1993 depiction of how viewers engage with art. Lanham argues that much of twentieth-century art is a self-conscious reflection on two kinds of engagement with the viewer: looking *at* and looking *through*. In painting, looking through means accepting the illusion that the painting is really a window on to a perceived world. Looking at means focusing attention on the painting as an artefact, a surface covered with paint, a manipulation of colour, shape and texture. In literature, looking through means losing oneself in the story. When the reader is called back to the text and examines it for its rhetorical and structural properties, she is looking at rather than looking through the text. In most cases, the viewer or reader must oscillate between looking at and through. Even in the most effective illusionist painting or in the most compelling narrative, readers and viewers are occasionally reminded that they are looking at paint on a canvas or at ink on paper. The twentieth century has many examples of verbal and visual art that establish a vigorous oscillation between looking at and looking through and so reminds the reader–viewer repeatedly of the painting as painting or the novel as novel.

Today, certain works that oscillate in this fashion – for example, hyperfictions like *afternoon* (Joyce 1991) – are bound to be unpopular. The common view is that art or writing should aim at realism – that is, create a compelling illusion. Hyperfiction, however, fosters both passive and active reading (Snyder 1996). When reading an episode, the reader–viewer–user–screener may succeed in looking through the text to an imagined world. Formal structures are both visible and operative in hyperfiction because they are embodied in the links between episodes. At each link, the text offers a series of possibilities that the user can activate, moving backwards and forwards between the verbal text and the structure. In *afternoon*, the user may get lost in Peter's engaging story of his search for his son. But the need to make choices about which link to activate never lets the user forget that she is participating in the making of a fiction.

By contrast, Howitt's 1998 film *Sliding Doors*, which also shunts the viewer between the experience of looking at and looking through, has enjoyed wide popular acclaim. But the viewer is never made to feel at a loss – neither confused nor uncomfortable – as to what is happening. The shifts in point of view are signalled literally by the image of sliding doors. Although the viewer moves between engrossment with the narrative line and forced acknowledgement that the film is a construction, the shifts are regular, even predictable. Whereas hyperfictions such as Joyce's *afternoon* take risks, a film such as *Sliding Doors* is careful to ensure its commercial appeal by not extending the boundaries too adventurously.

Overall, Bolter and Grusin's theory of remediation provides a contrast with the claims initially made for hypertext – that its use would fundamentally change learners' reading and writing practices and education systems (Burbules and Callister 1996; Snyder 1996; Landow 1997). They argue that the new media draw on established media practices, incorporating and refashioning them, rather than radically transforming them. In many ways, they build on McLuhan's observation (1964) that older media end up becoming the content of newer ones. Indeed, the sub-title of their book – *Understanding New Media* – pays homage to McLuhan's 1964 title: *Understanding Media*.

Other theoretical approaches are useful for teachers in their encounters with multimodality. Kress and van Leeuwen's 1996 book, *Reading Images: The Grammar of Visual Design*, provides a systematic account of the ways in which images communicate meaning. The authors examine how visual depictions of people, places and things are combined into a meaningful whole. It seems that the time is ripe for a book that concentrates on the grammar of multimodal texts: a theoretical examination of the grammar of verbal–visual language: how both words and images combine to create multimodal statements of greater and lesser complexity and extension.

At the beginning of *All Tomorrow's Parties* (1999), William Gibson's final book in his cybernoir trilogy, Rydell is still a security guard at the Lucky Dragon convenience store in LA. As he does his routine kerb check outside the store, Rydell notices

> a Japanese girl standing out there with a seriously amazing amount of legs, running down from an even more amazingly small amount of shorts. Well, sort of Japanese. Rydell found it hard to make distinctions like that in LA. Durius said hybrid vigour was the order of the day, and Rydell guessed he was right.
>
> (1999: 10)

With his inimitable verbal inventiveness, Gibson submits the idea of 'hybrid vigour' to explain the constitution of the stunning female product he beholds in the street. It seems that the Japanese girl is so breathtaking because of her mixed racial and ethnic origins. 'Hybrid vigour' also encapsulates an intrinsic component of the new forms of communication and representation discussed in this chapter. It is the very hybridity of the textual formations that gives them their force. Coming to understand the nature of this 'hybrid vigour', while at the same time allowing it to flourish in the context of curricular and pedagogical practices, provides a major challenge for teachers.

IMPLICATIONS FOR CURRICULAR AND PEDAGOGICAL PRACTICES

Teachers are now part of what Street (1998) calls 'a new communicative order'. Drawing on the work of Kress and van Leeuwen (1996) and Lankshear (1997), Street suggests that what characterises the new order is a mix of text and images. Indeed, if we heed Kress (1997a: 67), the visual is becoming so prominent in public communication that it 'cannot be ignored by school curricula'. To prepare students to participate effectively in this new order, teachers need to be aware of the semiotic range implicit in a variety of communicative practices. In the new communicative order, the task for teachers alters. They need to conceive of each curriculum area in terms of a broad framework that takes account of a wide range of communication practices. Without doubt, to be well educated students will have to understand more than they do at present about the communicative choices available to use, and about which media and what forms are more appropriate at a particular moment.

Given the reality of a networked world and electronic texts, the task for communication theorists also alters. They need to resituate notions of communicative practices. Understanding these texts requires an interdisciplinary range of methods of analysis. Reading and writing are only part of what people are going to have to learn in order to be able to communicate effectively in the future. They are also going to have to handle the kinds of icons and signs in computer displays with all their combinations of symbols, boundaries, pictures, words, text and images (Street 1998). Teachers need to turn to researchers such as Kress and van Leeuwen (1996) who are working in the area of semiotics and visual design to help build theoretical perspectives. When Kress and van Leeuwen talk about the grammar of visual design, they mean the ways in which the people, places and things depicted in images are combined into a meaningful whole. They are talking about the construction of meaning within the new communicative order.

As far as school curricula are concerned, a number of things are essential. It is likely that writing will remain an important medium of communication, indeed culturally the most valued form of communication. However, it also likely that writing will become increasingly the medium used by and for the power elites of society (Kress 1997b). Issues of equal access to power and its use make it essential therefore to ensure that all students have the opportunity to achieve the highest level of competence in this mode and its possibilities. Print and writing must not be sidelined.

At the same time, it is evident that other forms of communication are becoming prominent. All curricula will have to deal with that fact. Students require opportunities to use a number of modes. They need to recognise that there are deep and long-term changes taking place which it is essential that they understand, and that the form of the changes offers possibilities and resources which are available for their own use as makers of texts. They need to understand that the boundaries of generic form are breaking down: familiar genres are changing and new ones are emerging.

With the increased use and presence of multimodal texts, there will be a need for a broader repertoire of skills. Students will need to learn to ask certain questions about how multimodal texts function:

*   What kinds of information are best handled through visual display?
*   What are the available forms of visual display?

- What does each form permit the text-maker to communicate?
- What can the visual do that the verbal cannot?
- Are graphics and video as informative as, or even more informative than, verbal text?
- Is it possible to determine whether the image, the sound or the word is the principal carrier of meaning in the text?
- Can we continue to assume that the images are used to illustrate the main message that is conveyed in words?
- How do the words, pictures and sound interact to make meaning?
- How can ambiguities created by that interaction be identified and interpreted?

There may be gains and losses in the shift from the verbal to the visual. It may be that something will vanish in the move, but lamenting it does not seem very productive. Rather, the aim should be to understand the new modes and their possibilities.

It might seem that I have presented the challenge for practitioners and researchers–theorists as two separate enterprises. Such a division of labour is of course problematic. It both suggests a hierarchy – that theory building is somehow more important than working with students in schools – and it fails to acknowledge that theory and practice are intimately interconnected, each informing the other. Questions about the new communicative formations and practices associated with multimodal texts have important implications for curricular and pedagogical practices. These questions are best explored in partnership: a collaboration between researchers, teachers and students.

Researchers, teachers and students are now dealing with a range of media in their work. As Burnett (1996) puts it:

> [A]ll media now interface in a sometimes fascinating and sometimes perplexing manner. This information bricolage means that in the long run we will have to change the discourse that we use in relation to images. The challenge will be a profound one – how to work through this labyrinth of material to interpret and personalise its many different meanings, how to map out a direction and yet be ready to shift from one point to another and back again, how to make sense of twists and turns, learn and remember at the same time. The integration of video, film, and still photography into the computer means that we will have to be more aware of the individual histories of these media. We will also have to understand their aesthetic differences and in particular how those differences might affect the ways in which these media are used.
>
> (Burnett 1996: 71)

Teachers need to be aware of the potential and limitations of each medium. And if it is the case that texts are becoming more intensely multimodal, characterised by Gibson's hybrid vigour, teachers need to understand that the production and 'reading' of such texts involve distinctly different perceptual, cognitive and affective modes, all at the same time. In the final analysis, the notion of 'all at the same time' may pose the greatest challenge – but a challenge with which all teachers need to engage.

REFERENCES

BBC Shakespeare (1995) *BBC Shakespeare: Macbeth*, London: Attica Cybernetics, HarperCollins.

Bigum, C. and Kenway, J. (1998) 'New information technologies and the ambiguous future of schooling – some possible scenarios', in A. Hargreaves, M. Lieberman, M. Fullan and D. Hopkins (eds), *International Handbook of Educational Change*, Hingham, MA: Kluwer Academic Publishers.

Bolter, J. (1996) 'Ekphrasis, virtual reality, and the future of writing', in G. Nunberg (ed.), *The Future of the Book*, Berkeley, Los Angeles: University of California Press.

—— and Grusin, R. (1999) *Remediation: Understanding New Media*, Cambridge, MA: MIT Press.

Burbules, N. C. and Callister, T. A. (1996) 'Knowledge at the crossroads: some alternative futures of hypertext learning environments', *Educational Theory* 46: 23–50.

Burnett, R. (1996) 'A torn page, ghosts on the computer screen, words, images, labyrinths: exploring the frontiers of cyberspace', in G. Marcus (ed.), *Connected: Engagement With Media*, vol. 3, Chicago: University of Chicago Press.

Castells, M. (1996) *The Rise of the Network Society. The Information Age: Economy, Society and Culture*, Vol. 1, London: Blackwell.

Gibson, W. (1999) *All Tomorrow's Parties*, London: Viking.

Howitt, P. (1998) *Sliding Doors*, Los Angeles: Mirimax and Paramount.

Joyce, M. (1991) *afternoon, a story*, Cambridge, MA: Eastgate Press.

—— (1999) 'Beyond next before you once again: repossessing and renewing electronic culture', in G. E. Hawisher and C. L. Selfe (eds), *Passions, Pedagogies and 21st Century Technologies*, Logan, UT and Urbana, IL: Utah University Press and National Council of Teachers of English.

Kress, G. (1995) *Writing the Future: English and the Making of a Culture of Innovation*, Sheffield: National Association for the Teaching of English.

—— (1997a) 'Visual and verbal modes of representation in electronically mediated communication: the potentials of new forms of text', in I. Snyder (ed.), *Page to Screen: Taking Literacy into the Electronic Era*, Sydney: Allen & Unwin.

—— (1997b) *Before Writing: Rethinking the Paths to Literacy*, London: Routledge.

—— and van Leeuwen, T. (1996) *Reading Images: The Grammar of Visual Design*, London: Routledge.

Landow, G. P. (1997) *Hypertext 2.0: The Convergence of Contemporary Critical Theory and Technology*, rev. edn, Baltimore, MD: Johns Hopkins University Press.

Lanham, R. (1993) *The Electronic Word: Democracy, Technology and the Arts*, Chicago: University of Chicago Press.

Lankshear, C. (1997) *Changing Literacies*, Buckingham: Open University Press.

—— and Snyder, I., with Green, B. (2000) *Teachers and Technoliteracy: Managing Literacy, Technology and Learning in Schools*, Sydney: Allen & Unwin.

McEwan, I. (1998) *Amsterdam*, London: Jonathan Cape.

McLuhan, M. (1964) *Understanding Media: The Extensions of Man*, London: Routledge & Kegan Paul.

Moulthrop, S. (1997) 'Pushing back: living and writing in broken space', *Modern Fiction Studies* 43(3): 651–74.

Postman, N. (1985) *Amusing Ourselves to Death: Public Discourse in the Age of Show Business*, New York: Penguin Books.

Selfe, C. L. (1999) 'Technology and literacy: a story about the perils of not paying attention', *College Composition and Communication* 50(3): 411–36.

Snyder, I. (1996) *Hypertext: The Electronic Labyrinth*, Carlton and New York: Melbourne University Press and New York University Press.

Strand, P. (1993) *Myst*, Novato, CA: Broderbund Software.

Street, B. (1998) 'New literacies in theory and practice: what are the implications for language in education?', *Linguistics and Education* 10(1): 1–24.

Ulmer, G. (1999) 'Foreword/forward (into electracy)', in T. Taylor and I. Ward (eds), *Literacy Theory in the Age of the Internet*, New York: Columbia University Press, pp. ix–xiii.

Part II

Pedagogy and ICT

Chapter 4

Something old, something new . . .

Is pedagogy affected by ICT?

Avril Loveless, Glenn L. DeVoogd and Roy M. Bohlin

What are teachers *for* in the Information Society? What do we understand by the term 'pedagogy' and its place in the definition of the teaching profession? Which roles might information and communications technologies (ICT) play in both the expression and development of pedagogy? Will the teaching profession be able to articulate and embody these debates in their practice in ways that reflect, challenge and extend learners' engagement with new technologies?

These questions do not evoke quick and easy replies. Indeed, posing the first question to teachers and students involved in initial teacher training usually provokes lively discussion. It highlights the range of beliefs, experiences, understandings and anxieties that underpin the day-to-day work of teachers – in classrooms with pupils; in staffrooms with colleagues; preparing work at school and at home; and evaluating professional practice and development with peers.

A suitable title for this chapter might have been 'Technology doesn't change practice – people do'. The chapter will discuss ways in which ICT can affect pedagogy and the interaction between learners and teachers in many of today's classrooms. The first part argues that we are developing our understanding of the complexity of pedagogy and that the growing use of ICT by teachers provides an opportunity to look again at what teachers do and why. It gives a brief overview of some of the current perspectives on pedagogy and presents a model that provides a useful framework for further discussion. Understandings and descriptions of pedagogy differ in continental Europe from those in the USA and UK. These are briefly discussed and a European perspective is considered to be more useful in developing an approach to the questions presented at the beginning of the chapter. The second part of the chapter examines some of the implications for the change in the 'norms and routines' in classrooms in the USA which might be underpinned by the use of new technologies. It highlights some of the areas in which there is tension between the cultures and the context of contemporary classrooms and the potential of ICT to challenge and change the time, place and general endeavour of teaching.

Leach and Moon (1999) acknowledge that current reflections and debates about pedagogy imply a re-creation of the profession. We argue that the use of ICT by teachers and learners provides a catalyst for stimulating an evaluation of what is required of 'networked' teachers – identifying both new teaching strategies and those qualities of teaching which will not change, but will need to be honed and refined. The effect of ICT on the factors that influence pedagogy is considered, and we highlight the central importance of an understanding of 'information literacy' across and within subject domains. The impact of these issues on the norms and routines of classroom life are then discussed in terms of the shifts in roles of teachers and learners. These roles relate to an altered view of 'knowledge' in the light of the changes in access, authority, time and place of information available to learners, whether they be children, young people, students or teachers. The view is not, however, seen through rose-tinted computer screens, but discussed in the context of the competing forces that can shape curriculum, resources and pedagogy in schools.

A SCIENCE OF THE ART OF TEACHING OR CRYING FOR THE MOON?

Identifying a shared understanding of the term *pedagogy* is not immediately straightforward but is a worthwhile and important task, similar in some ways to that of a choreographer attempting to communicate the breathtaking complexity of expressive dance. One definition commonly given is 'the science of the art of teaching' (Gage 1985), a phrase which presents tremendous scope, but does not clarify interpretations and assumptions about the nature of science, art or teaching. It can also be described as a cultural practice (Giroux 1997) and defined as the 'transformation of consciousness that takes place in the intersection of three agencies – the teacher, the learner and the knowledge they together produce' (Lusted 1986 in Lather 1991: 15). Although acknowledging the wider interactive context in which teaching and learning take place, this does not provide a clear focus on the strategies that teachers adopt, nor their reasons for developing and refining them. Brian Simon, writing twenty years ago about the historical lack of prestige of education as a subject of enquiry in England and recognising the cultural impact of the English public-school system, commented: 'The concept of pedagogy . . . is alien to our experience and way of thinking . . . so disparate are the views expressed that to resuscitate the concept of a science of teaching which underlines that of "pedagogy" may seem to be crying for the moon' (Simon 1981: 125).

Understandings and debates about pedagogy have been more catholic and analytical in recent years, informed by the theoretical approaches of writers identifying a range of pedagogies (for example, Bruner 1996) and the empirical studies of researchers observing and describing the classroom behaviours of teachers (for example, Galton *et al.* 1999). Mortimore (1999) describes four main phases during the last thirty years in the research and development of a more complex understanding of pedagogy:

- a focus on different types of teachers and styles;
- a focus on contexts for teaching in classroom life;
- a focus on teaching and learning within a learning community which acknowledges the importance of pupils as thinkers and knowledgeable; and
- a focus on the views of practitioners and policy makers and their conceptions of learning, knowledge and the purpose of education.

He highlights the need for a view of learning communities in which learners and teachers are co-constructors of knowledge, and defines pedagogy as 'any conscious activity by one person designed to enhance learning in another' (Mortimore 1999: 17).

There is still, however, a significant difference in the approaches to pedagogy in the USA–UK and in Europe. Recent developments in the debate in the UK still lack the strong theoretical basis that can be found in continental Europe, where pedagogy is considered to be a subject domain taught within universities.

> [A] key characteristic of the different traditions was how the model for teaching in the United States came to be based on a business model. Under such a model teachers are perceived as a 'labour force' which is to be motivated and managed through narrowly conceived systems of control and accountability. It is further noted how such an atmosphere was not encouraging to independent and autonomous action.
>
> (Hudson *et al.* 1999: 8)

The German traditions of *Bildung* and *Didaktik* can provide a useful framework for further consideration of issues raised in this chapter, although the brief discussion cannot do justice to the complexity of meaning in translating these words. *Bildung* can be translated as 'erudition' – the qualities of learning which contribute to the overall aim of the growth of an 'educated personality' who can participate in and contribute to the social and cultural context. *Didaktik* can be understood as 'the science whose subject is the planned . . . support for learning to acquire *Bildung*' (Hudson *et al.* 1999: 7). An approach to pedagogy and 'information literacy' in the spirit of *Didaktik* and *Bildung* is useful in highlighting the interaction between 'action' and 'purpose'.

It is recognised that pedagogy is influenced by the interaction of a range of factors for teachers and learners. Teachers' performances in classrooms

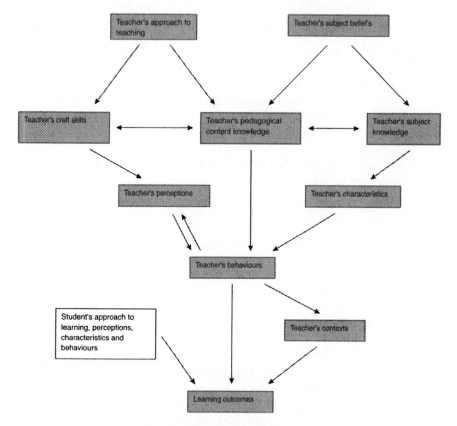

Figure 4.1 Factors relating to teaching and their interrelationships

and other learning environments are affected by their approaches to teaching, their beliefs about the subject matter, their subject knowledge, their pedagogical content knowledge (ways of representing subject knowledge appropriately for learners), their 'craft' skills in organisation and management, their personal characteristics, their perceptions of the current situation, their teaching behaviours and the context in which they are teaching (Mosely *et al.* 1999). The Learning and Instruction Group at Newcastle University developed an interactive model of teaching and learning which drew upon the work of other writers in highlighting the nature of teachers' subject and pedagogical knowledge (Shulman 1986); learning processes (Biggs and Moore 1993) and teachers' beliefs (Askew *et al.* 1997). This model is adapted in Figure 4.1 to focus on the interrelationships between the different factors relating to teaching.

Are we still left crying for the moon, as Simon lamented in the 1980s? The understanding of and approach to pedagogy have developed from a theoretical and external study of elements of teaching to a view of an interactive and evaluative process in which both teachers and learners are involved – a process more akin to 'action research' in which practitioners, policy makers and researchers in our society have a stake. We would argue that we are now in a much better position to approach our pedagogy with ICT, recognising the need to acknowledge the role played by culture and beliefs, representations of subject knowledge, the learning environments and the interactions between learners and teachers.

PEDAGOGY AND ICT?

Does it make sense to consider 'pedagogy and ICT' any more than it would make sense to consider 'pedagogy and pencils' or any other general resource? Are there characteristics of the wide range of information and communication technologies which make a distinctive contribution to teaching as tools, as resources and as catalysts for new ways of working? How does the previous discussion of pedagogy illuminate consideration of the first question posed at the beginning of this chapter – What are teachers *for* in the Information Society? One of the purposes of this chapter is to provoke discussion about the teacher's role in adopting strategies which enhance the learning of others, where that learning involves deep knowledge of how to deal with information.

In the UK there is much discussion about whether 'information technology' (IT) is a subject in its own right, or a description of the tools and resources used to support the teaching and learning of other subjects in the curriculum (ICT). A full discussion of the nature of this subject domain is beyond the scope of this chapter, but there is little disagreement that there is a conceptual framework which underpins a person's knowledge of 'how to deal with information'. Constructing knowledge from information requires far more than the ability to use a variety of ICT techniques or skills with the latest range of software applications: it relates more to an ability to question, access, interpret, amend, analyse, construct and communicate meaning from information. This may be called 'IT capability' (Loveless 1995) or 'information literacy' (Loveless and Longman 1998), and the discussion continues in an attempt to define the qualities and capabilities required in order to recognise the distinctive contribution which ICT might bring to a learning situation and know when and how to use digital technologies appropriately.

The National Curriculum for ICT in England requires that pupils develop the knowledge, skill and understanding to

- find things out from a variety of sources, selecting and synthesising the information to meet their needs and developing an ability to question its accuracy, bias and plausibility;
- develop their ideas using ICT tools to amend and refine their work and enhance its quality and accuracy;
- exchange and share information, both directly and through electronic media;
- review, modify and evaluate their work, reflecting critically on its quality, as it progresses.

Each of these four aspects of ICT capability should be developed within the wider context of a critical evaluation of the impact of ICT on their own and others' lives, considering the social, economic, political, legal and ethical issues. Pupils should also develop an approach to the use of ICT that demonstrates initiative and a preparedness to work with others to explore, develop and pass on information (DfEE–QCA 1999).

If this capability is a quality of *Bildung* – of being an educated person – then how do we as teachers develop *Didaktik* to enhance this learning? Returning to the adaptation of the model of pedagogy described in Figure 4.1, what impact might ICT have on the different elements of this model? These involve teachers'

- approaches to teaching
- beliefs about the subject matter
- subject knowledge
- pedagogical content knowledge
- 'craft' skills in organisation and management
- personal characteristics and perceptions of the current situation
- teaching behaviours
- context in which they are teaching.

Despite the long-standing caricature of the teacher as 'Chalky', standing belligerently at the front of a class with cap, gown and cane at the ready, teachers actually adopt and refine a variety of *approaches* to roles in their work. Instructor, demonstrator, project manager, consultant, resource provider, questioner, explicator, observer, model learner and co-learner are descriptions of the wide range of roles demanded of teachers and reflect their understandings of models of learning. In 1995 Loveless reflected on the ways in which teachers need to think about how ICT might support or alter their approaches to teaching strategies:

> It is by knowing when and how to intervene to encourage pupil autonomy and contributions that influence the quality of the learning experience for both child and teacher. Knowing when to stand back

in order to allow children time to work through uncertainty to solutions; knowing when to provide new information or skills to equip
the children in their task; knowing when to ask a question to challenge or divert; knowing how to balance guidance and sharing of
expertise with providing opportunities for children to think and work
things out for themselves – such knowledge implies 'intelligent action'
on behalf of the teacher. It is this intelligent action that lies at the
heart of effective teaching skills, and which reflective teachers develop
throughout their teaching careers.

[. . .]

There is a variety of research evidence to indicate that teachers do
in fact alter their roles and ways of working with IT, from shifting
the management and control of the activity to the children and
computer, to varying the nature of the interventions according to the
technical experience and cognitive needs of the children.

[. . .]

This requires careful thought, sensitivity and willingness to let go
of confidence and competence whilst becoming familiar with new
resources and working styles. It is also exciting and encouraging in
identifying the distinctive roles and responsibilities of the teacher in
moving into the twenty-first century instead of using new technology
to reinforce the activities and methods of the classrooms of thirty years
ago.

(Loveless 1995: 150–1)

Five years on, as the profile of ICT has been raised in the curriculum and
resources have become more widespread and accessible, it is interesting to
note that the demand for these roles is not much altered. Indeed they can
now be considered to be the requisite qualities of an 'expert learner'
working with novice learners as they progress to maturity (Carroll 2000).

Askew *et al.* (1997) highlighted the influence of teachers' beliefs about
the nature of mathematics on their effectiveness in teaching the subject.
Indeed, these beliefs about the subject were shown to have a more significant impact than did teachers' initial level of academic achievement in
subject knowledge. Teachers using ICT in their teaching need to be aware
not only of their beliefs about the subject and their knowledge of its
'content' but of their beliefs about ICT capability and their knowledge of
its underlying conceptual framework.

There needs to be a recognition of the role of *beliefs* about the place
and purpose of ICT in education, as well as an understanding of the ways
in which *subject knowledge* of ICT capability can be developed. Why does
ICT have such an impact in cultural, social and economic contexts?
How does this relate to the drive to raise the profile of ICT in education? What is its purpose in schooling? To raise current standards in pupil

achievement, to make teachers more efficient or to prepare young people for participation in a 'knowledge economy'? If these purposes can be identified, what are the knowledge, skills and understanding that teachers themselves need in order to demonstrate their own ICT capability within their work? In the UK, a National Curriculum for ICT in subject teaching has been developed to address some of these issues; it applies both to initial teacher training (DfEE 1998) and to the expected outcomes of New Opportunities Fund training for all practising teachers (TTA 1999).

The development of *pedagogical content knowledge* is central to the discussion of the ways in which teachers represent the knowledge, skills and understanding of the curriculum context and ICT capability to learners of different ages, styles, motivations and interests.

- How do teachers help learners to develop their understanding of organising and searching for information – whether they be 6-year-old children building a simple database of dinosaur facts, or 16-year-old students interrogating the World Wide Web for information on the latest findings that some dinosaurs might have been warm-blooded?
- How do teachers help learners to develop an understanding of the ways in which word processors might assist in the editing, redrafting and reformatting of text for a particular purpose and audience, while a web page might be a more appropriate form for linking together related elements of information in text, image and sound?
- How do teachers help learners to build 'microworlds' that support the exploration of the question 'What would happen if . . .?' in order to see the consequences of their decisions and actions – from giving instructions to a programmable toy to using a spreadsheet to predict the effects of changes in costs and charges on a small business?
- How do teachers enable learners to develop the models of information and knowledge which they construct from a variety of sources expressing different points of view, different voices and different authorities?

Teachers are part of networked communities – human and virtual – and need to be able to draw upon the experience, expertise and enthusiasm of colleagues in order to develop and share pedagogical practice. Pragmatic approaches of the 'tips for teachers' and the 'this worked for me' kind do not promote lasting change unless there is also a consideration of the principles and purposes that underpin activities in particular contexts. ICT can certainly support communication between teachers wishing to set up professional networks, but a model of a 'Virtual Teachers' Resource Centre' needs to be more than a centre for the broadcast and delivery of resources and lesson plans. It should attempt to model and reflect the very concepts on which pedagogical content knowledge needs to draw – using the speed, automatic functions, capacity, range, provisionality and interactivity of ICT to support capability in researching information, developing ideas and trying these out, exchanging and sharing information and critically reflecting on the quality of the process of developing knowledge from a variety of sources of information.

The *craft skills* of teachers are observable in their planning and preparation, and in their performance in the classroom, and can be identified and discussed between colleagues. Indeed, the standards for the Award of Qualified Teacher Status in England and Wales detail the areas of planning, teaching and class management, monitoring, assessment, recording, reporting, accountability and other professional requirements which form the basis of initial teacher training (DfEE 1998). These standards – such as maintaining a purposeful working atmosphere, effective questioning, careful listening and providing pupils with opportunities to consolidate knowledge – do not change substantially with the integration of ICT. Lessons and activities still need to have a clear purpose, structure and pace, and to elicit participation. Yet there needs to be an awareness of the range of resources and ways of working which ICT makes available to support teaching in curriculum areas. This requires clear understanding at the planning stage of

- the learning objectives for the curriculum subject area;
- ICT capability which can either support or be developed through the learning experience;
- ICT skills or techniques required to realise the activity;
- the range of teaching strategies required within the structure of the lesson – direct instruction or explanation, interactive whole-group work, guided collaborative group and individual work, whole-class plenary sessions and opportunities for differentiation and consolidation;
- the focus and balance for assessment in the subject, and of ICT capability and ICT skills or techniques.

The *context* in which this teaching takes place clearly influences the purpose, pattern and pace of activities. Teaching a whole class in a computer suite, while requiring similar attention to lesson structure, demands a different set of management skills from using a single machine or cluster of desktop machines in a classroom, a set of portables or palmtops or an electronic whiteboard. The sheer physicality of the equipment and the skills and techniques required to operate it have an effect on the movement and level of interaction in the room and needs careful creative consideration.

Are ICT resources seen as a 'bolt-on' extra to existing teaching resources and strategies, or do they offer both a challenge and an opportunity not only to assimilate new technologies into tried and tested practices, but also to explore and evaluate different structures and models of access to learning experiences? A recent study of pedagogy using ICT for literacy and numeracy in English primary schools highlighted patterns in the links between teachers' approach to teaching, some aspects of their *characteristics* (such as number of years in teaching) and their observable *behaviours* in the classroom. Teachers who were more positive about the use of ICT in their teaching tended to have well-developed ICT skills themselves and to value pupils' collaborative working, enquiry and decision making. Teachers who expressed reservations about using ICT were more likely to be highly directive and to organise pupils' individual work in the classroom (Mosely *et al*. 1999). If most teachers see a reflection of their existing practice and beliefs in the characteristics of ICT, teacher education and continuing professional development face complex challenges in approaching the changes required to meet the demands of teaching in the 'Information Age', where technologies act as a catalyst for radical educational change and in which 'locating, collating and summarising information and identifying connections and contradictions within a body of information all need to be explicitly moved to the centre of the classroom curriculum' (Scrimshaw 1997 : 112).

WHAT'S NEW? WHAT'S NOT NEW? HOW MIGHT ICT CHANGE PEDAGOGY?

In a recent informal discussion in an MA programme for lecturers in higher education, colleagues were asked how they would wish to use ICT to improve their teaching, without immediate constraints of limited or inappropriate access to resources. The subject areas in which they were involved included nursing, business studies, information technology, education and training and professional development, each integrating a range of traditional curriculum subject domains. Four imaginative and contrasting roles were described:

- A *manager of collaborative teaching and learning* – using the technologies to increase connectivity between information, teachers and learners and assist in overcoming restrictions of location and timetable. The teacher had a vision of being able to provide easy access to resources for research, preparation and presentation and then to use the technology to develop the materials collaboratively with students who contribute their own annotations and ideas.
- A *director–actor* – using the technology to support teaching by linking high-quality texts, images and sound to structure, illustrate and represent ideas in formal lecture instruction.
- A *facilitator* – using the technology to improve the students' quality of life in their learning experiences on part-time and distance-education

courses, by ensuring interactive communication between the course leaders, teachers and learners and building up an ethos appropriate to a learning community.

A *designer* – working in a team to produce high-quality interactive learning materials which enable students to engage with the subject 'content' and demonstrate the ways in which they had made connections and constructed their own understanding of the field.

What might be our image of the teacher in five, twenty-five and fifty-five years time? What will be taught? By whom? When? Where? Will the time, place and models of teaching have altered to reflect the needs of the learners on the other side of the 'cultural airlock' described by Sanger in the first chapter in this volume? Will teachers have an understanding of the complex conceptual framework for a pedagogy that demonstrates highly skilled teaching strategies that integrate the use of ICT in purposeful curriculum contexts? Are these images and perceptions shared by the children, young people, parents and politicians of today?

NEW PEDAGOGY WITH ICT? A VIEW FROM CALIFORNIA

By focusing on one element of the factors which influence pedagogy – *beliefs about subject knowledge* – this section highlights the role that ICT can play in supporting learners in constructing knowledge from a variety of information sources and experiences. Teachers need to have an understanding not only of the ways in which information sources can be accessed and used but of the teaching strategies which frame different learning experiences with these sources, from direct instruction to supporting collaborative and collective work.

'Technology doesn't change practice; people do' – as their knowledge, understanding, skills, beliefs and goals change. If practice in the use of ICT in schools changes, it will be because educators are being deliberate about shifting to a new pedagogy by changing the norms and routines that shape the daily work of learning environments. The heart of this section describes some of the shifts in the character of knowledge facilitated by digital technology and the pedagogies that will have to be adapted in order to take advantage of the new ways of knowing. It would be naïve to think that these technologies will be used in a vacuum with no other forces that will attempt to shape teaching. Hence, the final section describes the competing forces that shape the curriculum at school and, consequently, the uses of technology.

Currently, classrooms are steeped in cultural norms and practices, many of which have been constant for many decades. Using ICT doesn't necessarily change the norms and practices in the classroom unless the teacher or some other force establishes and guides new habits. For example, in mathematics some teachers in California have the practice of teaching multiplication facts by requiring all students to complete a timed test figuring all the facts on a page of simple one-digit multiplication problems. The use of technology doesn't necessarily change that norm. If students are simply practising their facts in a computer program such as *Number Crunchers*, while it may be more motivational for the students, there is little change in the shift to new knowledge, or in understanding the interaction between teacher, learner, teaching resources and knowledge.

However, if ICT could be used to help make the multiplication facts more memorable by exploring skip counting with the aid of a calculator, the pedagogy and knowledge undergo a dramatic shift. Accordingly, in contrast to the skill-and-drill on number facts done in the more traditional classroom, the new pedagogy would have the teacher practising differently, relying more on explanations and on students' construction of knowledge. And so it is not enough merely to use technology to do the same types of activity: the educator must also consider the new ways of thinking that the technology affords. The way that ICT is used reflects the teacher's beliefs about pedagogy, which in turn relate to knowing and learning.

Knowledge as revisionary, creative, personal and multisensory

Schools currently focus most of their efforts in advancing the telling and accrual of knowledge. They incorrectly view knowledge as a static, impersonal and unchanging entity. They view their purpose as that of transmitting knowledge to others. By treating knowledge as static and unchanging, schools are misrepresenting the true character of knowledge, which is revisionary, creative, personal and pluralistic in nature (Schwab 1982). In the recent past, knowledge was represented in a fixed form on paper. Paper has so mediated people's experiences that knowledge, like ink on paper, has been conceived of as fixed. Its true nature has been distorted. In some ways, using the tools of ICT allows us to represent the fluid character of knowledge by its ability to revise and represent experiences in sound and image.

One of the joys many people experience when starting to write using a computer after using a typewriter is the ability to revise and edit texts. In a similar way, digital sound and image are relatively more revisable and provisional than a child's painting that has been done on paper or a recording made with the previous technology such as an audio tape. Traditional pedagogy focuses on the finality of a text, image or sound, whereas the new pedagogy allows for revisions to improve the product or changes to make it into a new product. Users' choices in the revision represent the personalised and pluralistic nature of knowledge.

Whose knowledge? An exploding base of accessible information

One way to initiate an examination of the potential impact on classrooms of the rapid increase of access to knowledge would be to describe the stages in the evolution of sources of information in classrooms in the last 150 years. In the first stage, the vast majority of the population made their living by agriculture and lived in rural areas where one-room school-houses served to provide basic literacy and mathematical skills. Schooling was in session when the community could find an itinerant teacher and when there wasn't much work to do on the farm. People at the time rarely saw much text, so literacy and schooling were considered to be more a luxury than a necessity. Newspapers and libraries were still uncommon in everyday life for most people and letter writing was unnecessary because most friends and family could be visited. Children read the very few books available in the class and wrote on little slates with chalk. Science and social studies were studied only to the extent to which the teacher remembered information, which he or she shared orally with the class. In effect, with the exception of a few books, the teacher was *the* source of information, and the norms and routines in the organisation of the classroom reflected the need for students to receive the information stored inside the teacher's head.

The second stage, which still exists in many classrooms around the world, was in many ways similar to the first, except that students were able to get information from a textbook designated appropriate for that age level (Cuban 1986). Children were expected to stay in their seats reading their books, writing or listening to the teacher. Desks were separated to ensure students did not speak with each other. Since the sources of information were somewhat limited, students were expected to be able to repeat all or most of the information spoken by the teacher or presented in the textbook.

The third stage in the evolution of the sources of information came with the proliferation of books, charts and other visual aids in libraries and in classrooms. An extension of this stage included access to a range of data that is electronically stored and communicated, such as information on the web, on CD-ROM or hard drives, via the telephone and by e-mail. Although this stage demonstrates diversity in both media and formats for information storage and presentation, the dominant model is still of one-way delivery or broadcast in which learners are collectors and consumers of information.

The fourth stage is characterised by the introduction of interactive communications technology, such as the internet, CD-ROM, DVD and telecommunications. The technologies are similar, but learners and teachers can also be creators and collaborators in both the access and the construction of sources of information. Practice in classrooms exploiting this fourth stage would provide opportunities for students to access and manage a wide range of information using only the portions necessary to synthesise a unique and personal product. In such schools, students would be moving around the classroom or school to access information available on computers, in books, on videotape or on the telephone. With a clear purpose in mind, students would decide what information to store and then, in collaboration with other students and the teacher, students would write, edit and publish information perhaps in some electronic form such as a web page, a *PowerPoint* presentation or as hypermedia. Access to the resources for research and presentation would reflect the ways in which the teacher understands the contribution of 'information literacy' to the students' learning within different subject contexts. Such a view of literacy would underpin an approach to helping students to learn how to become mature learners.

Time and place for teaching and learning: strategic reading and writing

The interactions between teachers and learners need no longer be confined within the classroom walls and in a particular slot of the timetable. Electronic texts pass across continents and through office walls in the form of web pages and attached files, at speeds and in ways that are not possible for paper documentation. When the 'document' arrives at its destination, it can be edited and within moments returned to the sender. Because this technology moves text so fast, electronic transportation has extended the classroom beyond the specific place and dimensions of its four walls. Texts can be transformed for a variety of purposes. A teacher's lecture notes are easily printed for the students to use in making their own notes, and are equally easy to integrate with other information into presentation software to show to others in the class. That same text can be posted on the internet for students who are absent from the class at that time, and the annotations and feedback included to develop the work for future preparation.

The interactive features of ICT enable teachers and learners to make meaningful and convenient choices about the texts. The random accessibility and digital nature of disk technology such as CD-ROM and DVD allow the user to search, locate and access the correct song or film section more quickly than one could with the tape technology. Hypertext of today on the internet, and the new digital television of tomorrow, will allow teachers and students to make more choices. The old pedagogy would use whole-class 'turn-off-the-lights-and-everybody-watch' method. However, today's increased interactivity allows individual students to select an expository or narrative text and watch it, just as others might be reading their books. They could examine particular parts of the movie by stopping the action or by 'jumping' back to review a section. This type of strategic watching would allow students time to contemplate the ideas of the video, hence providing opportunities for reflection and greater growth and the reading of a multiplicity of texts.

Publication of information: costs, ownership and diversity

When information had to be stored on paper there was a major cost associated with the print production, distribution and sale of information. The ability to store information electronically on tapes, disks or computers, information which is sometimes accessed on the World Wide Web, led to the development of rather inexpensive low-end production and distribution. The cost of access to information is a political issue. In the USA immediate access to telecommunications in some regions is free or relatively cheap, whereas in other areas of the world the tariffs and regulations of telecommunications differ. The issues of the 'digital divide' in access to resources within and between communities at local, national and global levels need to be acknowledged and addressed through policy and practice. The rise and development of e-commerce will also have an impact on access to the network of information sources as the location of costs, profits and services associated with information digitally stored and accessed is causing debate and change in practices in the publishing world. MIKSIKE, for example, is a site for educational resources based in Estonia – the materials are available to be freely downloaded from the Web, while the services of educational consultants who assist in the customisation and development of these resources can then be negotiated. (MIKSIKE is at: http://www.miksike.com)

How does access to the internet have an impact on teachers' and students' understanding of authority, validity, ownership, sharing and collective development of knowledge? Newsgroups, online journals and listservs, especially when archived, can reflect a range of views. One example is the International Reading Association's *Reading Online Journal*. Not only can one read an article and the associated links online, but one may also explore and even write alternative points of view in response to the articles which are archived for readers to peruse. For children, whose interests and reading ability are different from adults, there are fewer online sites that demonstrate and provide such opportunities to construct diverse opinions.

One example of such an approach from social studies is described as 'historians do history'. The Virtual Centre for Digital History (VCDH) at the University of Virginia has set up a website that exploits the capacity and interactivity of ICT to make available primary and secondary sources of information relating to two counties that were involved, one on either side, in the American Civil War. The site provides access to newspaper archives, reproductions of documents, copies of letters, military reports and links to thousands of specialised sites about relevant individuals or events. Students learn to research information, analyse what they find and challenge their understanding as they reach conclusions about history. It demonstrates not only the collection and presentation of 'subject content knowledge', but also the development of 'pedagogical content knowledge' in the associated resources for lesson plans and activities for schools. These encourage students to experience working with such diverse materials, using ICT as a tool in developing a line of enquiry and presenting findings and ideas about the lives and times of the people caught up in the Civil War. (VCDH is available online at: http://www.vcdh.virginia.edu

Technology has made it easier to select books and other resources that represent particular perspectives. For example, at Amazon, one can limit book searches to a particular age-range and topic. In a recent search for books on the Civil War for students aged 9–12, 179 books were displayed for review. Among them there was a wide range of perspective on the American Civil War: *Bull Run* (Fleischman 1995), for example, gives several first-person accounts of that battle by participants and onlookers with differing points of view; *Abraham Lincoln the Writer: A Treasury of His Greatest Speeches and Letters* (Holzer 2000) describes the President's point of view; *Soldier's Heart* (Paulsen 1998) describes a typical enlisted soldier's experience; *Undying Glory: The Story of the Massachusetts Fifty-Fourth Regiment* (Cox 1993) describes the experiences of a black regiment; and *Behind Rebel Lines: The Incredible Story of Emma Edmonds, Civil War Spy* (Reit 1991) gives a woman's viewpoint on the Civil War. It is relatively easy to select from a wide range of books to cover the many curricular interests for particular grade-level groups.

Online booksellers such as Amazon also provide opportunities to read book reviews from sources like Horn Book, Booklist, major newspapers and readers. Though having many sources doesn't ensure diversity of opinion, the possibility for diverse opinions exists when varied sources are present. The first Harry Potter book listed at Amazon, for example, had fifteen editorial reviews and 2,291 customer reviews.

Shifts in classroom management in the Information Age

Is knowledge now viewed as a quality of memory or an understanding of how to access information stored in a variety of forms and places? Whereas at one time a scholarly person was expected to have a good general knowledge, today's professionals must have enough working knowledge to perform their roles, and must also be skilled at accessing reliable sources of information. Traditional pedagogy focuses on remembering as much as possible; the new pedagogy helps students focus more on knowing what to know and where to find and how to store knowledge.

This focus on the sifting of information is not common in schools. The texts used in traditional US schools contain information compiled and organised to provide just what students need to know to pass state assessments. Real life is not that simple. To perform a complex task, a person needs to explore the reasons for finding specific information; what it is important and valuable to know; the extent to which material provides a different perspective; what makes one perspective different from another perspective; and how knowing different perspectives makes the individual more knowledgeable and effective. These processes of sifting through information and making decisions about the purpose of information gathering – which information to use; decisions about the use of text, image and sound – all reflect the preferences and the voice of the child as an author. Pedagogy which develops effective and purposeful use of ICT will require that teachers spend a great deal more time establishing purposes for the learning, helping students to identify a credible body of information and create an author's voice that nurtures and represents their intellectual identity.

Table 4.1 highlights some features of 'old' and 'new' pedagogy that might be features of a classroom or learning environment where there has been a shift in the view of knowledge and the role that ICT might play.

The potential for curricular reform, as discussed in this section, is often lost to the many forces that press on the curriculum to shape it. Much to the disappointment of educators with a vision for the use of ICT, what is 'new' in pedagogy is often not defined by the scholarly community or by the practitioner. School officials, commercial forces seeking to sell their products, special-interest groups, state officials and voters have, however, all had an influence on the educational system and its pedagogical principles.

Commercial forces have sought to define the market by selling computer programs that claim to manage and guide student learning all by themselves. Teachers and school officials are encouraged to purchase this software so that they don't have to manage the students' work on computers. In this way, teachers simply rotate students through the computer stations with some kind of chart; the pedagogy is left up to the program and is ignored by the teacher. Yet, most scholars are concerned because the skills learned are discrete and not integrated into what would be genuine practice. The computer manages all that you have to do so that the learner never has to manage his or her own learning. In effect, then, learners do not acquire important strategies that allow them to learn on their own. This type of program leads to dependence on the computer learning system, hence limiting life-long learning.

Table 4.1 'Knowledge': the differing perspectives of 'old' and 'new' pedagogies

Old pedagogy	New pedagogy
Know as much as there is in the book and as much as the teacher says	Use strategies to decide what is worth knowing in the head and what needs to be stored: not all information should be learned
Teacher uses lecture to pass on his or her knowledge to the students	Teacher helps students access, select, evaluate, organise, and store information coming from a wide range of sources
Students dump information or organise information by categories	Students organise by categories and according to a range of perspectives
Students put information on paper for the teacher to see or the paper is posted on the wall for the school to see	Students write to disks or publish on the web for parents, relatives and a wider audience to see
Paper journals and books as the source of knowledge	Online journals and books replacing established protocols for writing and publishing
Texts are set	Texts are editable
Students have limited choice of sources	Students' personal choices are expected
Goals using technology are not integrated or not present	Integrating classroom goals with the power of technology
Intellectual products such as reports are fixed on paper and finished	Intellectual products are revisable living documents subject to addition, subtraction and change

Though California once boasted one of the best school systems in the world, in the past twenty years, its voters have passed referendums limiting property taxes, requiring that bond issue votes receive a two-thirds' majority, and limiting bilingual education. All of these voter initiatives have had a profound effect on the pedagogy of the schools. Lack of funds has caused classroom numbers to swell into the thirties for children older than 9, making the teachers shift towards more conservative whole-group activities in the interests of class management.

With three or fewer computers in a classroom and whole-group instruction, the pedagogical strategies are somewhat limited. For example, recently graduated teachers are still going to be primarily concerned about class-room management. With thirty or more students combined with difficult situations (e.g. split-age classrooms, fewer materials) new teachers are not

Table 4.1 (continued)

Old pedagogy	New pedagogy
Report form texts with no connection to the persons producing them	A range of creative multi-sensory electronic forms, such as web pages, with movement, charts, and pictures with personal connections
Neat hand-written reports with every appearance of being produced by children	Intellectual product has a professional look printed with colour and attention to design
Students hide papers from each other, allowing only teacher to read the paper	Students exchange tips about editing and revising their products
Texts are brought home and shared with parents or others in person	Teacher asks students to share their products with friends and relatives in an attachment or on the web as a way to revise and publish for an audience
Knowledge is displayed in one form only	Knowledge is written in a range of forms such as web pages, paper reports, *PowerPoint* presentations, by cutting and pasting the information into different programs
Knowledge is displayed only in a linear form	Knowledge is displayed in linear *and* hypertext formats. Class discusses advantages of each
Students who don't use technology at a young age don't have facility with electronic tools	Students use technology early and often, and discuss strategies for using tools

likely to be adventurous by using small groups, thematic study with literature, or portfolios. Even if a new teacher does know of a few ways to use technology in whole-group lessons, it is unlikely that he or she would have the resources to use it effectively. The instructional methods would more likely to be those that substitute for a chalkboard.

Almost every state in the USA requires students in certain grades to take a state assessment test which measures the achievement of students using multiple-choice questions. In most places information on schools' performance is made available to the public and printed in the newspaper or, in the case of California, the comparative performance of each grade level in every school is listed at a website. For low-scoring schools, many state legislatures have raised the stakes by threatening to tie the amount of money and control that their schools have to their ability to improve on the assessment. For other schools, there is pressure to achieve well on the assessment to keep the property values high. For purposes of maintaining high home property values and facilitating passage of bond levies, there is pressure to keep stories critical of a school's performance out of the media. Therefore, schools have shied away from allowing students to address issues from a wider range of perspectives that may be viewed as divisive or unconventional. This context promotes assessment and instruction of discrete knowledge and skills such as those measured on the standardised tests.

So when educators begin to articulate what is new and what is old in pedagogy, especially when methods are pushed by the uses of new technology, they must admit that much of what is new is still in the minds of mavericks and enthusiasts. It has not been diffused into the majority of classrooms because the pressures to create a different kind of pedagogy are too strong. In order to have an impact, educators will have to become active as change agents in influential sectors of society educating, not just beginning teachers, but also local communities, professional associations, curriculum developers, inspectors and policy makers.

Most of the new ways of knowing discussed in this section require teachers to establish new classroom routines and procedures that reflect these evolving epistemologies. Since learning teaching involves learning to establish and manage such routines, any shift in practice will be risky in the eyes of any established teacher who is already comfortable teaching in a particular way. Any shift in routine costs teachers dearly. It costs them time to learn the new approach, time to plan differently, time to gather new materials, and time to convince principals and parents of the value of this new approach. We have to be prepared to provide organised, thoughtful and long-term continuing professional development which acknowledges not only the demands of change on teachers' beliefs, knowledge and practice, but the high cost of a failure to address the purpose of the profession in the Information Society.

REFERENCES

Askew, M., Brown, M., Rhodes, V., Johnson, D. and Wiliam, D. (1997) *Effective Teachers of Numeracy: Final Report*, London: King's College.

Biggs, J. B. and Moore, P. J. (1993) *The Process of Learning*, 3rd edn, Melbourne: Prentice-Hall.

Bruner, J. (1996) *The Culture of Education*, Cambridge, MA: Harvard University Press.

Carroll, T. G. (2000) 'If we didn't have the schools we have today – would we create the schools we have today?' Keynote lecture given at the Society for Information Technology and Teacher Education 11th International Conference, San Diego, CA, 9 February 2000.

Cox, C. (1993) *Undying Glory: The Story of the Massachusetts Fifty-Fourth Regiment*, New York: Scholastic Press.

Cuban, L. (1986) *Teachers and Machines: The Classroom Use of Technology Since 1920*, New York: Teachers' College Press.

DfEE (1998) *Initial Teacher Training National Curriculum for the Use of Information and Communications Technology in Subject Teaching*, Circular 4/98, Annex B, London: Department for Education and Employment.

DfEE–QCA (1999) *The National Curriculum: Handbook for Primary Teachers in England*, London: DfEE–QCA.

Fleischman, P. (1995) *Bull Run*, New York: Harper Trophy.

Gage, N. (1985) *Hard Gains in the Soft Sciences: The Case for Pedagogy*, Bloomington, IN: Phi Delta Kappa.

Galton, M., Hargreaves, L., Comber, C. and Wall, D. with Pell, A. (1999) *Inside the Primary Classroom: 20 Years On*, London and New York: Routledge.

Giroux, H. A. (1997) *Pedagogy and the Politics of Hope: Theory, Culture and Schooling*, Oxford: Westview Press.

Holzer, H. (2000) *Abraham Lincoln the Writer: A Treasury of His Greatest Speeches and Letters*, New York: Boyds Mills.

Hudson, B., Buchberger, F., Kansanen, P. and Seel, H. (1999) 'Didaktik/Fachdidaktik as science(s) of the profession?', *TNTEE Publications*; online (available: http://tntee.umu.se/publications/publication2_1.html), October.

Lather, P. (1991) *Getting Smart: Feminist Research and Pedagogy with/in the Postmodern*, London: Routledge.

Leach, J. and Moon, B. (eds) (1999) *Learners and Pedagogy*, London: Paul Chapman Publishing Ltd in association with the Open University.

Loveless, A. (1995) *The Role of IT: Practical Issues for Primary Teachers*, London: Cassell.

—— and Longman, D. (1998) 'Information literacy: innuendo or insight?', *Education and Information Technologies* 3(1): 27–40.

Lusted, D. (1986) 'Why pedagogy', *Screen* 27(5): 2–14.

Mortimore, P. (ed.) (1999) *Understanding Pedagogy and its Impact on Learning*, London: Paul Chapman Publishing Ltd.

Mosely, D., Higgins, S., Bramald, R., Hardman, F., Miller, J., Mroz, M., Tse, H., Newton, D., Thompson, I., Williamson, J., Halligan, J., Bramald, S., Newton, L., Tymms, P., Henderson, B. and Stout, J. (1999) *Ways Forward with ICT: Effective Pedagogy Using Information and Communications Technology for Literacy and Numeracy in Primary Schools*, Newcastle: University of Newcastle.

Paulsen, G. (1998) *Soldier's Heart: Being the Story of the Enlistment and Due Service of the Boy Charley Goddard in the First Minnesota Volunteers*, New York: Delacorte.

Reit, S. (1991) *Behind Rebel Lines: The Incredible Story of Emma Edmonds, Civil War Spy*, New York: Harcourt.

Schwab, J. (1982) *Science, Curriculum, and Liberal Education*, Chicago: University of Chicago Press.

Scrimshaw, P. (1997) 'Computers and the teacher's role', in B. Somekh and N. Davis (eds), *Using Information Technology Effectively in Teaching and Learning*, London: Routledge, pp. 100–13.

Simon, B. (1981) 'Why no pedagogy in England?', in B. Simon and W. Taylor (eds), *Education in the Eighties: The Central Issues*, London: Batsford.

TTA (1999) *The Use of ICT in Subject Teaching: Expected Outcomes of the New Opportunities Fund ICT Training Initiative for Teachers in England, Wales and Northern Ireland*, London: TTA.

Chapter 5

Technology as material culture

A critical pedagogy of 'technical literacy'*

Donna LeCourt

The history of information and communications technologies (ICT) in education, albeit a brief one, tells what we might easily see as a predictable story. Like any new 'invention', change in 'paradigm' or large cultural 'shift', the introduction of technology to the classroom seems both inevitable and fortuitous. As ICT becomes more and more central in various aspects of cultural life – in both the professional and leisure realms of the middle class – education necessarily follows with the now recognisable mantra, repeating the importance of 'technical literacy' for its students' future success in educational, professional and civic realms of society. As technology is touted in the social realm as both a 'time-saver' and a 'change agent', education, not surprisingly, imports similar arguments into its own discussions about how best to employ technology in the classroom. Either technology will 'make our jobs easier', providing new and multiple alternatives for teaching the same information, or (the argument goes) technology will 'revolutionise' education, altering how we imagine its goals and function in the new century. In this binary, either practice changes with no alteration in pedagogical goals, or the educational project itself is re-envisioned. Yet, I want to suggest here, the relationship between technology and any other aspect of culture, particularly one as central to the reproduction of culture as is the educational institution, is not easily reducible to this cause–effect scenario.

Rather than technology being reduced to a function of education (a tool we might employ to our own ends), or the instigation of a revolution (leading, proponents tells us, to more democratic educational practices), the links between educational discussions of pedagogy and social claims about the values of technology point instead to a more important connection: the inextricability of educational practice and cultural practice in the social real. This connection is, of course, one that has been consistently made about schooling: recognising the ideological function of the school

*Portions of this chapter are reprinted from D. LeCourt (1998) 'Critical pedagogy in the computer classroom', *Computers and Composition* 15: 275–95 with permission from Elsevier Science.

is certainly not a new insight. It is, however, an insight that is rarely explored when we discuss how to employ technology in our pedagogies and practices. The uses of technology in classroom settings have been limited mainly to augmenting instruction in content areas or to teaching the technical skills necessary for employment in an increasingly technological world. Technology has, in short, been 'imported' into classrooms as yet another ideologically neutral tool to support the teaching of 'skills' deemed central to professional certification.

This perspective on technology, not surprisingly, has a corollary position in education: the teaching of functional literacy skills. In light of the increasingly textual nature of our society and professions, the teaching of reading and writing skills is no longer seen as the sole province of English teachers. Instead, the centrality of reading and writing acts to the 'information age' has highlighted the need for a highly literate worker who can synthesise large amounts of information and communicate this information clearly and concisely to others. Literacy, like technology, has been 'sold' as one of the most important skills for the twenty-first-century worker, and the importance of such skills in the professional realm has led to a wide-ranging concern in education with literacy skills across the curriculum. In fact, literacy has become so inextricably linked to education that, at least in the USA, cries of 'literacy crises' in the popular press emerge almost annually, leading to governmental responses such as state-mandated literacy testing across grade levels as one determiner of school funding. The cultural currency of functional literacy and technical writing–reading 'skills' carries great weight if for no other reason than that functional literacy seems such a logical response to the demands of the marketplace.

The demands for functional literacy become, then, inextricable from the market function education has come to be aligned with in capitalist societies, a link which is strengthened as global capitalism becomes more pervasive, with English as the *lingua franca* of the market close behind. In this light, the links between schooling and preparation for the workforce cannot be denied. Within a democratic capitalist culture, such demands for literacy and technology skills become further aligned with the class mobility necessary for such societies to maintain their myth of a free citizenry possessing equality of opportunity. The cultural imperative that schools serve as the institution which ensures both class mobility (for the poor and the working class) and class stability (for the already privileged) becomes almost inseparable from the benefits 'literacy skills' are purported to deliver. Such an appeal becomes even stronger when aligned with technology: if literacy skills ensure success, then technical literacy skills can only be better.

Although literacy's presumed function in alleviating class difference is part of its mythos within the social real – that is, the objectively real, material dimensions of our lives that create our social reality and the social being of individual consciousness – literacy's actual ability to ensure class mobility is much more questionable. The role of literacy education in both promoting a certain kind of docile worker throughout history (see Cook-Gumperz 1986; Graff 1987) and ensuring the stability of class distinctions (see Brodkey 1989; Trimbur 1991) has been well documented. Given the role that literacy instruction has played in further instantiating class structures, while purportedly ameliorating the very same, it would be difficult to assume that 'technical literacy' – i.e. functional competence with technological processes and literacy practices – is not to follow the same path. The 'literacy myth' that Graff (1987) points to in the USA – the assumption that literacy will, in and of itself, improve the lives of literate citizens – is no less connected to what might easily be called the technical literacy myth. As Wysocki and Johnson-Eilola (1999) have argued, linking technology with the term 'literacy' makes a not-so-innocent connection between technology and ideological reproduction. As they put it, such a linkage allows us to presume that technology will provide 'everything' about literacy 'we think worthy of our consideration: the term automatically upgrades its prefix. If "literacy" is already closely tied to our sense of how the world was colonised and settled and tamed, if "literacy" is already (deceptively) tied to political and social and economic improvement, if "literacy" already is the boundary of our sense of who we are' (p. 360), then tying literacy to technology seemingly ensures that the benefits of 'literacy' will be conferred via new media with the same effect.

If we see technology as more than a 'tool' and literacy as more than a neutral 'skill', however, we also need to enquire into their cultural function both within the social real and in educational practice. Literacy itself, as we have come to recognise due to the work of researchers like Brian Street (1984) and Shirley Brice Heath (1983), is no less imbued with cultural and ideological traces that circumscribe (and circumvent) its function and uses than is the educational project itself. Literacy, in this view, rather than being a neutral tool, becomes inseparable from culture itself. Whereas functional literacy links reading and writing to operational skills which can be generalised across the curriculum (i.e. a decontextualised form of literacy), a more cultural concept of literacy would distinguish particular kinds of reading and writing acts (e.g. genres, styles, purposes, etc.) and connect such literate acts to the forms of knowledge and value found within the cultural and disciplinary communities from which they emerge.

With such research into *multiple literacies*, whether cultural or disciplinary in nature, we have learned that reading and writing are never neutral acts; instead, they emerge in close relation to a community's ways of thinking and knowledge making. As we come to recognise the diversity of cultures within a given country – whether these be linked to ethnicity, race, class, gender, or even disciplinary differences – we have also been forced to recognise that ways of using language cannot be separated from the values of such cultures. Learning to read for particular kinds of meanings and learning to write particular kinds of forms must also be seen as learning a particular culture's ways of knowing – its ideology. Technology is similarly situated. As an artefact of culture, it comes with its own locatedness within that materiality, suggesting particular functions, uses and possibilities, while simultaneously being subject to the ideology of the cultural contexts (or academic disciplines) within which it is employed.

It is within this cultural understanding of schooling and technology, which I elaborate below, that this chapter seeks to explore how educators concerned with the literacy of their students might best make use of technology for other than functional, or even only cultural or disciplinary, means. In this chapter, I focus on the role ICT might play in supporting a more humanist, civic, educational function: our responsibility to train citizens capable of participating fully in a democratic society. Relying upon theories of critical pedagogy and their emphasis on training students to be both critical of and active participants in culture, I explore how teachers might exploit the new opportunities technology offers for examining culture and the new venues it offers for providing citizens with a public voice. Through a critical pedagogy of reflection on both literacy and technology, and *action* via the new writing spaces offered in ICT, I argue that teachers can construct a practice which encourages students to question the functional role of technology in culture and particular knowledge-making communities in order to use ICT's potential to produce alternative meanings.

A CRITICAL PEDAGOGY OF ICT: LITERACY EDUCATION AS CRITICAL CITIZENSHIP

When we problematise the role that functional literacy education plays in reproducing dominant ideology in favour of creating a more docile worker invested in the hegemonic practices of his society, seeing technical literacy as democratising (i.e. providing equal access to communication technologies) can no longer seem the logical response to the cultural changes ICT seems to be bringing about in cultural practice. Schooling, of course, can never be separated from cultural ideologies, but it need not be seen as their servant either. Instead, I argue, we need to begin to look to another model of education, one which might offer us a less functional, technocratic alternative to the teaching of reading and writing and which might also be relevant to the educational project as a *whole*, despite disciplinary differences: that of critical pedagogy. From the perspective of critical pedagogy, the goal of schooling would be figured much differently to include not only participation in the workforce but also critical participation as a citizen. Such a goal presumes that the ability to question ideology, to engage in the social real as a critical citizen, is more appropriately the function of education. This perspective, emerging from the critical pedagogies of Paulo Freire, Henry Giroux, Peter McLaren, Michael Apple and many others, does not extricate education from its ideological situatedness as the cultural institution whose chief function is preparing the young to be acceptable subjects within culture.

Critical pedagogy has many manifestations, but arguably what holds them all together is simply this focus on the critical capacities of students and our obligation to do more than reproduce cultural norms in our pedagogies. Critical pedagogy, in short, seeks to engage students in cultural critique, in a critical reading of the forms of knowledge, thinking and expression that culture makes available to them. Guiding such a critical reading is the presumption that the human subject is cultural rather than individual, a subject whose ways of thinking and acting are prescribed by the cultural contexts he or she has internalised. In this way, culture is seen as hegemonic, wherein hegemony represents the perspectives of the dominant ideology in such a way that its interests are taken on as the interests of other social groups. As Gramsci (1971) explains, hegemony exploits the commonalties in ideologies between the dominant classes and subaltern groups such that the ideology of the dominant is taken up by the marginalised as an act that seems to be in the best interest of the subaltern. Given the way culture inscribes us via such hegemonic practices, critical pedagogy presumes that our first response to a given situation will be a hegemonic one, a response designed to reproduce, and thus reinstantiate, the dominant ideology of a given culture. We enact, in short, the subject positions culture has already made available to us, seeing them as the only 'logical' alternative because of the power and validation they receive in multiple cultural contexts.

Critical pedagogy seeks to intervene in this process. Rather than seeing individuals as inevitably the 'dupes' of culture, this perspective argues that through critical acts of reflection, we can come to see our positions in culture differently and thus imagine alternatives to the subject positions our culture currently offers. Imagining such alternatives is the key to any critical pedagogy since the goal of these pedagogies is inevitably social action – an action taken to alter the oppressive conditions of society at the level of individual experience. Its focus, thus, is always local, situated in the experience of students who critically reflect on how those experiences have been internalised so that they support forms of ideology which may not function in their own (and others') best interest. Such critical reflection upon how culture has 'written' their subjectivities leads to the search for other alternatives, for new forms of cultural expression and action which can *act upon* the world rather than only react to it in already proscribed ways. As Giroux explains:

pedagogy deepens and extends the study of culture and power by addressing not only how culture is shaped, produced, circulated, and transformed, but also how it is actually taken up by human beings within specific settings and circumstances. It becomes an act of cultural production, a form of 'writing' in which the process by which power is inscribed on the body and implicated in the production of desire, knowledge, and values begins not with a particular claim to postdisciplinary knowledge but with real people articulating and rewriting their lived experiences within, rather than outside, history.

(Giroux 1995: 8)

This combination of reflection and action defines critical pedagogy's focus on *praxis* as a practice of self and social transformation. As Giroux (1992) argues, a pedagogy of *praxis* focuses upon both self-criticism, an interrogation of how one's thinking and acting reflect dominant ideologies, and social criticism of how such positions were created for the individual and how they might be transformed through different actions taken by the self. The first step to mobilising the possibilities for the student to act as social agent, then, is to deconstruct the subject positions created for her to occupy by engaging in ideological critique. These acts of 'social criticism' set the stage for constructing new concepts of agency by examining what such contexts silence within the self and what other meanings within the context they suppress. Giroux (1992: 223) makes this point clearly when he explains agency as a critical engagement with the 'languages that are made available in helping [subjects] to understand their everyday experiences' such that they can 'envision new cultural forms, [and] modes of subjectivity'. Promoting alternative ways of being, thinking and acting thus becomes the role of pedagogy.

This overarching goal of critical pedagogy is particularly apparent when contrasted to 'technical' literacy education. While technical literacy education focuses on the *skills* necessary for participation in certain aspects of society and more cultural concepts focus on gaining the knowledge of particular academic disciplines, a critical pedagogy focused on text would seek to make the ideological effects of literacy more apparent, opening up avenues for social action through written expression. Critical reflection becomes an act of examining how reading and writing acts reinforce specific ideologies. Although critical pedagogy is by no means a monolithic perspective, what holds its different manifestations together is the guiding presumption that textual spaces are always already ideological spaces. As Knoblauch and Brannon (1993: 15) argue (via Volinsonov), 'the domain of ideology coincides with the domain of signs'. Since language and text are one of the primary ways in which we understand our experience and constitute our thought, interrogating the role of language in reproducing ideology and internalising hegemonic subject positions becomes, for critical pedagogy, a concern of *all* critical educators, not just those of us in English education. In more particular terms, a critical pedagogy of textuality is concerned with the ways in which readers and writers internalise and produce text, and the ideological effects of such textual acts, particularly the impediments readers and writers encounter in creating any alternative meanings which might challenge the ideological status quo. In sum, critical literacy pedagogy is simply a critical pedagogy of text wherein literacy is refigured as civic responsibility rather than only a way to ensure individual success.

This critical pedagogy perspective is essential as we consider the technical literacy *needs* of our students in the new century. As technology becomes more pervasive, textual interactions will permeate almost all aspects of ordinary citizens' lives: the workplace and the home, consumerism, politics and government. Providing our students with the ability to interact critically with this overwhelmingly textual environment as well as to produce alternative meanings that can affect culture is not only a necessity in functional terms but a responsibility if education is to operate as more than a servant to the needs of the marketplace. The very newness of ICT as a cultural artefact, in this light, further points to more than the need for technical literacy as a functional element of society: it highlights a historical moment wherein the possibilities of this new literacy form have yet to be circumscribed.

The ways in which technology provides a more 'leaky' site in the current historical moment than many other cultural artefacts can be seen in the sheer diversity of claims made about the educational benefits of technology. This diversity is especially apparent in the research specifically on ICT, suggesting that the functions and uses of *literacy* in this environment are particularly open to change. In this work, we see images of power hierarchies being replicated in chat and asynchronous discussion technologies (e.g. Faigley 1992), at the same time as other research points to a more democratic discussion space (e.g. Jessup 1991), or even forms of text which challenge current constructions of identity (e.g. LeCourt 1999). ICT is seen both as that which will open new doors for those traditionally marginalised in culture, particularly women and people of colour (e.g. Jessup 1991; DeWitt 1997; Taylor 1997), and that which reinstantiates current power hierarchies (e.g. Janangelo 1991; Kaplan 1991; Takayoshi 1994). Similar arguments are made about hypertext – the type of writing found most often on the WWW – with some researchers claiming a new form of thinking emerging from this differently ordered text (e.g. Bolter 1991), while others see the textual form as being reinscribed within current linear modes of reading and thought (e.g. Charney 1994), and still others envision hypertext as a challenge to current conceptions of self (e.g. Johnson-Eilola 1993; LeCourt and Barnes 1999). What such divergent arguments point to is how unclear the future of technology will be; its newness, even as its history and meanings are being encoded, point to its potential to make other and related encodings more visible. Any artefact that can generate claims as diverse as ICT's seems like a rupture in ideology's ability to 'hide' itself from its subjects, a rupture of which we must take advantage.

The rest of this chapter takes up this possibility in more specific pedagogical terms, reproducing and expanding upon practical suggestions I have made elsewhere (see LeCourt 1998) and offering examples from my own teaching practice in higher education. In particular, I argue that ICT offers us a way to explore many critical elements of textual acts, both computer-mediated and print:

- the effects of writing contexts on the meanings made by student writers, particularly in educational writing contexts;
- the normalisation of meanings created through discourse communities, particularly the dominance of some communities over others and the effect of such privileged forms of literacy on the multiple literacies students bring with them to our classrooms.

The thrust of the pedagogical suggestions in these areas is one of critique – of making the ideology of textuality visible, and thus more open to manipulation by our students. As a result, the chapter closes by pointing to some possible uses of ICT in aiding our students in creating new meanings, ones that might lead to forms of public voice in culture that need not simply reproduce the status quo.

INTERROGATING CONTEXT'S INFLUENCE ON WRITING PRODUCTION

Beginning writers typically do not consider context a key aspect of writing. In fact, more attention to context – and acceding to its demands in terms of audience, purpose, and appropriate topics – is something we all try to teach. While creating texts that meet the demands of context is a key aspect to writing successfully, it comes at an ideological cost. Since rhetorical situations do not emerge neutrally, but instead reflect particular kinds of literacies and the social functions and meanings that come with them, the types of response they seem to proscribe also ensure that the meanings inscribed in text by individual writers will correspond to normalised meanings within the discourses from which the writing context emerges. By creating the 'norms' of communication within specific rhetorical contexts, a particular discourse ensures that individual writers will reproduce the forms of thinking and the worldview that its textual practices support. As Clifford (1991) has argued, student writers (and perhaps most writers) typically do not recognise discursive contexts as ideological but instead see their writing as an appropriate means to successful communication, or, in school, to success itself in the form of a grade. As Clifford, using Althusser, puts it: 'the "good" subject who comes to internalise the ideology of academic success decides, because it is the normal course, to write "appropriately", presuming that such a choice will not affect his ability to "inscribe his own ideas as a free subject in the action of his material practice"' (1991: 43).

One key function ICT might serve to a critical pedagogy of text, then, would be to aid in making the influence of context on a writer's *thought* as well as the form of his text more apparent and open to scrutiny. Discussion technologies are ideally suited to such enquiries. Because of the speed with which they occur, particularly in real time, and the seeming openness of the types of response that are acceptable, students typically do not see context as a factor in these discussions. Yet, their very speed and flexibility make context an even larger factor because so little reflection time – i.e. time to 'plan' what one wishes to say – is allowed. The effect of context in a fast-moving discussion (as in real time) or in an open form of text (as in asynchronous discussions) thus is not typically felt by the writer during the process of writing, but can easily be analysed through the textual artefact that both types of discussion allow the teacher to produce.

Typically, I use real-time discussions in class to begin a discussion of a reading, to continue a boisterous or politically sensitive discussion in a space where students feel less threatened than speaking directly to one another, or occasionally as an open discussion where students can bring up any class-related issue they wish. This type of written discussion in place of oral discussion can be adapted to almost any educational level. As anyone who has used real-time chat in a classroom knows, however, students rarely stick to the topic originally proposed. One of the great advantages of real time for the critical teacher is also what frustrates many of us about its use: how quickly topics change and how easily seemingly inappropriate topics come up. Students frequently express discomfort with this format for precisely that reason as well; they feel that their voices are not heard or that the conversation moves too fast for them to collect their thoughts. Discussing this form of discomfort can reveal many of our students' assumptions about writing itself: that it is a monologic form of communication where the writer should be in control, that it needs reflection time, and that it frequently is difficult to predict how an audience will respond.

Beyond a mere discussion of how this form of textuality challenges assumptions about text, real time also allows us to produce a transcript of such sessions immediately, affording a rich opportunity to return to the discussion and critically read it for how the context of others' comments affected what an individual student wrote. Such discussions in my own classes frequently lead to disturbing realisations on the part of the students: not only do they see how their classmates' comments change the direction of the conversation in ways they feel they must respond to (or else be a 'bad' interlocutor), they also frequently notice that what they wrote in a particular post is, disturbingly, not necessarily what they believe they thought. That is, they begin to reflect on how the context elicited a certain thought that they otherwise would not have had and, frequently, not one they want to lay claim to even ten minutes after the discussion is completed. Such quick changes in position happen often in oral conversation, but we rarely have the means to reflect on how what others say led to such changes. Reflecting on my students' discomfort with such changes in their real-time conversations, however, helps illustrate how context can 'inscribe' a certain position so that students, upon reflection, frequently want to disavow their own comments. The context of a very visible intertextuality has created a position for them that does *not* always reflect what they believe to be their 'true' self. This recognition provides an ideal starting-point for a more thorough consideration of how a particular ideology emerges from the discussion that can 'catch students in its web' without their conscious recognition of it.

As Faigley (1992: 183) points out, however, real-time discussions are never simply about the move to consensus as highlighted above; instead, 'the movement of discourse . . . is more wavelike, with topics ebbing and flowing intermingled with many crosscurrents'. It is this very movement which allows a critical enquiry to extend not only to how the context might have influenced an individual's contributions but to the nature of the discursive context itself: how it gets constructed, what contributions get attended to and why, which get silenced and why. That is, the real-time discussion presents in microcosm the ways in which a given discourse gains (and loses) the ability to silence and exclude or provide voice and power to a given contributor within a given moment. Thus, questions of context can be complicated in such analyses to include not only the effect of context on individual voice but actually the ways in which authority is constructed and how context influences the authority a single comment is granted to begin controlling the discourse.

This question of authority allows the class to examine whose position gets taken up and recirculated and why a particular comment, phrased in a certain way, is granted authority in this discussion. For example, my students quickly realise that some comments receive more attention because they 'sound like the teacher', or, conversely, because they reflect our culture's sexist or racist discourses so vehemently that they silence any other possible comments. As in these examples, the context-laden nature of the discourse provides a means by which students begin enquiring into the reasons why they tacitly granted some topics more authority by their willingness to continue them. Such enquiries begin an examination of how seemingly individual posts invoke the contexts they find more persuasive: how discourses within society and school gain power over defining their reality such that they willingly inhabit these views. The anonymity possible in most real-time discussions, in fact, makes introducing the influence of social discourses easier since students are more likely to express reified positions of racism, sexism, etc., in such discussions than in face-to-face discussion in an academic context.

Acknowledging their own embeddedness in ideology in such a short space of time, however, also brings with it the attendant protests we might have predicted. For my students, the time element so useful to highlighting the context's effects also becomes the 'out' for seeing their language use as inscribed by context. The pace of the conversation becomes the cause of such influences rather than the nature of writing and discourse themselves. As a result, an examination of context must also include elements where time cannot be relied upon as a causal factor. Asynchronous conversations (discussion groups, listservers, WWW forums, etc.) provide an ideal means for removing the time element while still allowing for an examination of writing within the intertext that helped to create it. Again, in this venue, what topics are 'picked up' and which never receive a response can become a key site for critical enquiry. As I have seen in my own classes, the reasons for ignoring a certain comment can be wide and varied: sometimes the students simply claim that it was uninteresting to them, leading naturally to probing how we determine 'interest' within the context of the classroom discussion or within culture; other times, students seem to respond more actively to comments which rely on forms of authority we use in class (e.g. textual proof; phrases which echo ones I have used in class, etc.), bringing up a discussion of how authority is formed and why we attend to some forms and not others.

Perhaps the greatest benefit of using asynchronous discussions for such analyses is its ability, like real-time communication, to highlight the effects of context not only materially but consciously, because of the text's unfamiliarity. Although seemingly more similar to composing a print text, since the writing can be done alone, allowing for the types of reflection and revision unavailable in real time, asynchronous discussions are also frequently disturbing to students because they are unsure how to write within such a discourse. Particularly important are the ways in which asynchronous discussions seem separate from the classroom space, and thus a more 'free' space, while still being embedded in academic discourse. The lack of the typical discourse cues provided by the teacher and the classroom context, as well as unfamiliarity with the genre, forces students to consider more explicitly how to present themselves in this space. As Theo, a student I interviewed for another study (LeCourt 1999), noted:

I could respond to someone, but since everyone's using a pseudonym I won't know who it is. This makes me uneasy! What if I get really vehement in my disagreement and then I find out that person I disagree with is someone who, in person, intimidates me? And then what if they found out who I was? Our relationship would change in a way it wouldn't otherwise.

(Article 44)

Theo's discomfort, and the echoes of it in other students' posts, seem to emerge precisely because she cannot rely on the same cues about appropriateness provided in other contexts (e.g. knowledge of audience, reactions of individuals, politeness norms, etc.).

What these expressions of ambiguity highlight so well is how the students seem to almost immediately sense the defamiliarisation such groups cause. By disturbing their easy sense of how to communicate successfully, context becomes an issue the writer must consciously consider rather than something that resides much in the background when one writes in forums with which one is already comfortable. The students find it much more difficult to assume that their writing is simply what they 'think and wanted to say'. Such critical reflection on how context and audience affect their own writing is so successful using ICT because online discussion technologies invite students to literally 'see' how context affects *their* writing, opening up possibilities for critique at the local level of the students' own experience, the most fruitful site for critical pedagogy's goals.

Extending such work beyond the classroom, though, also has significant benefits. Asking students to participate in chat rooms offered on the internet (although choices might need to be monitored, depending on the age level), or simply to analyse a print-out of one such room, can illustrate how the effects of context function even in seemingly less constrained spaces than the classroom. One of the great cultural myths surrounding new communication technologies is, after all, the premiss that ICT spaces on the web are 'open' and provide one of the last vestiges of 'truly free speech' in the Western world. Our students, particularly those who engage in chat rooms outside of school, no doubt have heard these claims and, more than likely, believe in them themselves. Thus, in addition to providing a critical distance students appreciate (i.e. examining the effect of context on others rather than themselves), moving beyond the classroom typically will allow a more thorough discussion of cultural influences on chat-room discourse. Further, given the seemingly free public space these rooms offer to so many, the nature of the discourse will often explicitly invoke forms of cultural authority – gender stereotyping, the authority of the media, references to money as the ultimate authority – that provide essential insights into the contexts to which many adults in our culture are subject. While students will not frequently see these influences on themselves (only examining their own discourse can do that), public chat rooms typically offer more explicit examples for a critique of ideology where students feel less self-implicated.

Public chat rooms also provide intriguing possibilities for role playing. One limitation of analyses of students' own discourse is typically that they take their own positions to be self-evident, particularly in terms of how they respond to those who are different from them. Through role-playing the positions of their cultural others (e.g. another gender or race) in chat rooms, students come to see how the discourses employed situate those others in a way that is very 'real' since within the 'mask' of the chat room they are the ones receiving the responses they may have made to others. As Alexander (1997) points out, 'role playing is the quickest way for one individual to experience another's social positioning' in the 'fairly safe' context of anonymous online discourse. The transcripts of such role-playing activities allow students to reflect upon how their writing and language 'stereotype and categorise each other' in ways that are 'heavily inflected by social and cultural forces' (Alexander 1997: 212). Such activities emphasise how cultural identities are 'constituted only in relation to otherness' (McLaren 1995: 109), demonstrating how that self–other relation is, then, also open to change. Students can further look at how their own lived experiences are partial and inscribed by discursive contexts such that they execute power over other identities, thus mobilising their potential to rewrite such positions in a practice of self-transformation.

It is this practice of self-transformation, particularly as it is figured discursively in response to the contextual interactions imposed by others' comments, which will hopefully open the path to agency so key to critical pedagogy. Examining the ways students invoke other cultural discourses (even those of flaming) to disrupt the academic context of a given task can be used to help them see that there is always more than one discourse available for textual interaction: acceding to the context need not be the only response. Students quickly recognise such violations of context as other students begin to foreground positionality in their conversations online – speaking as 'an African-American', for example – to lend authority to their ability to speak about race in juxtaposition to the presumed racelessness of their white classmates. Others invoke media authority – television shows, movies – to question the academic authority of our readings. In these examples, we see students taking on agency within discursive spaces, although they may not recognise their discourse as serving such a function. Extending discussions of context's influence beyond critique, then, and into an examination of how self becomes figured in discussion can lead to a more productive sense of how we all choose subject positions within textual contexts which both accede to those contexts and try to work against them to produce alternative meanings.

NORMALISATION OF COMMUNICATION VIA DISCOURSE COMMUNITIES

The discussion above limits the influence of context to a very local form of interaction. ICT, however, also provides opportunities to examine more closely how 'norms' for communication, already devised and out there in our culture, affect their own texts and their assumptions about 'good' writing. In particular, ICT provides a variety of venues through which students can come to see the influence of discursive norms on what they can write and the meanings they can create. Students typically recognise such influences already, but only in terms of 'rules' about school writing imposed by their English teachers. ICT provides the opportunity of opening up how such rules come to be, their effect on meaning making, and the marginalisations of alternative meanings and writers they execute.

One of the most obvious ways to begin an investigation into the effect of rules is to have a class examine a MOO or a MUD. These venues usually lay out specific rules for participation when one first attempts to join. Further, in their frequently complex norms for interaction, students quickly discover that not following the rules can lead to being 'kicked out' of a room, being ridiculed online by more experienced members, or being relegated to only parts of the MUD, while other dimensions have restricted access until they can discover the correct code. Having students reflect on being marginalised from the group through their inability to access the 'correct' language can, then, lead into discussions of more 'real' ways in which language has marginalised them in certain situations, including at school.

Looking at the normalisation of language within MOOs and MUDs, however, has its limitations. While the unfamiliarity of this environment poses significant advantages in how it similarly situates almost all students in a powerless position, students frequently see it as too removed from the real world. Once again, the best way to get at the influence of discourse communities on their own writing is to perform an ideological analysis at the site of their writing itself. Asynchronous groups provide an ideal venue for such an investigation. The ways in which asynchronous groups create their own discourse communities and form their own consensus about topic and discursive norms (Cooper and Selfe 1990; Butler and Kinneavy 1991) offer the critical teacher a microcosm of communities in action.

The ideological importance of consensus about discursive norms and content cannot be overemphasised. Research into and theory about discourse communities have shown us that discursive norms have significant influence on the relationship between thought and writing: such research points to how disciplinary discursive norms function to ensure similar ways of knowing through proscribing expectations for what can count as proof (e.g. textual citation v. personal experience), how prescriptions about genre limit the types of knowledge which can be made (e.g. research report v. personal narrative), or how norms for appropriate voice and ethos allow the writer only particular subject positions from which to speak (e.g. the use of passive voice v. the objective 'I' v. the culturally situated 'I'). These observations lead some researchers to theorise that joining a new discourse community must involve a process of 'reacculturation' wherein the student writer must loosen his or her ties to other discourse communities – since their ways of knowing conflict with those of the new community – in order to join the more 'powerful' one (see Bruffee 1984). This is particularly true with academic literacy (see Berkenkotter, *et al.* 1988; Villanueva 1993). Yet students are frequently unaware of the influence that becoming academically literate might have on their other cultural literacies. In sum, Bizzell's 1986 contention that discursive forms may inscribe certain ways of thinking, rather than contain thought in a certain form, is something largely invisible to our students for whom school ways of writing seem 'correct' and inevitable: after all, school determines which literacies count and which do not – it is school, presumably, that will make them literate.

Discourse communities, however, also provide a way to achieve critical insight into their own effects. As Trimbur (1989) has argued, interrogating the consensus formed within communities – by looking at what kinds of dissensus are not allowed within them – can provide a means of examining how consensus works ideologically. By highlighting the workings of such communities in microcosm, in the form of momentary 'communities' formed in online discussion groups, asynchronous conferencing again provides a way of examining the effect of community on student writers' own textual productions. In my experience, the way context influences the 'rules' of the conversation is frequently recognised by the students themselves without as much teacher intervention as is necessary with real-time chat. In many such groups, the students themselves remark on this. In a project analysing an asynchronous group from one of my graduate classes (LeCourt 1999), for example, I asked Hatless Cat (an online pseudonym) why she had posted less often than any other class member. Her response is telling: 'In the beginning, I waited quite a while to post because I wanted to see what other people had posted first; see what was okay to say.' Here, Hatless Cat voices what I heard continually in class early on: the need (and the desire) for me to provide more direction for the group. In the absence of such direction, most students reported that they turned to other posts for cues on how to participate. In a post late in the group's discussion, Andromeda begins to intuit not only the effect of the group itself but the effect of the academic context in which the group is situated on her own and others' writing: 'Have you ever noticed that although it has never been mandatory, almost every single newsgroup entry has had something to do with what we've discussed in class? Personally, I don't always feel like writing about something related to class discussion, but a lot of times feel pressured to' (LeCourt 1999: Article 345).

Responses such as these set the stage for a thorough analysis of how context is creating positions for writers that go beyond individual desire for self-expression into the realms of both the immediate (the group itself) and related (classroom discussions) discursive contexts. Although my under-graduates sometimes need more prompting in face-to-face discussions to acknowledge how their online contributions become normalised, once their attention is turned to it, they frequently express shock that their contributions are so easily influenced and 'controlled' without their aware-ness. Having students critically analyse the group as a class project, further, frequently shows what forms of difference the group's discourse is silencing in this way, providing a means for validating that difference rather than silencing it. In short, critical reflection on context also quickly motivates students towards action.

CONCLUSION: FROM REFLECTION TO ACTION

Although the ideological influence of context and community exposes how easily writers and readers can be controlled by the textual semiotics which surround them, such critiques are not the goal of a critical pedagogy of text. Instead, these critiques should serve the ends of social action in some way. In terms of critical pedagogy, these forms of social action are best imagined as the production of resistant and alternative meanings in textual venues that would exclude them. In sum, the penultimate goal of educating a *critical* citizen needs to provide the opportunity for that citizen to act upon the world to change oppressive cultural realities, and, just as impor-tantly, to communicate those alternative senses to other citizens. The role of literacy here is key in so far as literate acts provide a way not only to produce alternative meanings but to make them available, as part of the social, for others to take up, as part of their construction of identity and/or in favour of collective action.

What specific route such calls to action might take is difficult to predict as they must always, of necessity, be located in the student's experience of self and her particular interpretation of what action is necessary. No two students will take action upon their critical work in the same way, and some may choose not to act upon their critical reflection at all – a choice which must be validated by the critical educator if she is dedicated to the concept of education as making critically informed choices rather than following the political prescriptions of the teacher. By way of closing, however, I would offer a few examples of the forms such textual action have taken in univer-sity classrooms. Each of these examples, not coincidentally, takes place in

ICT environments. One of the chief benefits of pairing ICT and a critical pedagogy of text is the opportunities it opens up for students to negotiate ICT spaces differently – as socially active subjects – and for them to take advantage of ICT's ability to provide an immediate public forum.

One of the more intriguing results of critical approaches to ICT – at least for me, given my interests as a feminist educator – has been the ways in which students might take up the challenge to provide different negotiations and conceptions of gender in these spaces. For example, Romano's 1999 work illustrates how students, in real-time discussions, make productive use of the multiple-subject positions offered them in the comments of other students and their instructors. In one such discussion, for instance, women's 'natural' shyness becomes the topic, offering women students a place to respond as women who protest this characterisation. Such a discussion, however, also opens up opportunities for considering the differences female and male students experience in online discussions and their possible relationship to the 'shyness' factor, allowing ICT textuality and gender to be interrogated. In another such discussion, women students are offered the multiple positions of women, ethnic women and women business executives. Rather than taking only one of these positions up, one of Romano's students, Angelica, uses all three to re-open a space for Latina women in the class to respond which had previously been closed off. While these examples are seemingly small instances of 'social action', they do point to the possibilities of a critical pedagogy. In Romano's class, students were already, mostly unconsciously, making use of the opportunities for the kind of multiple meanings and subject positions offered in real-time discussions considered above. Adding the critical element to such a pedagogy, I hope, would make such manipulations of the discursive space – manipulations specifically designed to alter the spaces provided for women to speak only particular meanings – more apparent to students like Angelica.

In more explicitly critical classes, in fact, students do take up these very opportunities. For example, Sullivan (1999) writes of a class where she focuses on examining gendered representations on the internet, and in other venues, ending with an action-oriented assignment asking students to write 'autobiographical hypertexts and activist hypertexts'. In the autobiographical assignment, for example, Sullivan asks students 'to interrogate their positions within social history and entertainment narratives' (p. 30). What the students produce are extremely provocative hypertexts, then published on the internet, both interrogating current conceptions of gender and offering alternative visions. In one such hypertext, 'Angels of desire', Doray Fried uses the cultural artefact of bras to explode gendered identity, creating links to bra advertisements which show desire to be the model while also questioning that desire. Other links recount vignettes of experiences with bras – one where she enters a famous lingerie store only to be told they do not make 'bras that large' – or conversations with friends about body image (see Sullivan 1999: 32–3). The overall result is a text which demonstrates both the construction of the 'breast' in popular culture and everyday life and its connections to one woman's experience while simultaneously critiquing the 'culture of the breast' through one woman's search for a different relationship to this highly encoded part of her body.

In my own experience, students have similarly used hypertext to critically examine representations of self and their relationship to social forces. For example, in 'Fabric of voices' (http://www.colostate.edu/Depts/WritingCenter/assignments/e630d/voices/home.htm) Luann Barnes uses the non-linear nature of hypertext to explore the multiple subject positions she feels she occupies. Just as significantly, this exploration is not merely personal: instead, she hopes that her own autobiographical text will help open up concepts of identity for her readers. As she explained in an article we co-wrote on this text:

> By both blurring genres and making them collide, never allowing a reader to be totally comfortable with a single genre, a hypertext writer can make a reader see genre as artificial and subject positions as dynamic. I hoped ultimately to encourage the interrogation of text rather than the pursuit of stable meaning. . . . By disrupting the academic genre, I hoped to give voice to multiple subject positions and expose the fallacy of a unified self. In a way, this was my attempt to show what drives logical choices, but does not end up in a final text.
>
> (LeCourt and Barnes 1999: 61)

Barnes, then, imagines her text as a form of action – as a self-reflection meant to provide alternative possibilities for her readers. Similarly, in Sullivan's class she analyses texts which deliberately try to invoke alternative cultural meanings, as in her example of Laura Adams' text which rewrote a Calvin Klein advertisement (the 'CK Be' campaign) to read:

> Just Be . . . a lesbian.
> Just Be . . . a battered wife.
> Just Be . . . what others expect you to be.
> Just Be . . . a sex object.
> Just Be . . . a slave.
> Just Be . . . a woman.
>
> (Quoted in Sullivan 1999: 41)

These texts are provocative, political and public. The ideal of textual action in a critical pedagogy, they offer alternative visions of the world and invite others to construct their own conceptions of gender in alternative ways. Not all our students, particularly the younger ones, will construct such obviously critical texts, however, that need not negate the attempt. As we move further into the new century, we will need citizens who will 'Just Be . . . something other than culture dictates' if we are to realise the benefits of the 'Technological Age'.

REFERENCES

Alexander, J. (1997) 'Out of the closet and into the network: sexual orientation and the computerized classroom', *Computers and Composition* 14(2): 207–16.

Berkenkotter, C., Huckin, T. and Ackerman, J. (1988) 'Conversation, conventions, and the writer: case study of a student in a rhetoric Ph.D. program', *Research in Teaching English*, 22.

Bizzell, P. (1986) 'What happens when basic writers come to college?', *College English*, 37.

Bolter, J. D. (1991) *Writing Space: The Computer, Hypertext, and the History of Writing*, Hillsdale, NJ: Lawrence Erlbaum Associates.

Brodkey, L. (1989) 'On the subject of class and gender in "the literacy letters"', *College English*, 51.

Bruffee, K. (1984) 'Collaborative learning and the "Conversation of Mankind"', *College English*, 46.

Butler, W. M. and Kinneavy, J. L. (1991) 'The electronic discourse community: God, meet Donald Duck', *Focuses*, 4.

Charney, Davida (1994) 'The effect of hypertext on processes of reading and writing', in Cynthia L. Selfe and Susan Hilligoss (eds), *Literacy and Computers: The Complications of Teaching and Learning with Technology*, New York: Modern Language Association.

Clifford, J. (1991) 'The subject in discourse', in P. Harkin and J. Schilb (eds), *Contending With Words: Composition and Rhetoric in a Post-Modern Age*, New York: Modern Language Association.

Cook-Gumperz, J. (1986) 'Literacy and schooling: an unchanging equation?', in J. Cook Gumperz (ed.), *The Social Construction of Literacy*, Cambridge: Cambridge University Press.

Cooper, M. and Selfe, C. L. (1990) 'Computer conferences and learning: authority, resistance, and internally persuasive discourse', *College English*, 8.

DeWitt, S. (1997) 'Out there on the web: pedagogy and identity in the face of opposition', *Computers and Composition*, 14.

Faigley, L. (1992) *Fragments of Rationality: Postmodernity and the Subject of Composition*, Pittsburgh, PA: University of Pittsburgh Press.

Giroux, H. (1992) *Border Crossings: Cultural Workers and the Politics of Education*, New York: Routledge.

—— (1995) 'Who writes in a cultural studies class? or, Where is the pedagogy?', in K. Fitts and A. France (eds), *Left Margins: Cultural Studies and Composition Pedagogy*, Albany, NY: SUNY Press.

Graff, H. (1987) *Professing Literature: An Institutional History*, Chicago: University of Chicago Press.

Gramsci, A. (1971) *Selections from the Prison Notebooks*, ed. and trans. Quiten Hoare and Geoffrey Nowell Smith, New York: International.

Heath, S. B. (1983) *Ways with Words: Language, Lie and Work in Communities and Classrooms*, London: Cambridge University Press.

Janangelo, J. (1991) 'Technopower and technoppression: some abuses of power and control in computer-assisted writing environments', *Computers and Composition*, 9.

Jessup, E. (1991) 'Feminism and computers in composition instruction', in G. E. Hawisher and C. L. Selfe (eds), *Evolving Perspectives on Computers and Composition Studies: Questions for the 1990s*, Urbana, IL: National Council of Teachers of English.

Johnson-Eilola, J. (1993) 'Control and the cyborg: writing and being written in hypertext', *Journal of Advanced Composition*, 13.

Kaplan, N. (1991) 'Ideology, technology, and the future of writing instruction', in G. E. Hawisher and C. L. Selfe (eds), *Evolving Perspectives on Computers and Composition Studies: Questions for the 1990s*, Urbana, IL: National Council of Teachers of English.

Knoblauch, C. H. and Brannon, L. (1993) *Critical Teaching and the Idea of Literacy*, Portsmouth, NH: Boynton–Cook.

LeCourt, D. (1998) 'Critical pedagogy in the computer classroom: politicising the writing space', *Computers and Composition*, 15.

—— (1999) 'Writing (without) the body: gender and power in networked discussion groups', in P. Takayoshi and K. Blair (eds), *Feminist Cyberscapes*, Norwood, NJ: Ablex.

—— and Barnes, L. (1999) 'Writing multiplicity: hypertext and feminist textual politics', *Computers and Composition*, 16.

McLaren, P. (1995) *Critical Pedagogy and Predatory Culture*, London: Routledge.

Romano, S. (1999) 'On becoming a woman: pedagogies of the self', in G. E. Hawisher and C. L. Selfe (eds), *Passions, Pedagogies, and 21st Century Technologies*, Logan, UT: Utah State Univeristy Press, pp. 249–67.

Street, B. (1984) *Literacy Theory and Practice*, Cambridge: Cambridge University Press.

Sullivan, L. (1999) 'Wired women writing: towards a feminist theorization of hypertext', *Computers and Composition*, 16.

Takayoshi, P. (1994) 'Building new networks from the old: women's experiences with electronic communications', *Computers and Composition*, 11.

Taylor, T. (1997) 'The persistence of difference in networked classrooms: non-negotiable difference and the African-American student body', *Computers and Composition*, 14.

Trimbur, J. (1989) 'Consensus and difference in collaborative learning', *College English*, 51.

—— (1991) 'Literacy and the discourse of crisis', in R. Bullock and J. Trimbur (eds), *The Politics of Writing Instruction: Post-Secondary*, Portsmouth, NH: Boynton–Cook, pp. 277–96.

Villanueva, V. (1993) *Bootstraps: From an American Academic of Colour*, Urbana, IL: National Council of Teachers of English.

Wysocki, A.F. and Johnson-Eilola, J. (1999) 'Blinded by the letter: why are we using literacy as a metaphor for everything else?', in G. E. Hawisher and C. L. Selfe (eds), *Passions, Pedagogies, and 21st Century Technologies*, Logan, UT: Utah State University Press.

Chapter 6

Science beyond school

Representation or re-presentation?

Roy Hawkey

> I never let my schooling interfere with my education.
>
> (Mark Twain)

It may seem perverse, in a section about pedagogy that is aimed largely at education professionals, to include a chapter concerned with matters beyond the classroom. Yet, whether or not they are the best days of their lives, those spent in school comprise only about 10 per cent of UK citizens' lives. By coincidence, approximately 10 per cent of visitors to The Natural History Museum come in organised school groups (although this is much less than the total number of children, many of whom visit the Museum with their families at weekends and in holidays). Of course, the near equivalence of these figures has no real meaning, since they measure very different parameters. But they do serve to remind us that much learning of science – or, at least, the opportunity for doing so – takes place outside the formality of school and classroom. In any analysis of learning science it is important to consider the opportunities available to those beyond compulsory schooling. This applies not only to those 'outside' spatially but to those who are temporally removed from the reach of formal education.

Viewed from the outside, from the informal and post-compulsory sector, what is for many the straitjacket of the National Curriculum in England can appear rather as a supportive skeleton. Without a statutory framework, inherent assumptions cease to be valid and a fundamental reappraisal becomes possible, even essential. 'Back to basics' acquires new meaning, as the opportunity arises to evaluate not only issues concerning the role of ICT but the very nature of science itself and of science education. Whatever the context, in or out of school, learning science through ICT is primarily about learning, secondarily about science and only then about ICT: purpose, content, method.

It is easy to categorise science-learning provision on dimensions both of formal–informal and of real–virtual (see Figure 6.1) but this is likely to

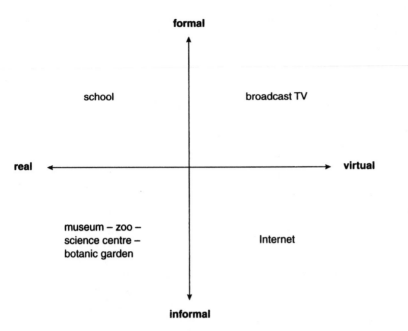

Figure 6.1 Persistent dichotomies or blurring the boundaries?

be, at best, simplistic and, more probably, obsolescent. We are entering an age where the relationship between formal and informal learning is rapidly and irrevocably changing. No longer is it a simple dichotomy, but more of a continuum that is moving increasingly towards identity. With distinctions between real and virtual learning environments also becoming less and less discrete, the *status quo* is certainly dynamic. Drawing upon a range of examples, this chapter will argue that the widespread availability of powerful ICT applications not only makes possible but rather *demands* a radical reappraisal of education in science.

ICT, SCIENCE, EDUCATION: ISSUES AT THE INTERFACE

It is possible (if simplistic) to differentiate into three groups those concerned with the role of ICT in the development of informal science education, according to their perspective on ICT. One group's focus is primarily on the technical aspects. Another regards ICT as a means of delivering the conventional public understanding of science messages more rapidly, more effectively and to a much wider audience: better delivery of unquestioned answers. The third regards ICT as a new opportunity to reconsider fundamental questions about what it means to be scientifically literate, about the nature of science and the relationships between practising scientists, their work and the public.

An actual exchange at a recent conference[1] provides a good example:

Q: The web gives fifteen different values for the melting-point of bismuth! How are students expected to cope with that?
A: How many values would you find in 1,000 books? And how long would it take to find them?

The initial question came from a teacher whose overriding concern was that his students could more readily access and recall the correct answer essential to pass an examination and achieve a good grade. The respondent (a librarian), while operating in broadly the same epistemological and pedagogic framework, was quick to highlight the variability of other secondary-source data. Her reply was, however, very different from that of the technophile, who would want to know which search engine was used. It differed also from my own reaction: I found myself thinking about the use and accuracy of measuring instruments, the adoption of particular scales – whether 0°C is the same as 273K – and so on, to errors of measurement, variation, chaos, objectivity, why melting- and boiling-points rather than freezing- and condensation-points, and so on?

While this chapter is not concerned with wholly technical questions – and will make some reference to novel approaches to conventional activities – its primary purposes fall into the third category, re-presenting the whole domain of the public understanding of science, rather than perceiving ICT as a delivery mechanism representing a particular establishment view.

The intimate association of ICT with science itself is hardly new. Yet, so rapid has been the development of ICT in science education that it is easy to forget that the World Wide Web began as a communications tool for research physicists at CERN in Geneva. Within the science research community it is certainly more ubiquitous than ever was the Bunsen burner, for long the icon of the school science laboratory. It is, perhaps, unfortunate that in schools, at least, the initial excitement generated by early applications of ICT in the learning of science – see, for example, Kahn (1985) and Stewart (1985) – was rapidly overtaken by the introduction of the National Curriculum. The different priorities that this brought about were certainly contributory factors in the subsequent reduction of creativity and innovation in this area.

Science, education and ICT are each beset by their own particular issues, but, in addition to their mutual interfaces (see Figure 6.2), they share a common problem. Each is fraught with a set of naïve and simplistic notions about the very nature of the domain, many – if not all – of which

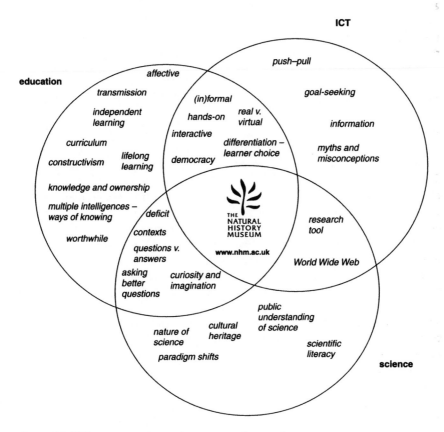

Figure 6.2 ICT, science, education: issues at the interface

are assumed to be canonical by pupils, parents and politicians alike (see Table 6.1).

To the uninitiated it may appear that

- *science* is a body of knowledge about the world and how it works, as discovered and revealed by experiments (predominantly in laboratories by middle-aged Western men wearing spectacles and white coats);
- *education* takes place in schools, and is principally the efficient and effective transfer of knowledge and understanding from teacher to student;
- *ICT* is a state-of-the-art means of delivering information on demand.

It is a series of timely coincidences, concerning each of these domains, which, more than ever before, makes it appropriate to challenge these

Table 6.1   Naïve notions of science, education and ICT

Science	Curriculum	Education	ICT
Body of knowledge	'Essential' part of scientific knowledge	Transmission (Assessment = checking deficit)	Efficient transfer mechanism

assumptions. The reader will perhaps be aware of the far from radical revision of the National Curriculum (DfEE 1999). Despite exponential growth in ICT applications and possibilities, this 'new' National Curriculum shows less imagination, and with less enthusiasm than was evident in the earlier establishment perspective presented in *Highways for Learning*. There the value of access to raw data to provide evidence for experimental and investigative use is highlighted (Shaw 1995: 14) even if the predominant focus is one of knowledge acquisition.

Within the science education community, there have been calls for a completely different philosophical stance to be adopted, and a number of alternative models have been proposed (see, for example, Millar and Osborne 1998). Interestingly, in the context of this chapter, there are parallel concerns among science communicators, including suggestions that the very phrase 'public understanding of science' be replaced with a more inclusive notion that relates more generally to scientific literacy (House of Lords 2000). Jenkins (1996) would certainly concur with any attempt to move away from the current and inappropriate model, one of identifying and rectifying a perceived cognitive deficit, to present science more as a quarry from which resources are extracted as required, rather than as a cathedral at which worship is expected.

Official publications in the United States – from the American Association for the Advancement of Science (AAAS 1993) – have proposed a similar reassessment of the direction in which to try to take public perceptions of science. They recommend a change in emphasis, from the impression of science as a series of unquestioned answers presented by the school curriculum to the reality of unanswered questions that form the essence of scientific research. There are official documents in the UK, too, that have recently begun to question more broadly many of the assumptions pertaining to education. Publication of *The Learning Age* (DfEE 1998) has begun to re-define the nature of informal education, 'away from the rigid, supply-side model of the past, and towards individual choice and responsibility for learning in a diversity of contexts' (Anderson 1999:19). It is rapidly becoming more acceptable to ask critical questions, such as:

- What is knowledge?
- What, in particular, is scientific knowledge?
- Who owns such knowledge?
- Can scientific ideas be presented as models or paradigms?
- Who decides what learning is worthwhile?

To a large extent, it is recognition of the educational power of ICT that has brought about this radical reassessment. The key to ICT in this context lies in its ability to democratise learning and to provide differentiation on demand. In moving away from a deficit model of the curriculum and towards independent learning, ICT has substantive echoes of lifelong learning. Many of these critical issues also mirror those of concern within the public understanding of science movement.

Not that this is new. Postman and Weingartner (1971) asked key questions about knowledge some thirty years ago:

> Consider, for example, where 'knowledge' comes from. It isn't just there in a book, waiting for someone to come along and 'learn' it. Knowledge is produced in response to questions. And new knowledge results from the asking of new questions; quite often new questions about old questions. Here is the point: once you have learned how to ask questions – relevant and substantial questions – you have learned how to learn and no one can keep you from learning whatever you want or need to know.

This 'subversive' theme was picked up by Kahn (1985) in what appeared to be a timely link between Kuhn's analysis of scientific progress by paradigm shifts and the then embryonic use of ICT in science education:

> We use them [computers] because they allow us to do things better than we could before. But for this same reason they are subversive; computers will bring about significant change in the way we teach and do science, they will challenge accepted ideas and alter hallowed methods of education.

BEYOND SCHOOL: LEARNING SCIENCE INFORMALLY

Science beyond school has both spatial and temporal dimensions. The former applies to those who are in formal education but are encountering material relating to science outside the framework and control of the school. The latter is equivalent to lifelong learning, used here to mean learning for its own sake throughout life, rather than any more vocational interpretation. Both groups, however, have access to informal science education in similar modes and media:

- museums, science centres, zoos and botanic gardens;
- books, magazines, newspapers and other printed materials;
- ICT, from broadcasting to the internet.

The UK has in recent years seen a proliferation of centres for informal hands-on or interactive science learning. A few of these, such as The Natural History Museum's *Earth Lab*, are aimed at adults, the majority at children and their families. They include both special galleries in major museums and also a variety of independent centres.

Not that they necessarily present a consistent or coherent view of science. Durant has highlighted the tendency of both museums and science centres to display different – but equally flawed – perspectives on the nature of science:

> The image of science that I find in most science centres is one of clear, elementary principles waiting to be discovered by anyone with sufficient child-like curiosity and adult patience to search them out. By contrast, the image of science that I find in most science museums . . . is one of sure and solid mastery of nature. In both cases, science itself emerges as a fixed body of knowledge and practice, more or less totally beyond either doubt or dispute.
>
> (Durant 1992)

Many of these centres for informal science now also have websites. Some of these present what is essentially only visitor information, some represent a virtual visit, while others have unique online resources. Some centres, especially in the USA, appear to use a different educational approach in the virtual world. Those of the American Museum of Natural History (www.amnh.org) and the Exploratorium (www.exploratorium.edu) – the original hands-on science centre itself in San Francisco – are of particular interest in this regard. The website of the Singapore Science Centre (www.sci-ctr.edu.sg/sciorg/sc_onnet.html) provides a valuable annotated reference list of such sites (other useful lists will be found at www.ase.org.uk, www.icom.org and www.big.uk.com).

A number of fundamental questions are inherent in the debates over learning in informal environments, such as museums:

- How can learners be engaged actively and constructively?
- How can emphasis be given to transferable skills rather than knowledge acquisition?

- How can alternative ways of knowing be encompassed?
- What is the contribution of the affective domain?

The Natural History Museum is the UK's national museum of natural history. Well known for its exhibitions and its prime position on the tourist agenda, it is also a world-renowned scientific research institute, incorporating research on the life and earth sciences, the envy of many a university. Significant for our present purpose, it was also one of the first to establish a website (www.nhm.ac.uk). Initial developments were largely ad hoc, but an underlying rationale evolved to encompass elements relating to ideas about science and about learning.

Although itself unique, The Natural History Museum has much in common with other museums. All museums – and zoos and botanic gardens – have a split focus: they have an introverted focus on the maintenance of their collections while simultaneously reaching out, sometimes extravagantly so, to engage the interest of the public. They sit not so much on the fence as uncomfortably on a tetrahedron, balancing concern for their collections with research, and with their roles as educators and visitor attractions in the leisure and tourism industry (see Figure 6.3).

Publicly funded museums have existed in the UK for longer than publicly funded schools – the British Museum as early as 1753, with universal primary schooling dating from the Education Act of 1870. However, the

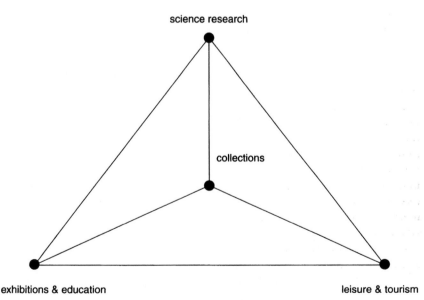

Figure 6.3 Relationships between the activities of a natural history museum

heyday of museums was very much the late Victorian era. The national museums of art and design (Victoria and Albert Museum), of technology and industry (Science Museum) and of the natural sciences (Natural History Museum) – all in London's South Kensington district – were established in this period, with an apparently straightforward educational mission. The knowledge of the time, under the guardianship of the museums' curators, was to be transmitted to a grateful public. Museums were seen, beyond their primary functions of conservation and curation, as a means of providing controlled access to knowledge. The attitude of the Victorian curators seems to have been, if the visitor did not understand, then it was the visitor's fault (Miles *et al.* 1982).

Museums rather missed out the twentieth century, or at least the first three-quarters of it. Very little changed for almost 100 years, until, in the 1970s, The Natural History Museum developed '*Human biology*', the first modern exhibition, which had a completely new perspective and emphasis. The educational needs of visitors as learners were considered; members of the public were even consulted, their interests and knowledge (or lack of it) taken into account. Exhibitions became vehicles for science communication, rather than simply for the display of museums' wares, and a variety of methods and a range of media were employed. These included the then 'state of the art' ICT, the BBC Microcomputer, with its 32k RAM and cassette-tape data storage system!

Such a quantum leap inevitably generated considerable controversy, but – with the benefit of hindsight – it is possible to identify two key issues of significance. First, although presented as an approach that kept the visitor in mind, the direction of subsequent developments rather tended to put more emphasis on matters such as 'storyline' and visitor flow. Exhibitions became, both conceptually and geographically, much more linear, and more overtly didactic. Second, with the arrival of the microcomputer and video recorder, audio–visual and multimedia 'interactives' threatened to supplant objects in museums. Ironically, the almost universal penetration of ICT is now enabling museums to reassert their primary roles of collecting and providing access to real objects – and in celebrating those aspects of the affective learning domain for which museums are uniquely advantaged. They are also more easily able to give intellectual freedom to visitors, empowering them to pose their own questions, and to find answers to them for themselves.

Today, centuries on, considerable debate continues as to how the educational role of museums is best interpreted. Government departments define the parameters from different perspectives. The Department for Education and Employment (DfEE) tends to regard museums as places where school students can enhance their test performance – and raise standards. It also displays a tendency to (mis)appropriate the notion of 'lifelong learning' so that its principal foci are utilitarian and economic, in relation to competitive needs for training and retraining for different types of employment. Responsibility for museums falls to the Department of Culture, Media and Sport (DCMS), which emphasises reliability as it anxiously sets performance targets for education, while uncertainty remains over exactly what to measure and how to measure it.

Whatever the political climate, there is undeniably an already extensive and continually expanding role for ICT to play in the learning of science in informal settings. This is not, however, to imply that ICT is the sole means of providing particular preferred outcomes. Other contexts, such as learning directly from objects in museums, may contribute to the realisation of many of these goals. However, one effect of these rapid developments in ICT has been to raise a series of issues that question many of our pedagogic assumptions.

These are best explored through a detailed examination of a particular example.

QUEST:[2] A CASE STUDY

Figure 6.4 shows the 'interactive' index of The Natural History Museum's website. The site contains a number of very different ICT applications, all intended to promote informal science learning, but for different audiences, with different learning intentions and employing different strategies:

- AntCast
- Dinosaur data files
- *Earth lab*
- Eclipse
- *Investigate*
- Science Casebook
- QUEST
- Walking with woodlice.

QUEST – Questioning, Understanding and Exploring Simulated Things – aims to provide opportunities for students online to

- explore natural objects;
- investigate in the manner of a scientific expert;
- discuss findings and their interpretation.

(QUEST can be found on the internet at: www.nhm.ac.uk/education/quest2/english/index.html)

QUEST itself declares that it matches the approaches taken by scientists in the Museum and the process of science as exemplified in school curricula.

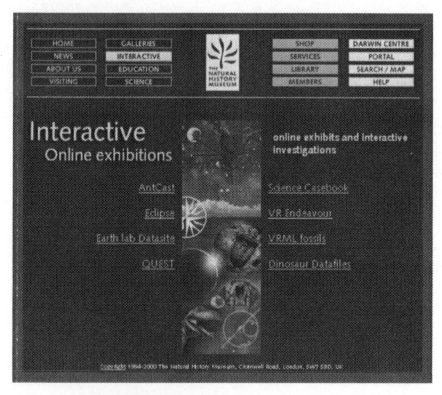

Figure 6.4 www.nhm.ac.uk/interactive/index.html
(© The National History Museum, London)

This it hopes to achieve by placing emphasis on

- first-hand enquiry;
- exploring and investigating;
- asking questions;
- methods and techniques.

Although QUEST is an innovative development, it was not conceived purely on the basis of functionality, but has a clear underlying educational philosophy and rationale. In many ways it appears to be the very antithesis of the conventional approaches taken by museums in providing access to objects and educational programmes (Hawkey 1999a). Its intended learning outcomes are clearly stated and relate to scientific exploration and investigation, to the internet itself and to the work of the Museum.

Although the provision of virtual tools for exploration of the virtual objects is essential for basic functionality, the significance in terms of

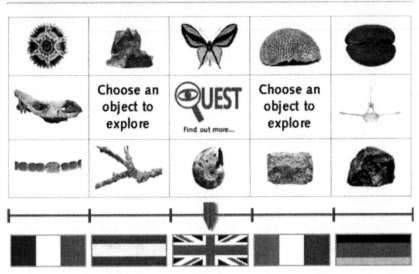

Figure 6.5 QUEST's opening screen
(© The National History Museum, London)

scientific methods lies in the nature of expert advice – more questions rather than answers – and, in the online notebook, to share findings and ideas.

The opening screen (see Figure 6.5) presents twelve disparate objects – rock, mineral, animal, plant, fossil, micro-organism – carefully chosen to represent not only the diversity of the natural world but the range of the Museum's scientific work. A selected object is then displayed full-screen, without supplementary information, not even an indication of scale. Tools selected from the visual menu can then be applied in turn (see Figure 6.6).

Any of the tools can be used, in any order. Application of the tools makes it possible for a student to build up her or his data set about each object, to interpret these data and to hazard inferences about them.

Most of the tools represent observation aids or measuring instruments, but three are significantly different. 'Ask a scientist' provides advice or prompts – further questions rather than answers – from an expert. The online notebook enables students to record their findings and thoughts and, crucially, to share those of others. Finally, the information page – accessible only from the notebook – gives background and further information, usually in a questioning style.

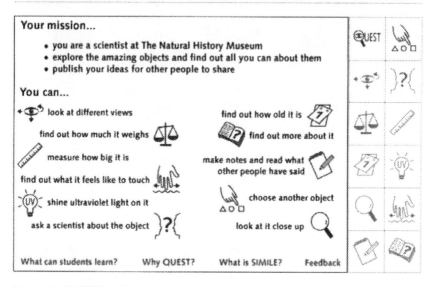

Figure 6.6 QUEST's available tools
(© The National History Museum, London)

Approaches to learning

Botanic gardens, zoos and museums rely heavily on the expert knowledge of keepers, curators and researchers for interpretation. In this respect, traditions in science and of natural history are not particularly different from those in other subjects. All of this – from notes to names – is the province of the expert. Similarly, in school science teaching, the predominant mode of discourse is the provision of expert knowledge and its transmission from teacher to student, a tradition reinforced by content-laden curricula. Underlying both situations are implicit assumptions, both epistemological and pedagogic, in which the hegemony, or power relationships, of teachers and curators and of their expert knowledge predominates.

   In contrast are approaches labelled 'constructivist'. There has been much work in school science in this area (see, for example, Driver *et al.* 1994), with the emphasis on the pedagogic implications. In the informal learning environment, however, the situation has been less clear. Hein (1995) has highlighted frequent confusion and contradiction over notions of constructivism. His model (see Figure 6.7) clearly distinguishes between perceptions of knowledge – from revealed truths to best-fit paradigms – and perspectives on learning – from *tabula rasa* to personal sense-making.

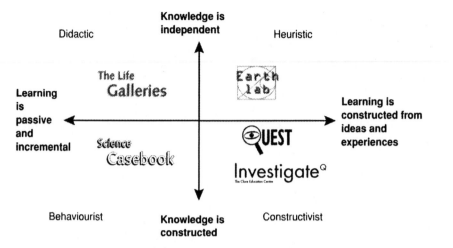

Figure 6.7 Hein's 1995 model applied to The Natural History Museum

From the outset, QUEST was designed to be constructivist on both of these dimensions, although it should be noted that Wild and Quinn (1998) have pointed out the importance of being cautious when applying labels such as this to multimedia products. Conventional strategies are more likely to follow Gagne's dictum (1986) that predetermined instructional goals are matched with artificially constructed learning events. QUEST aims to support different learning styles – by providing multiple paths for navigation allowing the learner to choose between them. It enables the learner to 'engage, explore and build', by providing information resources, deliberately facilitating cognitive processes and offering opportunity for 'scaffolded reflection' – an attempt at a coherent model of multimedia design.

Interactivity

During the last quarter of the twentieth century, museums and science centres embraced the microcomputer with considerable enthusiasm. Pearce (1998) suggests that there is an 'interactive continuum' which runs from 'pushing buttons and selecting choices' to 'touching, smelling, doing'. The implication is that computer-based interactives are *ipso facto* a good thing and, furthermore, that their role is to explain and illustrate. Indeed, as recently as 1998, voices from Naples to Nairobi were equating 'interactive' with electronic multimedia. Add to this the proliferation of hands-on science experiences – some of which incorporate ICT – and confusion and misconceptions abound (Hawkey 1999b). Caulton (1998) provides a useful working definition of an interactive museum exhibit, which can be readily extended to the virtual domain: 'A hands-on or interactive museum exhibit has clear educational objectives which encourage individuals or groups of people working together to understand real objects or phenomena through physical exploration which involves choice and initiative.' Key criteria, he asserts, certainly include those of physical interaction, clear learning objectives and a multiplicity of outcomes, depending on the visitor's individual explorations. Can this apply to ICT applications, without falsely introducing an inherent assumption that all computer multimedia are *ipso facto* interactive?

Although its interactions are clearly in the virtual realm, QUEST claims to be genuinely interactive, and, furthermore, that this makes it unlike many online science learning resources, which, lacking choice or feedback, are best described as 'operand' (Miles *et al.* 1982). When engaged in QUEST, students are involved in a series of active decision-making steps, such that the choice of routes using thousands of hyper-links is enormous. It is such mental activity – asking questions, collecting data, interpretative decision-making – leading to clearly defined learning outcomes that makes QUEST interactive. An additional layer of interactivity is provided by the exchange of ideas and information between students in the online notebook. Here, each contribution can be valued for its own sake, even if it is subsequently contradicted, and shows the potential for such sharing of ideas to lead to enhanced understanding.

Active learning

The Natural History Museum's education policy highlights active learning in terms both of learner participation and of the learner making his or her own sense of experiences. Emphasis in all activities, both real and virtual, is therefore given to observation and enquiry, to exploring and investigating. Teachers of science in the UK are very familiar with the notions of exploring and investigating, for they remain the basic tenets of a major element of the National Curriculum for science (DfEE 1999). The idea that the processes and methods of science should form an essential component of the school curriculum is, however, far from new. Darwin's champion, T. H. Huxley, was a strong advocate of the view that 'the true teaching of science consists, not merely of imparting the facts of science, but in habituating the pupil to observe for himself, to reason for himself on what he observes, and to check the conclusions at which he arrives by further observation or experiment' (Huxley 1875).

Many of these fundamental scientific processes are possible with museum objects and are reflected in QUEST: observing, measuring, identifying patterns, formulating and testing hypotheses, evaluating evidence, recording and communicating.

In QUEST, the 'Ask a scientist' function provides advice, encouragement or provocative questions from a specialist. Learners may expect expert knowledge, but instead find themselves being asked further questions. Learner-controlled exploration may begin to negate an innate preference for asking an expert over first-hand investigation (Hawkey and Clay 1999).

Exchange of views

QUEST assumes that learning prospers by asking questions and attempting to make sense of what is discovered. Testing ideas – against those of others and against further evidence – is a critical part of this process. So, although the 'expert' view is available, it is accessible only from the notebook and avoids simply presenting the 'right answer'. Emphasis on the processes of investigation and enquiry means that an officially sanctioned 'right answer' is certainly not given prominence. In some cases, no approved data are provided, and some objects are not named at all. One definite advantage of the virtual system is that it cannot be persuaded to become a mere transmitter of knowledge, unlike explainers in science centres or museums, who may 'view their function as being predominantly to provide information rather than stimulate conjecture' (Russell 1995).

In science there is often a complex mixture of evidence, interpretation, guesswork and assumption, yet this aspect – sharing findings, discussion and debate – is all too often absent from conventional learning resources. (It is rarely, if ever, included as a significant component of formal science education.) QUEST's powerful notebook function allows users to record their thoughts on the object, to share those of others and respond to them. This represents an exchange of views and ideas parallel to those of the scientific paper, poster or conference presentation.

Careful examination of students' comments in the online notebook suggests three broad categories:

- statements, suggestions or guesses
- observations, evidence and interpretations
- discussion and debate between learners.

(Examples of discussions can be found in Figure 6.8 and in Johns and Sanger 1998 and Hawkey 1998, 1999c, 1999d, 2000a.)

The 'right' answer can be obtained with only a few clicks of the mouse, but the challenge of discovery, of thinking, of communicating, seems to overcome this. Evidence of shared learning in such online dialogues abounds. We may speculate that it is the excitement of not knowing and

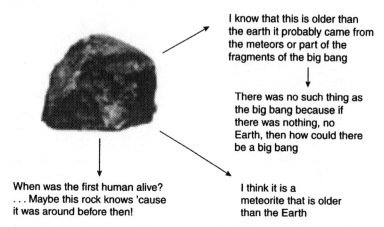

Figure 6.8 QUEST discussion in the online notebook

the vitality of the challenge of searching for solutions that provides stimulus and motivation for the scientists of the future.

There is much anecdotal evidence that knowing the name of a biological specimen actually inhibits close observation and enquiry. Adults, in particular, regard naming as a crucial outcome (often the only significant outcome) of an encounter with a natural object. Because of the potential limitation of students equating learning with the knowing of names, QUEST makes further information available only through the notebook. After offering an additional opportunity to carry out further tests this function gives background details, including a category or common name for the object and/or an image of the object in context.

Given that the Natural History Museum is one of the world's leading institutes for taxonomy and systematics, it is ironic that QUEST relegates the names of objects to such a lowly position. However, as Feynman (1989) has pointed out, knowing the name of something normally says more about people (the namers) than about things (the named). This is especially true for natural objects – rocks, minerals, fossils, animals, plants and micro-organisms – where the name is not a property of the object and can never be deduced by observation or experiment.

It has become axiomatic that it is in the nature of online learning resources to be either information-rich or goal- and reward-orientated. QUEST is neither of these, and yet it appears to be successful in providing a real representation of a field of scientific enquiry and in developing its philosophy, pedagogy and perspectives on science. Several issues merit further exploration. These include the earlier claim that ICT inherently facilitates democracy and differentiation – and whether the re-think instigated by the information revolution will catalyse change in the real world of informal science learning.

VALUE, ELATION, EVALUATION?

One suggested approach to evaluating ICT-based learning in science is the use of 'WISE' criteria (Hawkey 1999d). In attempting to avoid emotive responses – whether elation or fear – this requires activities to be worthwhile and interactive, and to be founded on appropriate models of both science and education. The QUEST case study has examined some of these factors, but further consideration may be useful.

'Worthwhile' is inevitably value-driven. What if Faraday had taken the advice to 'stop wasting time on worthless electricity' and had instead concentrated on improving the gas mantle? 'Worthwhile' is certainly not limited to the vocational or the utilitarian, but neither is it restricted to wholly academic or esoteric pursuits. Defining what is worthwhile is intimately associated with particular philosophical perspectives on education. For Peters (1966) education is essentially 'initiation into worthwhile activities'; for others, the essence of worthwhile educational activities is that they lead the learner to ask better, more appropriate, questions. For centuries, the predominant mode of formal education has been one of transmission. One of the consequences of ICT development has been to reassert the notion of independent learning at all levels. This shift of emphasis – from the transmission of facts to the asking of questions and from following a recipe to a research-led approach – can lead to learners becoming more autonomous (see Figure 6.9) (Hawkey 1993).

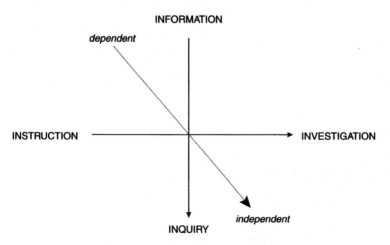

Figure 6.9 Shifting the balance from recipe to research

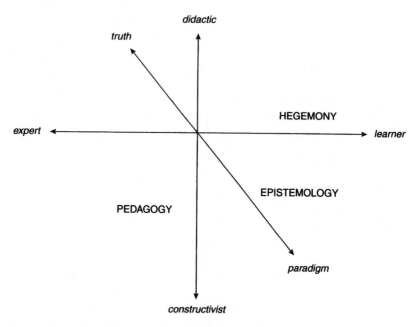

Figure 6.10 Dimensions of science knowledge: authority and learning styles

Critical in the information age is the ability to ask appropriate questions – and to seek one's own answers. Useful though it has proved, it can be argued that Hein's model (Figure 6.7) is deficient, and that it requires a third dimension (see Figure 6.10). To the nature of knowledge (epistemology) and perspectives on teaching and learning (pedagogy) should be added a dimension of power and authority (hegemony).

In this way, it is the capacity of ICT-based learning to empower learners – by providing choices that require decision making by the learners themselves – that is the most powerful. It is this element of self-determination that makes such learning potentially democratic and introduces a third type of differentiation.

Differentiation

Axiomatic in formal education is the notion that differentiation is a simple dichotomy: either the teacher selects the task to match the learner's ability, or learners respond to the same task by producing outcomes appropriate to their own knowledge and skills. Compare the task of writing a key to sort and classify a number of fossils from very different taxonomic groups with a similar task in which all the specimens are much more closely related, e.g. ammonites.

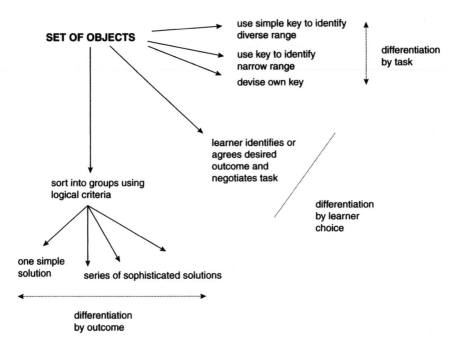

Figure 6.11 A third kind of differentiation

A major pedagogic contribution of ICT is that it facilitates an alternative way of approaching differentiation. It becomes possible to define differentiation by learner choice, a process that is both dynamic and iterative, and that has elements of both task and outcome differentiation (see Figure 6.11). Although Postlethwaite's analysis (1993) avoids such a simplistic approach, and does not consider ICT as such, it does include strategies such as mastery learning and flexible learning. Indeed, much of what can be considered to be almost inevitable elements of good website design underlies both his approach and traditional views of independent learning: 'In individualised work and with more relevant and socially conscious content, it may be possible to turn the tide against the "mass production" approach that has so much dominated science teaching' (Green 1976: 167).

The comparison between informal learning in museums and on the internet is readily drawn. This observation could as easily be made of websites as of museums: 'In contrast to classroom routines or film or television programs, museums offer the learner the opportunity to stop at will, to loiter and repeat, to ignore what does not stimulate, and to share what seems interesting' (Hein 1990: 126).

SITES FOR LEARNING

Papert (1980) presaged an image of the learning society long before it became an established perspective. His vision is of a computer culture that helps learners not only with their learning but with learning how to learn. The irony of Papert's view is that he sees ICT as humanising learning by permitting a more personal and less alienating relationship with knowledge. Furthermore, there will be 'complex interactions between new technologies and the recasting of subject matters' (Papert 1980: 184). What he doubts is that the social context for future learning will be the school.

Gardner (1991), a proponent of multiple intelligences, goes further. He believes that all children should attend an intensive museum programme rather than – or, at least, in addition to – school. Certainly, an analysis of learning in and out of school and with ICT speaks for itself (see Table 6.2).

Table 6.2 A comparison of learning in and out of school and with ICT

	School	*ICT*	*Beyond*
Why?	Convention and convenience; socialisation; imbue values, knowledge, traditions	Variety of learner-dependent motives	Learners desire to enhance and enrich their experience; learning for its own sake
What? (content)	Curriculum/deficit/ conformist	Provider content/ learner needs	Mission of provider/ desires of learner
Where? (location)	Classroom	Home/workplace/ informal setting/ classroom	Informal learning environment, e.g. museum/ home
Who decides?	Teacher (with students?)	Learner	Learner
Who learns?	Identifiable student cohort	Anyone with access	Anyone with motivation
When? (timetable)	M-F 09.00–16.00, term-time only	Any time	Varied, depending on provider and learner
How?	Organised sessions; may use 'push' technologies	On demand ('pull' technologies)	On demand (may include formal sessions, e.g. broadcasts or formal lectures)

Table 6.3 Changing perspectives on museum objects, ICT and visitors

	1880s	*1990s*	*2020?*
Museum objects	Exotic	Marginal	Essential
ICT	–	Alternative	Integral
Learners	Tolerated	Encouraged	Empowered

Source: Hawkey 2000b.

In recent years, museums (and other centres for informal science learning) have significantly changed their relationship with both visitors and objects. The future will see them continually re-evaluating their relationship with ICT (see Table 6.3), not only in the ways in which they make direct use of technology but in the impact that it has on the whole of their view of learning. More than facilitating the representation of science, advances in ICT have initiated and accelerated a fundamental reappraisal, a re-presentation from a very different perspective.

As Tawney (1979) pointed out at the dawn of the age of computer-based learning: 'The limitations of computer-assisted learning lie most probably in our ability to understand the learning process, and not in the ability to develop the technology appropriate to any learning situation.' There is undoubtedly an extensive and expanding role for ICT in the learning of science. As we have seen, one effect of this has been to raise a series of issues that question many of our pedagogic assumptions. This is not, however, to imply that ICT is the sole means of providing particular preferred outcomes. Other contexts, such as learning directly from objects in museums, may contribute to the realisation of many of these goals.

NOTES

1 M/SET 2000, International Conference on Mathematics, Science and Technology, San Diego, 5–8 February 2000.
2 QUEST was developed as part of the SIMILE project (Students In Museum Internet Learning Environments) with support from the Information Society Project Office of the European Commission.

REFERENCES

American Association for the Advancement of Science (AAAS) (1993) *Benchmarks for Scientific Literacy*, New York: Oxford University Press.
Anderson, D. (1999) *A Common Wealth: Museums in the Learning Age*, 2nd edn, London: Department of Culture, Media and Sport.

Caulton, T. (1998) *Hands-on Exhibitions*, London: Routledge.

DfEE (1998) *The Learning Age: A Renaissance for a New Britain*, London: DfEE.

—— (1999) *The National Curriculum*, London: QCA–HMSO.

Driver, R., Squires, A., Rushworth, P. and Wood-Robinson, V. (1994) *Making Sense of Secondary Science: Research into Children's Ideas*, London: Routledge.

Durant, J. (1992) 'Introduction', in J. Durant (ed.), *Museums and the Public Understanding of Science*, London: Science Museum.

Feynman, R. (1989) 'The making of a scientist', in *What Do You Care What Other People Think?*, London: Unwin Hyman .

Gagne, R. M. (1986) *The Conditions of Learning and Theory of Instruction*, 4th edn, London: Holt, Rinehart & Winston.

Gardner, H. (1991) *The Unschooled Mind: How Children Think and How Schools Should Teach*, New York: Basic Books.

Green, E. (1976) 'A new deal in science', in E. Green (ed.), *Towards Independent Learning in Science*, St Albans: Hart-Davis.

Hawkey, R. (1993) 'A mnemonic for the design of learning materials in science', *School Science Review* 74(268): 113–15.

—— (1998) 'Exploring and investigating on the Internet: virtually as good as the real thing?', *Journal of Education in Museums* 19: 16–19.

—— (1999a) 'Screen QUEST', *Museums Journal* 99(2): 31.

—— (1999b) 'Hands-on, minds on, interactive?', Paper presented at the Conference of the *European Collaborative for Science, Industry and Technology Exhibitions*, Prague, Czech Republic, 19–21 November.

—— (1999c) 'Learning from objects on-line: virtue and reality', *British Journal of Educational Technology* 30(1): 73–7.

—— (1999d) 'Exploring and investigating: Sc1 on-line', *Primary Science Review* 60: 4–6.

—— (2000a) 'Real education from virtual objects: active learning in science on-line', in R. Robson (ed.), *Proceedings of M/SET 2000*, Charlotte: Association for the Advancement of Computing in Education, pp. 202–6.

—— (2000b) 'Myths and models: making meaning in the modern museum', Paper presented at the Conference *Nature's Treasurehouses?*, London, 4–8 April.

—— and Clay, J. (1999) 'Science in context: changes in scientific perception from primary school to secondary school', *Education 3–13* 27(2): 27–35.

Hein, G. (1995) 'The constructivist museum', *Journal of Education in Museums* 16: 21–3.

Hein, H. (1990) *the exploratorium: The Museum as Laboratory*, Washington, DC: Smithsonian Institution Press.

House of Lords (2000) *Science and Society*, Third Report of the Select Committee on Science and Technology, London: Stationery Office.

Huxley, T. H. (1875) Evidence included in *Report of the Royal Commission on Scientific Instruction and the Advancement of Science* (The Devonshire Report).

Jenkins, E. W. (1996) 'Scientific literacy: a functional construct', in D. Baker, J. Clay and C. Fox (eds), *Challenging Ways of Knowing: In English, Maths and Science*, Basingstoke: Falmer Press.

Johns, N. and Sanger, J. (1998) *Evaluation of Educational Museum Web Sites: Report*, Norwich: Research Centre, City College.

Kahn, B. (1985) *Computers and Science: Using Computers for Learning and Teaching*, Cambridge: Cambridge University Press.

Miles, R. S., Alt, M. B., Gosling, D. C., Lewis, B. N. and Tout, A. F. (1982) *The Design of Educational Exhibits*, London: George Allen & Unwin.

Millar, R. and Osborne, J. (eds) (1998) *Beyond 2000: Science Education for the Future*, London: King's College.

Papert, S. (1980) *Mindstorms: Children, Computers and Powerful Ideas*, Brighton: Harvester Press.

Pearce, J. (1998) *Centres for Curiosity and Imagination*, London: Calouste Gulbenkian Foundation.

Peters, R. S. (1966) *Ethics and Education*, London: Allen & Unwin.

Postlethwaite, K. (1993) *Differentiated Science Teaching*, Buckingham: Open University Press.

Postman, N. and Weingartner, C. (1971) *Teaching as a Subversive Activity*, Harmondsworth: Penguin Books.

Russell, T. (1995) 'Collaborative evaluation studies between the University of Liverpool and the National Museums and Galleries on Merseyside', in P. Sudbury and T. Russell (eds), *Evaluation of Museum and Gallery Displays*, Liverpool: University Press.

Shaw, M. (ed.) (1995) *Highways for Learning*, Coventry: National Council for Educational Technology.

Stewart, J. (ed.) (1985) *Exploring Primary Science With Microcomputers*, London: National Council for Educational Technology.

Tawney, D. A. (1979) 'CAL and learning', in D. A. Tawney (ed.), *Learning Through Computers*, London: Macmillan, p. 109.

Wild, M. and Quinn, C. (1998) 'Implications of educational theory for the design of instructional multimedia', *British Journal of Educational Technology* 29(1): 73–82.

Part III

ICT and the curriculum

Chapter 7

Analogue clock/digital display
Continuity and change in debates about literacy, technology and English

Viv Ellis

Let me begin with a story that will illustrate some of the themes of this chapter. It is the story of my introduction both to computers and to the teaching of English, which occurred simultaneously in the mid-1980s at a state university in the Pacific northwest. As a teaching assistant, I was assigned three sections of freshman composition – the writing courses required of most first-year undergraduates – two of which were 'computer-assisted'. This meant that the class was to be taught in the computer laboratory, a traditional university seminar room now liberally furnished with Apple IIe computers donated by the largest local employer, the Boeing Corporation. The only expectations were that all the writing produced by the students would be word-processed and that we would make as much use as possible of the computers during class time. I had never used a computer before and, at first, I did not understand anything about these 'magic typewriters'.

The writing that my students produced was largely drafted in the pages of their spiral-bound writing journals – another important introduction for me – and then quickly transcribed during class time onto the word processor. As far as I recall, none of the students had a computer at home and time at the keyboard was at a premium during the hour booked for our class three times a week. Consequently, their assignments were well presented and the spelling was usually accurate. Indeed, students who were worried about their spelling, punctuation or sentence construction could opt to participate in the evaluation of a piece of software designed to improve these areas through a series of drill-and-practice routines. At the end of the semester, these students' scores, on the standardised tests helpfully provided by the software manufacturer, had gone through the roof. I received letters of thanks from parents who had been given the good news. Unfortunately, these families were to be disappointed by end-of-semester grades when the apparent gains in accuracy on the standardised tests were not carried over into the students' own writing.

At the same time, I occasionally found myself working for a professor of literature who was using computers to produce what he hoped would be the definitive edition of a Renaissance text. In the centre of the building that housed the English department, there was a highly secure, windowless, air-conditioned research centre. Inside, whirring and humming, was an enormous IBM mainframe computer. The room looked very much like the nuclear command centre of my imagination, with a small group of workers silently tapping away at keyboards. In fact, this poor machine was collating the different editions of the text and producing a detailed concordance. The research assistant 'workers' were turning the emerging document into camera-ready copy. The result was published at the end of the 1980s as a large gold-embossed volume by a major university press and it was launched at the Bodleian Library.

The next time that computers came to my attention I was a secondary-school English teacher in the West Midlands in 1991 when a student asked me if he could put a disk containing a multimedia text into his folder of GCSE English coursework. Using an Acorn computer, Longman's *Magpie*, and working during his lunch breaks, he had produced a hypertext about his beloved Aston Villa FC that incorporated sound and visual images. My answer to his question, after consulting with the examinations board, was 'no', but we eventually reached a compromise whereby a dismembered version of his work was printed off – without the sound and fury that signified a great deal – accompanied by a hand-written 'rationale'. This was good 'informative writing', but it wasn't anything like his original.

There are a number of reasons why I chose to begin with this extended personal anecdote (although I believe that, as a whole, it foregrounds a number of important issues). One is to show that there is a history of using digital technologies within the area of the curriculum described as English that goes back at least twenty-five years, and probably more if we include the efforts of the computer-aided instructors of the 1950s and 1960s. This isn't a new phenomenon. A second reason is to show the variations in use and integration of the technologies in education in the USA and the UK arising from differences in political and economic context and the resulting technological infrastructures. There is no reason to think that the priorities of those involved in English education in each of the anglophone countries will be identical, nor that they will share conceptions of the subject and 'appropriate' technologies. Third, that far from challenging the dominant ideologies of an education in the subject English, the technologies have been used in an attempt to make the subject's 'delivery' more efficient, effective and, perhaps, enjoyably attractive. Indeed, Richard Lanham (1993: 106) suggested that digital technologies would 'allow us to teach the classical canon with more understanding and zest than ever before'. And, finally, a platitude: the literacy practices of young people outside school are not necessarily the same as those of school, and the English classroom may not reflect or draw upon what students are doing elsewhere in their literate lives. Nevertheless, it is usually proposed that 'good English' makes connections between students' lived experiences and the curriculum (even if just as a 'bridge' to the canon or a nod towards vocationalism). Yet I would assert that most English teachers rarely plan opportunities to use or develop the knowledge, skills and understandings practised at home or in 'extra-curricular' digital literacy. These will be recurrent themes in what follows.

This chapter, then, explores some of the debates concerning literacy, technology and the subject English, principally in the context of the school and drawing upon research and scholarship from the UK, the USA, Canada and Australia. It reflects upon the ways in which the incorporation or integration of digital technologies in English and English teaching may render both subject to change. I then consider two specific examples of new opportunities and challenges to the subject presented by 'literacy technologies', before finally discussing a framework for thinking and teaching about English and ICT. Throughout, the term 'digital technologies' will be used to distinguish computers and their peripherals, networks and communications systems – the focus of this volume – from the older media technologies also included in the English and Welsh definitions of ICT (DfEE 1998a).

STORIES ABOUT THE FUTURE OF ENGLISH

Technology has long been one factor in debates about the future of English and English teaching although, of course, there have been and continue to be many others. For example, the relative importance of students' explicit knowledge of language structures – or, to use the current UK mantra, their knowledge of word, sentence and text-level grammar – and how this knowledge should be developed has been a continuous debate. The need for a prescribed canon of literary texts and what criteria to use in their selection has been another. Indeed, the maintenance of a relatively stable curriculum of aesthetic valuing, cultural heritage and the development of taste in 'good' books is an indication of the continuing success of literary studies as part of school English. The role of English in the aesthetic and expressive development of individual identities is another function of the subject that many have valued highly. Recent research (Peel and Hargreaves 1995; Goodwyn and Findlay 1999) would seem to indicate that many English teachers, both in the UK and in Australia, continue to subscribe to a 'personal growth' model of English over other paradigms, still based on opportunities for creative expression, reflection and exposure to suitable texts.[1] What Peel and Hargreaves (1995: 46) described as 'the multiplicity of roles for the subject' has led to a set of highly complex debates in which digital technologies have become implicated.

The use of drill-and-practice software to develop knowledge of language structures and 'secretarial' accuracy in writing, for example, has a very long history. In the mid-1980s I used software that accompanied the textbook adopted by my department for an undergraduate writing course. I found that the gains in accuracy and apparent knowledge my students demonstrated on the standardised tests were not carried over into their own writing and that this led to disappointment and confusion. There is a body of research from the USA that confirms my anecdotal experience (see, for example, Alderman *et al.* 1978; Hillocks 1986). Drill-and-practice software, now enhanced with stereo sound and colourful animation, has been morphed into the integrated learning systems (ILS) favoured by some UK schools in the drive to raise standards of functional literacy and reach national testing targets. Longman's *Tomorrow's Promise* and Research Machines' *Success Maker* are the two most popular packages that some primary and secondary schools have chosen to adopt, in some cases extracting students from English lessons in order to work with the ILS. Although extremely expensive (recently, one school I work with spent £60,000 equipping themselves with ILS hardware and software), photographs of children wired-up to teaching machines continue to be a powerful marketing tool for schools forced to compete with each other, and any gains that children make on standardised tests continue to be popular with parents. The evaluation of ILS software by the British Education and Communications Technology Agency (BECTA) was equivocal as to its effectiveness, to say the least (Wood 1998).

CD-ROM companions to Shakespeare's plays are a good example of digital technologies being used to support the traditional literary studies' aspects of school English. Blending the text of the play with notes on themes, characterisation and variations in language use, and the short video and audio extracts from the BBC's productions, these CD-ROMs have been held up as dynamic and interactive teaching aids. CD-ROM publishers have also produced complete editions of (out-of-copyright) poets' works on disk, the work of whole poetic movements and even attempts to capture the 'best' of English poetry. These disks often have editorial notes that are aimed at the school market and a search facility that enables the user to look for poetry with similar semantic fields or related themes. The internet is also full of out-of-copyright literature that can be downloaded, cut-and-pasted or bookmarked in readiness for classroom work. There are also many websites which offer resources for the study of literary texts, often based at North American universities, and, occasionally, academics offer to answer questions online via e-mail about their literary specialism or even in-role as a character. How long they will be able to keep this up as more students get access to e-mail is an interesting question.

The role of digital technologies in the personal growth model of English is more complex. Sometimes it appears that the teachers who value this model are those most resistant to or ambivalent about the place of technology in English. Andrews (2000: 23) points to the 'subversive,

humanities-based, liberal and book-dominated culture of English (the orthodoxy since the 1920s)' as one factor in what he sees as the slowness of
English teachers as a whole 'to take up the challenge of computers'.
Goodwyn, *et al.* (1997: 55–6) speculate that maybe nearly half of UK
English teachers are reluctant to embrace digital technologies either because
they are 'fearful' or 'unresolved' and feel a 'moving away' from the core
values of English. Conversely, there is a tradition of viewing the rise of
digital technologies as an opportunity for students to write more effectively, to publish their writing more widely and to write in the same space
as established authors. The successful 'Kids on the net' writing project is
a good example of this kind of work which continues the tradition of
personal growth, of aesthetic and expressive development through writing
in traditional print genre – but now published on the World Wide Web
(Kids on the net can be found at: http: //www. trace.ntu.ac.uk/kotn/
gokids.htm).

The ways in which the technologies are used is, of course, the key
question. In and of themselves they do not make existing English practice any better or any worse than it was before their introduction.
CD-ROM Shakespeare can be used to praise Shakespeare and to bury
him, or it can be used to enliven the ways his plays are read, to demonstrate their status as performed physical, visual and auditory texts. Digitised
literature from the Web can be used simply to make quotation easier in
word-processed academic essays or to enable students to 'write back' (Kress
1995), to make the kind of 'digital' textual interventions described by
Goodwyn (Goodwyn 2000b) familiar to those English teachers who have
already been working within the approaches documented by Pope (1994).
ILS can be used to replace interactions with books and other readers and
writers for whole classes of children or to supplement the interventions
of teachers and offer motivating activities and useful feedback for some
children at specific points in their learning. Presentational software like
Microsoft's *Powerpoint* will not in itself make students' oral presentations
more effective or worthy of higher grades. Indeed, it presents the speakers/
writers with a whole new set of complex textual demands that make the
task potentially much more difficult. The use of word processors and
the supposed benefits they offer writers and teachers, through the apparent
'provisionality' of text on-screen, is another very old debate. Goodwyn
(2000a: 15) offers one definition of provisionality as 'an ongoing dialogue
between writer (student) and reader (teacher) about improvability'. Again,
it is important to recognise that the perceived provisionality of text on-
screen is not a given: it can also be perceived as stable and fixed. As
Jeanette Harris pointed out (1985: 330), and as teachers of writing worldwide have surely come to recognise, 'word processing does not, in and
of itself, encourage student writers to revise more extensively'.

Models and metaphors

All of the above examples of the use of digital technologies in English are essentially continuations of mainstream traditions of English teaching. The technologies are advanced as offering more effective, efficient, motivating and attractive possibilities for students and teachers. The metaphor of the 'analogue clock' can be used to represent this approach to ICT, literacy and the subject English. The 'clock' is significant in that, for many UK readers, it will refer to the clock of the National Literacy Strategy and the rise of the Literacy Hour in primary schools (DfEE 1998b). This framework prescribes subject content in terms of 'literacy' (functional skills, familiarity with culturally important genres, knowledge of grammatical structures, etc.) and a teaching methodology that divides the recommended hour-long daily lesson into blocks of time with a particular teaching focus. Many have commented on the limited view of literacy presented by the framework and what they see as the restrictive nature of the methodology (see, for example, Cox 1999). Nevertheless, it is consistent with one tradition of English teaching in the primary school and has gained support from primary teachers. The strategy itself is clearly related to national targets for improvements in test results by students aged 10–11.

'Clock' is also meant to suggest traditional chronologies, both in terms of literary history, with its canon of culturally important 'classics', and in terms of text structures that are in one sense chronological or linear, based on conventional narrative or logical argument. These are aspects of traditional (and, in England, statutorily supported) constructions of English as a subject. 'Analogue' is intended to suggest that the aims and purposes of this approach to English can be achieved without the use of the digital. The process may not be as effective, efficient or enjoyable, and the products may not be as attractive, but the learning outcomes may still be the same.

However, there are also strands in the debate around technology and English teaching that propose new dimensions to the English curriculum, additions to the subject knowledge content and adjustments that should be made to existing constructions of the subject. An important precedent has been the gradual inclusion of media education in the school English curriculum in most anglophone countries – with its attention to media languages, institutions, audiences and means of production – as well as the development of media studies as a discrete subject. Goodwyn (2000b), for example, suggests that media education has changed the nature of literary studies within the English curriculum and has resulted in increased emphasis on psychological approaches and theories of representation. There is the possibility that there will be new elements to established school subjects such as English, and that the established subjects themselves may be subject to reconfiguration. The degree to which subjects can and will change is something with which other of the contributions to this volume are concerned.

However, the strand of the debate that proposes change and new content is sometimes marked by the discourse of technological determinism. We are told that this or that will necessarily happen simply because particular technologies make it a possibility. For example, it is frequently asserted that writing is becoming more like speech because of the prevalence of e-mail communication (see, for example, Andrews 2000: 27) or that e-mail has created a new communications genre (see, for example, Tweddle *et al.* 1997: 35). Doesn't this depend on the context for the communication, its audience, topic and purpose? Many e-mails, I am sure, are situated in the established genre of the memorandum, and the asynchronous nature of e-mail makes it possible (and often highly desirable) to carefully craft a message. I am not convinced that e-mail (a means of communication) is a good example of a distinctive consequent change in discourse or genre. This description is perhaps more appropriate when applied to synchronous computer-mediated communication such as internet relay chat (IRC).

Similarly, are we certain that there has been a movement from 'linearity to collage' in written texts (Stannard 1997: 9) as a result of hypertext technology? The most common form of hypertext organisation on the internet appears to be extremely hierarchical and sequential. Are we certain that digital technologies will 'entrench visual modes of communication as a rival to language' (Kress 1998: 55)? Kress claims that the growing importance of visual modes of representation and the efficiency of visual images at conveying 'dense information' in print genre are phenomena that are both mirrored in and 'entrenched' by the 'exponential expansion of the potentials of electronic technologies' (*ibid.*).[2] I will return to these questions later.

This approach to ICT, literacy and English we may characterise with the metaphor of the 'digital display'. 'Display' recalls Kress's use of the word to explain a change in textual organisation away from what he describes as the traditional linear virtues of 'narrative' to an altogether different relationship between elements of text that may be visual or verbal (*ibid.*: 72). Burbules (1998: 107) also describes a similar shift in textual organisation as the movement from 'outline and syllogism' (logical structures inherited from the classical rhetorical tradition) to 'bricolage and juxtaposition', in which readers are invited to make multiple interpretations of discrete textual elements that may be in an ironic relation to one another. According to Kress and Burbules, these are distinctive and characteristic features of digital hypertexts. Digital technologies allow high-culture texts and (to use Kress's description) 'mundane texts' to occupy the same space.

'Digital' is meant to indicate a view of text that is provisional and fluid, more readily open to textual interventions by readers, somehow more democratic and more innovative. 'Digital' has also become a high-status adjective in the discourses of education, technology and consumer culture, one that connotes superior performance and greater complexity. We are positioned within these discourses to prefer the digital without question – *if we can afford it*. The metaphor of 'digital display' applied to literacy and the English curriculum suggests the increased importance of the screen over that of the page, new forms of text and communicative practices, and the possibility of new, more critical, relationships between readers and writers. It should also heighten our awareness of the socio-economic context in which any changes or shifts are taking place.

Neither of these metaphors, of course, is entirely 'watertight'. However, they do characterise the dichotomous construction of literacy and technology in relation to the subject English. Perhaps, as the authors of *Digital Rhetorics* (Lankshear *et al.* 1997) suggest, the contradictions apparent in much of the thinking about digital technologies, literacy and English are because we as English teachers may seem to know what technologies we want or reject – and those we favour and those we don't – but we don't have such simple or powerful agreements about the kinds of literacy we think are important or the important developments in English as a subject. Digital technologies are often used to support and develop the 'analogue clock' construction of English; the 'digital display' is, at the moment, a contested model of literacy in which meanings are often realised and sense established in relation to notional 'analogue' values. The 'digital display' may come to be fully realised in the literacy practices of the home (the development of home pages, participation in online role playing and IRC, and console games, etc.) which then receive attention in schools, but the established organisation of compulsory schooling and national testing, and the political imperatives that drive educational reform, are such that English classrooms are still organised around the ticking and chiming of the clock.

CHANGING THE SUBJECT?

In this section I look very briefly at three instances of curriculum development in English and digital technologies, all of which have taken or are taking place as a result of political reforms. The first is the current UK initiative to develop all serving and pre-service teachers' ICT capability in subject teaching. For all those involved in initial teacher education, like myself, this means working with the *Initial Teacher Training National Curriculum (ITT NC) for the Use of ICT in Subject Teaching* (DfEE 1998a). Teachers already working in schools will also be expected to demonstrate the same standards expressed as 'expected outcomes' after a course of in-service training funded by the UK National Lottery and its New Opportunities Fund (NOF). To assist teacher educators, serving teachers and their

NOF trainers, the Teacher Training Agency has produced a series of exemplification materials to show how these standards or outcomes may be met in a variety of subjects. Among the first to appear were the secondary English materials (TTA 1999).

The document gives a series of 'need to know' statements that all secondary English trainees must demonstrate in relation to the contribution of ICT to children's learning in English (TTA 1999: 4). They range from 'enhancing and developing pupils' reading and writing' – by, for example, newsroom simulations and searching the internet – and 'supporting and enhancing the study of literary texts' through to 'allowing literacy skills to be extended beyond [the] reading and writing of chronological and linear texts to multi-layered, multi-authored, multimedia texts' (*ibid.*: 4). Yet in the new pupils' National Curriculum Programmes of Study for English, there is scant mention of digital technologies across the three attainment targets of speaking and listening, reading and writing. Digital technologies do not feature in the programmes for writing other than as an injunction that 'pupils should be taught to . . . plan, redraft and proofread their work on paper and on screen' (QCA–DfEE 1999: 37). There is certainly no recommendation that children should be taught how to compose 'multi-layered, multi-authored, multimedia texts'. In the programmes for reading, some attention is given to the selection and evaluation of 'ICT-based information texts' (*ibid.*: 33). In speaking and listening, there is one reference to the development of English as a language which should include 'the impact of electronic communication on written language' (*ibid.*: 32).[3] In addition, there are few possibilities for the inclusion of digital technologies in the proliferating system of national testing that accompanies the statutory curriculum. The dominance of 'pen and paper' terminal examinations seems assured, at least in the short term.

It would seem, then, that there are some aspects of the *ITT NC for the Use of ICT in Subject Teaching* (and the associated 'expected outcomes' for serving teachers) that will develop competences which English teachers will rarely have opportunities to demonstrate in a curriculum dominated by the twin ideas of coverage and testing.

The second example comes from Australia where the states of Victoria and Queensland have, over the last few years, implemented new English syllabus documents for the final years of secondary-school education. The Victorian Certificate of Education Literature Study Design and the Queensland Year 12 Literature Extension Syllabus have, to a degree, engaged teachers in a reconstruction of English and literary study. In a suggested course structure of a Queensland syllabus, the following activities are offered as exemplars: 'comparisons of hypertext reading logs; rewritings in the form of "genre busting" and complex transformations' (Board of Secondary School Studies 1997; cited in Corcoran and Beavis 1998: 2). In one school's response to the Queensland syllabus, presented by Corcoran and Beavis at the NCTE International Conference in 1998, a unit of work had the following focal points:

• Examining how computers and computer-mediated communication have changed the way we think and write.
• Visiting a range of sites on the Internet, 'reading' examples of hypertext and the on-line theoretical discussions on hypertext.
• Reading, writing and discussing hypertext as a 'new' genre.
• Rewriting (in groups) Ray Misson's meta-narrative, *Will and Jane*, as hypertext.

(Kelvin Grove High School; cited in Corcoran
and Beavis 1998: 25)

The assigned coursework for this unit was 'a complex transformation of a self-selected print text into an independently negotiated form of hypertext' (*ibid.*).

There are at least two major differences between the first example from the UK and this one. The first is that, far from being tokenistic inclusions in an essentially stable and prescribed English–literary studies curriculum, these explorations of computer-mediated communication and digital text arise out of a reconfiguration of the subject's epistemological boundaries and discourse. This reconfiguration was undertaken by a particular English department and stimulated and made legitimate by state-wide curriculum reform. The Victorian definition of literature is particularly interesting: 'what is considered literature is subject to shifting attitudes, tastes and social conditions. Accordingly the study encompasses works that vary in cultural origin, genre, medium and world view, and includes classical and popular, traditional and modern literature' (Corcoran and Beavis 1998: 2). This is a definition – within a curriculum structure offering some flexibility and options – that makes it possible for English teachers to go in the directions taken by those at Kelvin Grove High, if they so choose. It is a 'digital' definition in that it allows for fluidity, for the broad distribution and juxtaposition of texts – assembling an interrelated fabric that is not governed by a single chronology or authoritative history.

Second, at the time of these curriculum developments in both Queensland and Victoria, the systems of assessment and testing had at least significant proportions of 'decentralised' portfolio or coursework school-based assessment. Although this has recently changed significantly in Victoria (with a familiar shift to less school-based assessment), efforts have been made to maintain the principles of the course and the definition of 'literature' remains the same.

The third example comes from the Atlantic provinces of Canada where, once again, there has been a shift in the English curriculum for the later years of the secondary-education phase. In 'Technology and change in

Atlantic Canada's new Secondary English Language Arts Curriculum', Barrell (1999: 233–4) outlines a new curriculum framework that specifies three significant expectations to be made of 'literate' secondary students: information literacy, media literacy and visual literacy. This is not to say that these aspects or dimensions of literacy were never acknowledged and developed prior to the new framework, just that they are now given a greater and more explicit importance, and so appear almost as 'new' content areas. The framework makes the fundamental assumption that words now 'share space' with visual images and non-verbal sounds, suggesting a characteristically 'digital' definition of text.

It also recognises the importance of computer-mediated communication (CMC) in the development of students' subject knowledge, and teachers are recommended to encourage students to enrol in chat rooms, newsgroups and other forms of CMC in order both to undertake 'research' and to learn by forming new relationships with experts and peers (*ibid.*: 234). If these expectations are realised in the classroom, then a fundamental difference will be apparent in the approaches to CMC in Canada and the UK. In the UK, there is still considerable fear and suspicion about children communicating with others outside the physical boundaries of the school, and students and parents are often asked to sign 'contracts' which forbid the use of certain forms of CMC and access to areas of the World Wide Web in school. The commonest items of display I have observed during recent visits to computer classrooms in the UK are variations on 'No chat rooms'.

These three examples cannot, of course, be fully representative of the state of digital technologies in English as a subject. The Canadian and Australian examples cover only a specific age-range and were developed regionally rather than nationally. The curriculum frameworks have different status and the disciplinary boundaries of the subjects are also rather different: the Australian examples are from literature curricula and the Canadian example from English language arts/communication. The political and economic context from which each has emerged is also very different, as are the technological infrastructures. The relatively greater emphasis on the use of CMC in North America, for example, may have something to do with the long tradition of free local telephone calls. Nevertheless, these examples are instances of changes to subjects called English/literary studies/communication in which digital technologies are implicated, whether this is the significant change found in the Atlantic Canada Secondary English Language Arts Curriculum or the relatively minor accommodations found in the National Curriculum in England.

There are, of course, contradictions and complications inherent in each of the instances I have discussed. For example, in England and Wales, the students' *National Curriculum for English* (and its associated testing arrangements) and the *ITT NC for the Use of ICT in Subject Teaching* (and the related 'expected outcomes' for serving teachers) seem to have very different approaches to digital technologies and English. In all three, issues of access to the technologies are not fully addressed, and the technology can also appear as ideologically neutral or value-free. This is something that particularly concerns Barrell (1999) when outlining a technologically-saturated English Language Arts Curriculum for students from families who may have been made redundant from the great agricultural and fishing industries of Atlantic Canada by technological advances in productivity (*ibid.*: 237). He is particularly concerned about the relationship between literacy, technology and social justice — and the vital role of teacher education:

> As world cultures, pushed by superimposed technological imperatives, succumb to homogeneity; as trans-national companies, dependent on a constantly expanding market place, gain greater control over government decision-making worldwide; as public expression is enveloped by the synergy of media giants; and as the division between the rich and the poor of the planet widens, it is crucial to reconsider and debate what is to be expected of future teachers of English.
>
> (*Ibid.*: 246)

The need for English teachers to 'pay attention' to technology in literacy pedagogy has been made strongly by Cynthia Selfe. Arguing that we should not take technology for granted or consider it merely as a tool, Selfe proposes that technology must be the 'business' of the teacher of English if we are to confront the challenges of the 'digital divide' and avoid replicating familiar patterns of illiteracy (Selfe 1999: 431). An approach to English teaching consistent with a familiar critical literacy pedagogy is proposed whereby students are encouraged to reflect on the institutional aspects of text, ideology and means of production. Parallels with the traditional aims of media education curricula are obvious, although it is becoming clear that digital technologies also present challenges for the received wisdom on this subject (Sefton-Green 1999: 34).

The fragmentation of English as a subject — or the merging of English with other subjects — is often discussed. Lanham (1993: 11–14) speculated that 'digital equivalency' will lead finally to 'a new rhetoric of the arts'. Goodwyn (2000b) suggests the blending of ICT and media studies in the study of new texts and communicative practices. The authors of *English for Tomorrow* also suggest that English must learn from media studies and offer an interesting diagrammatic representation in which English, music and art intersect in an area they would like to see occupied by a new curriculum which blends the study of words, images and sounds in texts held together by the 'glue' of words (Tweddle *et al.* 1997: 44).

In the remainder of this chapter, I consider two aspects of digital technologies that currently offer particular challenges and opportunities for

English teaching, before moving on to a framework for thinking and teaching about literacy, technology and English.

DIGITAL LITERACIES/ANALOGUE VALUES?

Much has been written about changes to the way we read and write on-screen. The perceived provisionality of digital text is one theme; changes to the organisation of texts and a 'turn to the visual' are others. In this section, I look at computer-mediated communication and World Wide Web hypertexts as elements of digital technologies that have already been incorporated in English curricula, but that may in fact present different new challenges and opportunities.

CMC

Computer-mediated communication (CMC) can be either synchronous (that is, it takes place in real time; telephone conversations are synchronous) or asynchronous. Examples of asynchronous CMC are e-mail and newsgroups or bulletin boards. Messages are sent or, in the case of newsgroups, posted and can be read and responded to at any time. The intervals between messages and responses can be very short or much longer, depending on the social context and purpose of the communication. Thus, asynchronous computer-mediated text can be either carefully crafted and related to very traditional print genres such as the memorandum or the business letter, or less carefully crafted and related to less formal print genres such as the post-it note message or the marginal note. CMC can also include print symbols such as emoticons (or 'smiley faces') that can be viewed as attempts to replace the paralinguistic features of speech. They can also include image files and hyperlinks to the World Wide Web. All these language features can be studied in English in the same way as the language features of other media channels and genres.

Less attention has been paid to synchronous CMC, however, other than in the support of critical literacy pedagogy (see LeCourt, this volume) or as an opportunity to consider the 'hybridity' of synchronous CMC discourse. Other uses of synchronous CMC which offer extended textual experiences to readers are MUDS or MOOS. MUDS (or multi-user domains) are text-based virtual environments that can also be used for collaborative storytelling and role-playing. MOOS (multi-user domains object oriented) are MUDS that are programmed in a different way. There are thousands of MOOS and MUDS on the internet, some of them designed and developed by professional communities, others by groups of role-players or science fiction/fantasy enthusiasts. In some cases, stories have been told collaboratively for fifteen years or more by fluid groups of player–writers.

In *Hamlet on the Holodeck*, Janet H. Murray (1997: 280) claims that MUDS and other simulations are beginning to exploit fully the properties of digital environments and she uses the contrast between games/web hypertexts and MUDS to make an interesting distinction between agency and authorship. Responding to those postmodern theorists who have argued that digital texts, and hypertexts particularly, blur the boundaries between reading and writing, effectively making the reader a 'writer' of a new text, Murray argues that this is a 'misleading assertion' (*ibid.*: 152). Just as in print texts, readers bring their knowledge and experience (including those of other texts) to a digital text and make sense of it differently. This does not make them the writer of that text; they do not have 'authorship' (*ibid.*: 153). The same is true of computer games as texts: the player–reader may seem to have control over where and how the avatar moves and what it does, but these actions are only possible within the parameters set by the game's programmer. It is the programmer who has set the rules for how the game may be understood by allowing certain possibilities and limiting others. The same is true of hypertexts and even of hyperfiction (the very model of a postmodern genre) where the author has set the rules and possibilities – you go only where you are allowed to go. Readers of hypertexts/hyperfiction and players of console games are interactors, says Murray, and have greater flexibility for interaction, for the exercise of agency. Authorship of digital texts, however, is 'procedural' – it involves setting the rules by which the text may be understood (*ibid.*: 152). MUDS are a good example of how digital environments can increase the opportunities for procedural authorship, says Murray. The author begins to take on a role previously considered that of the programmer, and the role of the reader–interactor is also enhanced: 'The interactor is not the author of the digital narrative, although the interactor can experience one of the most exciting aspects of artistic creation – the thrill of exerting power over enticing and plastic materials. This is not authorship but agency' (*ibid.*: 153).

Bruckman and De Bonte (1997) have used MOO technology with children aged 8–13 learning how to read, write and program. Bruckman developed MOOSE, an easy programming language, that enabled children in Minnesota, Massachusetts and California primary schools to become procedural authors in simulation activities designed by their teacher. They created a structure and an environment for understanding narrative and made objects – places, rooms, characters – that displayed behaviours. In the California classroom, the children designed different rooms on a sinking ship described in verbal text and connected their rooms according to a common design. As examples of simple 'procedural authorship', children wrote scripts (or pieces of programming) that made the ship sink every time someone entered a particular room (*ibid.*: 6). MOOS and MUDS present opportunities for students to learn about language, narrative and the technology of making meaning of a kind that has scarcely been considered by English teachers. There is something different for English teachers to consider about the means of production of these texts and the ways that they are understood. They call into question our understandings of what it takes to be an author of digital narrative.

Web hypertexts

Another use of digital technologies that is found more commonly in English classrooms is hypertext, and a great deal has been said and written about the ways in which this text type is sometimes seen to challenge or even supersede conventional print genres. Earlier, I referred to the work of Kress and Burbules who point to shifts and turns away from traditional linear ways of organising texts to more distributed, juxtaposed structures sometimes described as collage (Burbules 1998; Kress 1998). There has also been a great deal written about the rise of visual modes of representation and their 'efficiency' in communicating information. Some of us may even have been engaged in teaching students how to write multi-form parallel stories or hypertextually glossed readings of literary texts using HTML (see the earlier examples I gave from Australia).

It is useful to note, however, that there is very little hyperfiction on the internet and very little that is commercially available from publishers such as Eastgate Systems. Michael Joyce's *afternoon, a story* (1987) (saved to disk and packaged and sold like a book) is the most famous example of a rather small collection. Rick Pryll's web-based hyperfiction *Lies* (1994) is perhaps one of the more satisfying examples on the internet.[4] Nevertheless, there isn't much of it around, and it doesn't seem particularly popular with readers (or with writers, who seem to prefer offering their work on the internet as downloadable *Word* files).

Nor do these hyperfictions exploit visual modes of representation. Following the title page of *afternoon, a story*, there are no visual images. The only self-consciously visual aspect of Pryll's *Lies* is the typography of the two key words, 'Truth' and 'Lies'. Indeed, even a casual browse of websites will confirm that it hasn't turned to the visual just yet and that the function of verbal text is not yet that of a gloss on or orientation to the visual image. Recently, I asked my students to search for web texts in which the visual images are the dominant and most efficient means of communicating information. After a very unscientific couple of hours, they agreed that they could only really say that this was partly true of one website out of the forty-five they had analysed. This was the Cadbury's Crème Egg site, designed by the confectionery manufacturer to promote its Easter treats to the children's market (http://www.cremeegg.co.uk/). However, they were only able to say that it was *partly* true that the visuals were most important as the sound that accompanied the images was also an important means of communicating information and making interaction with the site enjoyable.

It seems fair to say that most of the texts on the Web are information or non-fiction texts of one kind or another and that visual modes of representation do not yet dominate. Indeed, it would seem that many sites are becoming more verbal, as designers work harder to attract and retain readers/users. Jakob Nielsen, the doyen of web designers, and the person who developed the theory of 'web usability', has recently published what is seen as the state-of-the-art guide to website design (Nielsen 2000). One important piece of advice is to minimise the amount of graphics on a page (*ibid.*: 134) as long download times (more than ten seconds) have been shown to deter readers and make them move elsewhere. The possibilities for graphics outlined include cropping and scaling, and including as 'thumbnails' (very small images), rather than enlarging images to fill the screen. He also discusses the use of audio files in web texts, something not attempted very often, even though they are known to be very effective, consist of smaller files and are easier to produce than high-quality visual images (*ibid.*: 154). The overriding principles of web design for Nielsen are usability and utility:

> The Web is an attention economy where the ultimate currency is the user's time. What do they look at, where do they decide to stay, and where are they going to return at a later date? In traditional media, these questions are often resolved in favour of staying put. ... The Web reverses this equation: the cost of going to a different web site is very low, and yet the expected benefit of staying at the site is not particularly high.
>
> (*Ibid.*: 160)

One of the challenges for English teachers presented by web-based hypertexts is not simply to make texts more visual in order to chime with a particular theory but rather to encourage children to think about how the World Wide Web situates them as readers and writers and to allow their voices to be heard in its 'attention economy'.

CONCLUSION: BEGINNING TO PAY ATTENTION

The 'place' of digital technologies in English as a subject is a highly complex issue that is implicated in questions of what we think are the purposes of English and what we mean by literacy. Constructions of English, even when there is statutory curriculum prescription, vary between schools and among teachers in the same department. Where, over time, strong subject sub-cultures have developed that seek, for example, to perpetuate a high-cultural heritage model of the subject, technology will be used to support that model and 'the antecedent subject sub-culture in effect colonises the computer' (Goodson *et al.* 1998: 120). However, choosing to ignore or reject technology – or to regard it as somehow ideologically neutral – are particularly dangerous options, as Selfe (1999) and Barrell (1999) have pointed out. Even so, the debate has focused for a considerable time on the possibilities for *using* technology rather than on the construction of the subject.

The authors of the *Digital Rhetorics* report, drawing on the work of Bill Green, offer a framework for thinking about literacy which it is useful to consider when thinking about the future of English as the language responds to new literacy technologies (Lankshear *et al.* 1997; see also Green 1988). There are, they say, three dimensions to literacy that are 'equal to the demands of the information age' (Lankshear *et al.*: 17). The first is the 'operational', which 'involves being able to read and write within a range of contexts . . . employing conventional print and electronic media' (*ibid.*). This includes the level of skills – writing, spelling, keyboarding – that support effective interaction with the interfaces of literacy, whether pen and paper or mouse and screen. The second dimension is 'cultural', which involves 'understanding texts and information in relation to the contexts . . . in which they are produced, received and used' (*ibid.*). This includes knowledge of what makes particular forms of discourse appropriate or inappropriate in certain situations. I would suggest that it also includes knowledge of culturally important or valued texts. The third dimension is the 'critical', which involves innovation and transformation, making the difference 'between merely being *socialised* into sets of skills, values, beliefs and procedures and being able to make *judgments* about them from a perspective which identifies them for what they are (and are not) and recognises alternative possibilities' (Lankshear *et al.*: 17; emphasis in original).

This framework is useful, I believe, because it offers something which is open enough to allow for what we do not know and which may be yet to come. Literacy itself is a technological process whereby meanings are transformed into symbols and given some physical presence. The papyrus, quills, slates, quinkies, electronic personal organisers and interactive white boards are all examples of literacy technologies. There seems little point in developing an approach to English and ICT that takes account of the technical minutiae of where we think we are now or what we perceive to be future possibilities. Predicting the future of literacy technologies is, at best, a waste of time and, at worst, an extremely misleading, demoralising and frustrating experience for teachers and for students. The *Digital Rhetorics*–Green framework is concerned with values and processes necessary for the education of critically literate students. It encourages English teachers to pay attention to technology as an intrinsic part of becoming literate. It views technology not merely as providing us with a tool or a resource but as providing us with text (whether a newspaper or pages on the internet) and context (an environment in which we work which affects what we do, why and for whom).

The framework also allows for continuity with the traditions of critical literacy, and continuity is an important factor in the development of the English curriculum (Tweddle *et al.* 1997: 47). Choosing between the 'analogue clock' and the 'digital display' models of literacy is not an option; it can't be an either/or. It isn't the end of literacy or of English or of literature as we know it. Whether we describe the relationship between the two as an accommodation or a competition, it is clear that we will have to deal with both. As Catherine Beavis points out: 'Rather than "pressing the wrong buttons", our responses to the literacies of the new technologies need to be located within familiar cultural and pedagogical discourses: continuity, re-creation, critical literacy and responsibility' (Beavis 1999: 50–1).

EPILOGUE

In the first few months of 2000, the Microsoft Corporation began an advertising campaign for its latest technological innovation. Headed 'This is a story about the future of reading', some of the advertisements spread over four pages and contained a time-line predicting that all newspapers would publish their final paper editions by 2018 and that by 2019 paper books would retain popularity only as gifts or for specialist publications and with collectors (Microsoft 2000: 4). The leading-edge innovation being advertised, however, was *Microsoft Reader* with *Clear Type*, and the key visual image was of a laptop computer displaying the first page of Melville's *Moby Dick*, as if it had been ripped from an expensive hardback edition of the novel. This wasn't a 'non-linear' hypertext version, nor did the text exploit visual images. *Microsoft Reader* with *Clear Type* is software that allows books to be prepared for the computer screen and sold on the World Wide Web with security encryption that protects authors' copyright. Traditional print literacy technologies have for some time occupied the minds of Microsoft's researchers:

> For the past two years, Microsoft researchers have studied the influ-
> ence of typography on the process of reading. We came to a simple
> conclusion: the book is a perfect reading machine. Evolved over
> centuries, the well-designed book frees the mind to focus not on letters
> and words, but on the story and meaning. A good book disappears
> in your hands. So when we set out to design the optimal reading soft-
> ware, we didn't dismiss the book. Instead we embraced it as our
> blueprint.
>
> (*Ibid.*: 3)

The development of 'e-books' and their adoption of traditional print values and 'rejection of the distracting icons, buttons and bars that can clutter computer screens' (*ibid.*) is a good example of the interplay between 'analogue clock' and 'digital display' models of literacy. Digital technology is being used to make reading from the computer screen more like reading a book, while offering some added-value features (dictionaries, the ability to enlarge font size, annotation facilities, etc.); but fundamentally this is an attempt to replicate an 'analogue' technological experience (reading a book) that has become almost invisible.

And that is why English teachers must heed the words of those who, like Selfe, urge us to pay attention to technology. Rather than breaking down the walls of the library and the publishing industry, technological innovations can shore them up, as effort and expense is devoted to developing systems and protocols that replicate print copyright regulations and control in digital environments. A political and economic context in which digital technologies are available to some and not to others, in which access to information, play and imaginative literature may depend more than ever upon the social class and ethnicity of individuals and communities, is something about which all of us need to be concerned, especially those of us who are teachers of literacy and English. We cannot choose to reject or ignore technology, nor should we rush headlong into an uncritical embrace because we are told to regard it as a good and necessary thing. There is no reason to believe that English teachers will not eventually confront this challenge and draw on lessons learned during the introduction of older media technologies and from colleagues' experiences around the world. This will undoubtedly be a time of discomfort for all parties – including policy-makers and technology manufacturers – during which English teachers will continue their honourable tradition of principled, 'subversive' activity and begin to make digital technologies a critical feature of the literacy curriculum.

NOTES

1   The term 'personal growth', applied to one of five models of English teaching, was popularised by Brian Cox and his committee in the report that preceded the first National Curriculum in England and Wales in 1989 (DES 1988). The other four were: cultural heritage; adult needs; cross-curricular; and cultural analysis. The precise meaning of these terms is, of course, a matter for stipulation, and we cannot assume that individual teachers operate exclusively within a single paradigm or that their intentions will be realised in practice.

2   It must be noted that Kress spends the first part of the chapter from which these quotations are taken giving a very clear warning against technological determinism and the importance of viewing technology as 'socially-applied knowledge' (Kress 1998: 53).

3   There is a separate pupils' National Curriculum for ICT in England and Wales. It is left to schools to decide where and how this content is taught, however.
4   For a short annotated list of single- and multiple-author hyperfiction on the Web, see: http:// www. duke.edu/~mshumate/original.html

REFERENCES

Alderman, D. L., Appel, L. R. and Murray, R. T. (1978) 'PLATO and TICCIT: an evaluation of CAI in the community college', *Educational Technology* 18: 40–44.

Andrews, R. (2000) 'Framing and design in ICT in English: towards a new subject and practices in the classroom', in A. Goodwyn (ed.), *English in the Digital Age: Information and Communications Technology and the Teaching of English*, London: Cassell.

Barrell, B. (1999) 'Technology and change in Atlantic Canada's new Secondary English Language Arts Curriculum', *English Education* (NCTE) 31(3): 231–47.

Beavis, C. (1999) 'Pressing (the right?) buttons: literacy, technology, crisis and continuity', *English in Australia* 123: 42–51.

Board of Secondary School Studies (1997) *Trial Senior Syllabus in English Extension (Literature)*, Queensland: Board of Secondary School Studies.

Bruckman, A. and De Bonte, A. (1997) 'MOOSE goes to school: a comparison of three classrooms using a CSCL environment', Proceedings of CSCL '97, Toronto, Canada, December 1997; online (available: http://www.cc.gatech.edu/~asb/papers/cscl97.html), 26 April 2000.

Burbules, N. (1998) 'Rhetorics of the web: hyperreading and critical literacy', in I. Snyder (ed.), *Page to Screen: Taking Literacy into the Electronic Era*, London: Routledge.

Corcoran, B. and Beavis, C. (1998) 'Reconstructing the high school literature teacher: case studies of curriculum change', Paper presented at the Third NCTE International Conference, University of Bordeaux.

Cox, B. (ed.) (1999) *Literacy Is Not Enough: Essays on the Importance of Reading*, Manchester: Manchester University Press.

DES (1988) *English for Ages 5 to 16* ('The Cox Report'), London: HMSO.

DfEE (1998a) *The Initial Teacher Training National Curriculum for the Use of ICT in Subject Teaching*, Circular 4/98: *High Status, High Standards* – Annex B, London: Stationery Office.

—— (1998b) *The National Literacy Strategy: Framework for Teaching*, London: Stationery Office.

Goodson, I. with Anstead, C. J. and Mangan, J. M. (1998) *Subject Knowledge: Readings for the Study of School Subjects*, London: Falmer Press.

Goodwyn, A. (2000a) '"A bringer of new things": an English teacher in the computer age', in A. Goodwyn (ed.), *English in the Digital Age*, London: Cassell.

—— (2000b) 'Texting: reading and writing in the intertext', in A. Goodwyn (ed.), *English in the Digital Age*, London: Cassell.

—— and Findlay, K. (1999) 'The Cox models revisited: English teachers' views of their subject and the National Curriculum', *English in Education* 33(2): 19–31.

—— Adams, A. and Clarke, S. (1997) 'The great god of the future: the views of current and future English teachers on the place of IT in literacy', *English in Education* 31(2): 54–62.

Green, B. (1988) 'Subject-specific literacy and school learning: a focus on writing', *Australian Journal of Education* 32(2): 156–79.

Harris, J. (1985) 'Student writers and word processing: a preliminary evaluation', *College Composition and Communication* 36: 323–30.

Hillocks, George (1986) *Research on Written Composition: New Directions for Teaching*, New York: National Conference on Research in English, and Urbana, IL: ERIC Clearinghouse on Reading and Communication Skills, National Institute of Education.

Joyce, M. (1987) *afternoon, a story*, Cambridge, MA: Eastgate Systems.

Kress, G. (1995) *Writing the Future: English and the Making of a Culture of Innovation*, Sheffield: NATE.

—— (1998) 'Visual and verbal modes of representation in electronically mediated communication: the potentials of new forms of texts', in I. Snyder (ed.), *Page to Screen: Taking Literacy into the Electronic Era*, London: Routledge.

Lanham, R. A. (1993) *The Electronic Word: Democracy, Technology and the Arts*, Chicago: University of Chicago Press.

Lankshear, C., Bigum, C., Durrant, C., Green, B., Honan, E., Morgan, W., Murray, J., Snyder, I. and Wild, M. (1997) *Digital Rhetorics: Literacies and Technologies in Education – Current Practices and Future Directions (Executive Summary)*, Canberra: Department of Employment, Education, Training and Youth Affairs.

Microsoft Corporation (2000) 'This is a story about the future of reading' (advertisement), *Brill's Content* (January).

Murray, J. H. (1997) *Hamlet on the Holodeck: The Future of Narrative in Cyberspace*, Cambridge, MA: MIT Press.

Nielsen, J. (2000) *Designing Web Usability*, Indianapolis, IN: New Riders Publishing.

Peel, R. and Hargreaves, S. (1995) 'Beliefs about English: trends in Australia, England and the United States', *English in Education* 29(2): 38–50.

Pope, R. (1994) *Textual Intervention*, London: Routledge.

Pryll, R. L. (1994) *Lies* (hyperfiction on the World Wide Web); online (available: http://www.users.interport.net/~rick/lies/lies.html), 26 April 2000.

QCA–DfEE (1999) *English in the National Curriculum*, London: Stationery Office.

Sefton-Green, J. (1999) 'Media education, but not as we know it: digital technology and the end of media studies?', *The English and Media Magazine*, (Summer): 28–34.

Selfe, C. L. (1999) 'Technology and literacy: a story about the perils of not paying attention', *College Composition and Communication* 50(3): 411–36.

Stannard, R. (1997) *IT in English: A Report on the Colloquium – English and the New Technologies*, Coventry: NCET.

Teacher Training Agency (TTA) (1999) *Exemplification of the Use of ICT in Subject Teaching: Secondary English*, London: Teacher Training Agency.

Tweddle, S., Adams, A., Clarke, S., Scrimshaw, P. and Walton, S. (1997) *English for Tomorrow*, Buckingham: Open University Press.

Wood, D. (1998) *The UK ILS Evaluations: Final Report*, Coventry: BECTA.

Chapter 8

Information and communication technologies and representations of mathematics

Michelle Selinger

> The modern classroom computer has an unparalleled ability to imple-
> ment both graphical and procedural components of mathematics
> understanding in a single unified object. By their creation and utilization
> of mathematically relevant computer-based objects this dual encapsula-
> tion enables the students a unique opportunity to see both the form of
> representation and their actions utilizing this representation simultan-
> eously.
>
> (Connell 2000)

In 1985 Daniel, aged 4, enjoyed playing computer games, particularly space
invaders, on the BBC Micro, the computers that had been put into every
school by the UK Government in 1982. He wanted to beat his 6-year-
old sister and knew that the numbers in the corner of the screen indicated
who was winning. 'What's that number?' he would continually ask.
Some time after he had started school his teacher called his mother in to
tell her that his numeracy skills were extremely well developed. He was
reading a book about dinosaurs and had read to her that the dinosaurs
had lived 8 million years ago. What had amazed the teacher was that
he had read the number from the figure 8,000,000. He had also developed an understanding of place value without any formal teaching, as he
was also reading numbers like 6,458,234 correctly (see also Vaughn 1997).
At that time Reception children were, in the main, taught numbers only
up to 10.[1]

In September 2000 the revised UK National Curriculum came into
force. Each subject has been revised and new Orders have been produced;
yet, despite the increase in computers in school and the workplace, there
are few changes to the Order for mathematics that recognise the role of
ICT in developing students' understanding of mathematical concepts and
procedures earlier than was previously thought possible. It seems that either
little cognisance has been taken of the fact that ICT can change both the
access to and the way that learners approach mathematics, or it has been

recognised that some schools are still not equipped with sufficient technology to make the radical changes to the curriculum viable and accessible to all. Perhaps the next version will be written in a more ICT-conscious environment, and will be a proper reflection of the research that has been undertaken to show what access to a range of mathematical software can do to change what children learn, what they need to learn, when they learn and how they learn.

A primary-school IT co-ordinator described how she used a series of software programs to progress pupils through numeracy tasks. She used ICT in her mathematics teaching because she believed it was motivating and non-judgemental; it provided fast and reliable feedback; the method was not decided by the teacher; and if the wrong answer were achieved, children had to revisit their conceptions and their methods in order to obtain the correct answer. She also felt that children were more willing and able to test out their ideas with ICT than with pencil and paper or with a teacher. This matches the views expressed in the NCET publication *Primary Mathematics with IT* (NCET 1997: 1): 'A calculator or a computer can provide fast and reliable feedback that is non-judgmental and impartial. The facility to change things easily and try again encourages children to make their own conjectures and to test out and modify their ideas.'

There are aspects of mathematics and mathematical ideas that have only been recently made accessible through computers. At a recent seminar Tim O'Shea discussed how knowledge could now be expressed in computational forms.[2] He contended that with computers visual representations of polynomials (such as $y = 3x^3 - x^2 + 2x + 4$) can now be developed and manipulated on the screen. Therefore he questioned whether the 'how to' of yesterday's mathematics is still important. How much arithmetic do we need when calculators are given away at petrol stations? In what ways can a calculator support and/or change the way we think about or do mathematics? Just what mathematical learning is necessary? If the calculator can be considered to perform the role of a cognitive support, we need to be clear about how it acts to help learners develop cognitive structures.

Another feature of ICT in mathematics to which O'Shea draws our attention is object-oriented programming, which is now used to solve engineering problems. It provides a general way of describing interactions in the world. An example would be the use of object-oriented programming to develop a mathematical model which explains how the V shape in a flock of birds is formed. Before ICT there was no way of developing this model. Proof has changed too. The four-colour theorem[3], hitherto unproven, has now been proved using a computer. It is not simply a case of computers doing things faster: it is a case of the technology allowing us to do what we could not do before. Therefore, O'Shea argues, in the same way the curriculum has to change.

Some of these ideas and concepts, however, are not yet present in the school mathematics syllabus. In this chapter my focus is on those aspects of mathematics which are covered by the compulsory curriculum for the 5–16 age range. Three aspects are considered:

1   the ways in which ICT can challenge the 'ways of knowing' in mathematics and, therefore, the curriculum taught in school;
2   the ways in which the teacher's role is challenged by ICT, particularly the teacher's need to mediate between students and machines, and the importance of all teachers having a more robust subject knowledge;
3   the ways in which the use of ICT can mask the nature of students' learning or misunderstandings.

I shall focus on the role of visualisation, and how it might bring access to concepts earlier; how ICT can make use of multiple representations to link spatial and algebraic views of mathematics and so enhance understanding and help make connections; how the modelling of dynamic concepts develops understanding; and how the processing power of ICT can breathe new life into old methods of calculation. Additionally I shall highlight aspects of the mathematics curriculum that could be relegated to lower-order skills, leaving room for higher-order thinking, and how ICT can enhance collaboration and develop it in different formats.

CHALLENGING WAYS OF KNOWING IN MATHEMATICS

In this section I consider how students' thinking and ways of knowing can be challenged through simple software applications, spreadsheets and integrated learning systems for numeracy, and how calculators also can develop understanding in new ways. I then consider other aspects of mathematics. The role of the teacher in this process is fundamental and will be considered in the next section. But first I look at the UK Government's focus on and concern with numeracy.

Back to basics or forward to basics?

The Government has expressed concern about the national standards of literacy and numeracy in schools (DfEE 1997). As a result two strategies were developed: the National Literacy Strategy was launched in schools in 1998, and the following year the National Numeracy Strategy came into force. The definition of numeracy itself is a contentious issue. In the final report of the Numeracy Task Force (DfEE 1998) it is defined as:

a proficiency that involves a confidence and competence with numbers and measures. It requires an understanding of the number system, a repertoire of computational skills and an inclination and ability to solve number problems in a variety of contexts. Numeracy also demands practical understanding of the ways in which information is gathered by counting and measuring, and is presented in graphs, diagrams, charts and tables. This proficiency is promoted through giving a sharper focus to the relevant aspects of the National Curriculum programmes of study for mathematics. Numerate primary pupils should be confident and competent enough to tackle problems without going immediately to teachers and friends for help.

(DfEE 1998: para. 15)

The role of ICT in developing this confidence and an 'at homeness' with number is through aspects similar to the ways in which numeracy has traditionally been taught in schools, including:

* number recognition
* manipulation of number
* reinforcement
* drill and practice
* pattern spotting
* estimation
* visual imagery of number
* problem solving.

The Numeracy Task Force's consultation document *Numeracy Matters* had devoted a small section to ICT. This lack of attention to ICT was noted in the responses received, and was highlighted and discussed in the final report:

There was some concern that *Numeracy Matters* did not say enough about the way in which ICT can support the successful teaching and learning of mathematics. We feel it is important to stress in this context that whilst we see increasing benefits from the use of ICT to support mathematics, we are convinced that ICT must supplement, and cannot replace, an effective teacher. The whole thrust of our recommendation has been to ensure that all teachers are equipped with the knowledge and skills that they need to teach mathematics successfully, and this has been our priority in recommending how the money available for specific support over the years of the National Numeracy Strategy should be spent. We have, therefore, not had sufficient time or opportunity to study the use of ICT in mathematics in depth, and do not give detailed guidance in this report, although we do recognise the potential promise in this area.

(DfEE 1998: para. x)

The 'potential promise' provides the focus for much of this chapter. As illustrated above, ICT can help develop new forms of mathematics: it can challenge existing ways of knowing and it can bring about ways of knowing that did not exist prior to computers.

Learning the four rules of number, or becoming numerate

Recent publications have pointed to subject-specific software for developing pupils' numeracy skills (see, for example, Wadebridge 1996). Oldknow (1993) acknowledges the use of the calculator and the computer in resurrecting ancient algorithms for computation. He describes how computers can support the development of key skills, which he defines as 'the ability to formulate a problem, to choose the appropriate tool, to interpret the results, to check for accuracy, to make and test predictions, to communicate to others and so on' (*ibid.*: 98). Often spreadsheets are used to do this. Old algorithms, such as the Russian peasant algorithm shown below (*ibid.*: 92), thus become novel ways of looking at how numbers can be reconstituted in several ways to find the result of multiplying two numbers together. For example, to multiply 35×19

35	19★
70	9★
140	4
280	2
560	1★

$$35 \times 19 = 35 + 70 + 560 = 665$$

There are several ancient algorithms like this, and the act of setting up a spreadsheet to perform each element of the calculation could lead to an exploration of why the method works. This can help students come to a greater understanding of mathematics, together with the realisation that the traditional methods they have been taught are not the only methods by which to arrive at a solution. Learning a meaningless algorithm does not enhance mathematical understanding; nor does it promote relational understanding, which Skemp (1976) argued is essential for developing robust schemata. What is required in this example is an understanding of what multiplication is, and a spreadsheet can help this process. Spreadsheets have also allowed trial and improvement methods to be resurrected as ways of solving mathematical problems, since the drudgery of low-level calculation is taken over by the computer. Students can attend to patterns that are forming as they move towards the solution of a problem. The Maxbox problem that is discussed later is one such example.

Kurta (1997) suggests a number of other spreadsheet activities, one of which is setting up a 'think of a number' spreadsheet. He gives this example. Think of a number. Double it. Add four. Multiply by five. Add twenty. Divide by ten. Take away the original number. What is left? He asks the user to change the first number, then to try with decimals and negative numbers. The power of the spreadsheet allows children to develop an understanding of number at an earlier age than used to be the case, and this is entirely due to the ease with which the computer can perform the arithmetic. Encouraging children to conjecture what would happen and to try to explain the results they get will help them develop the 'at homeness' with number that McIntosh *et al.* (1992) define as 'number sense'. The ability to manipulate numbers is vital, but the ability to understand what is happening as you manipulate and change them is paramount to the essence of numeracy. Repetition of the four rules in the same way will never produce the same effect. Fuglestad (1997) also demonstrates how spreadsheets can be used to help develop a clearer understanding of decimals by experimenting with sums and products. Trial and improvement is another valuable mathematical skill which lends itself to the use of spreadsheets. The drudgery of calculation is removed and the pupil is introduced to the iteration process as a mathematical tool in a more transparent way.

Small software

'Drill and practice' software is another example of a type of 'small software',[4] which helps to reinforce concepts. In an interesting debate in *Micromaths* in 1991, several mathematics educators argued the pros and cons of small software as opposed to generic business applications like spreadsheets and databases or educational applications, for instance those using the Logo language. The argument for small subject-specific concept-focused software was that it needed little teacher input: it could be fitted in around the topic currently being taught and therefore integrated into the teaching. It also enabled reinforcement of concepts, and afforded those students who were struggling alternative entry points to an understanding of the concepts. Calculator games are also useful in teaching basic skills in the four rules of number; in developing an understanding of place value and decimals; and in demonstrating the link between decimals, fractions and percentages. Much has been written about the use of calculators in supporting numeracy development (e.g. Shuard *et al.* 1991), and despite recent bad press on the use of calculators, their limited use is encouraged in the National Numeracy Strategy.

Integrated learning systems

Integrated learning systems (ILS) can be used for drill and practice, and for teaching new concepts. These systems tend to use a 'mastery' approach to learning in which each student is provided with a series of tasks to master in order to make progress to the next series of tasks. The tasks are sequenced according to an expert's notion of hierarchical difficulty, and the assumption is that, with correct teaching and sequencing, the student will be able to master the concepts and hence make progress. There have been gains in numeracy across all levels of attainment, but one wonders, in the case of ILS, whether the computer has really helped in helping the child formulate mathematical concepts in a different way, and how much is attributable to teacher support around the ILS. This is discussed later in more detail in relation to the role of the teacher. ILS systems are basically teaching mathematics in old ways using new technology. The concept of mathematics being about correct answers and 'right' ways of performing certain mathematical procedures tends to be reinforced. Certainly ways of knowing in this instance are unchanged

Making mathematics visual and dynamic

Computer software can offer mediation between pupils and mathematics in the way it exploits mental imagery. In making use of ICT the question needs to be asked: what aspects of mathematics can be expressed with the software which are hard to express without it? Certainly the visual and dynamic can play an important part in developing students' understanding of mathematics. Too often teachers have grappled to teach dynamic concepts through static models or to teach about three-dimensional objects with two-dimensional representations. Much has been left to mental imagery, rarely taught and difficult to share as one's mental image can be substantially different from another's. Early attempts to address these problems made use of 8mm film and later video images, and some of these ideas have now been translated into computer-generated models, but ICT has also allowed much more to be developed.

My first inkling that ICT could support mathematical learning came to me when I was introduced to a motion sensor devised by Lawrence Rogers at the University of Leicester. I attended a very entertaining workshop in which a group of teachers were invited to copy a distance–time graph on the screen by moving towards and away from a motion sensor. At the time I was having great difficulty in getting students to understand distance–time graphs, in particular the fact that a horizontal line on the graph means that the object, a vehicle or person, say, is stationary. Here at last was a solution to my (or, rather, my students') problems. I did not have access to a motion sensor at school or the funds to purchase one, but I did discover a software program called *Traffic* that had a similar effect.[5] The software gave me a dynamic way to illustrate how distance–time graphs are generated, as well as a number of options to illustrate this. I could, for example, show snapshots of a car moving along a motorway over a period of time. These snapshots were laid horizontally across the screen and then the road was replaced by the distance–time graph, which followed the path of the snapshots. I could also show scenarios of cars travelling, overtaking or remaining stationary, and ask students to construct a graph, or I could show a graph and ask students to interpret the graph as a sequence of events that could then be replayed to see if their conjectures were correct. This dynamic representation of a dynamic situation previously represented by a static graph helped develop students' conceptions in a way that I had not found possible before. It also gave me ideas about how I might develop the concepts if the technology had not been available to me, thus increasing my range of teaching strategies.

Since then there have been developments in software. Geometrical drawing packages such as *Cabri-Geometry*[6] and *The Geometer's Sketchpad*[7] allow students to manipulate Euclidean forms in a dynamic way. With use of the internet, dynamic geometry can be incorporated into dynamic textbooks or interactive problems.[8] Instead of constructions being 'talked through', students can observe them being constructed, or shown how, as a triangle becomes equiangular, the sides all become the same length, and that the length of the sides can vary but the angles remain the same size. Students' conceptions of angles can be developed as the tools make them accessible and manipulable. Students can confirm the concepts themselves, and the tools can be set up in such a way as to give access to the youngest or least able of users.

Another example in this category is the teaching of place value with a recently developed piece of software (ATM 1999), based on Gattegno's model for teaching children about the number system using words for numbers. Gattegno aimed to make the learning of numbers as efficient as possible, and measured the learning effort in units which he called 'ogdens'. To learn the numbers one to ten takes ten ogdens. To then learn the numbers eleven to twenty as we currently teach takes another ten ogdens. However, if you can construct these numbers from the numbers one to ten, fewer ogdens are required. Eleven and twelve are special cases that have to be taught. Thirteen is the first of the 'teens' and has a slightly different rule from the other 'teens', but if children learn that the number fourteen is constructed from ten and four and is pronounced *four–teen*, fifteen, sixteen, seventeen, eighteen and nineteen can be easily constructed. Of course 'five–teen' is pronounced *fif–teen*, but the leap to that is minor – it is just a case of pronunciation. Twenty needs to be taught, as does thirty, forty and fifty, but from then on any number ending in 'ty' is easily built. The next number that needs to be learnt doesn't appear until one hundred. Compare this to the number of ogdens needed in teaching children to count from one to one hundred in succession. Once the rules have been learnt, constructing numbers is a case of putting words together. The ATM software *Numbers* helps children to do this

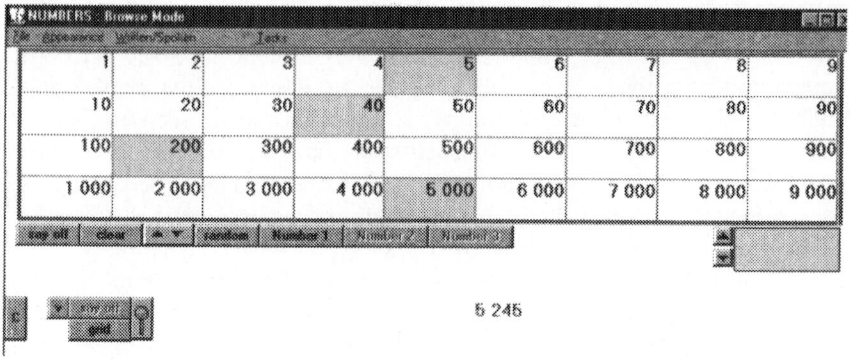

1	2	3	4	5	6	7	8	9
10	20	30	40	50	60	70	80	90
100	200	300	400	500	600	700	800	900
1 000	2 000	3 000	4 000	5 000	6 000	7 000	8 000	9 000

5 245

Figure 8.1 Screen from *Numbers*
(Reproduced by permission of the Association of Teachers of Mathematics)

by visually pulling numbers from a number grid and positioning them correctly on the screen. They can see it being constructed from its component parts. The software can 'speak' the number, write it in numeric and word format and the teacher can control what is seen and developed. The program has the capacity to teach decimal numbers also, using the same principles. Figure 8.1 gives a static representation of the software's capability. Research has demonstrated that the technique has proved successful with children who previously had problems understanding place value and reading numbers correctly (Hewitt and Brown 1998).

Cannon *et al.* (2000) are designing a web-based National Laboratory of Virtual Manipulatives for the learning of mathematics in elementary (primary) schools. Their design philosophy is guided by existing physical resources such as a geoboard, but they go beyond current objects to design new objects that are not easily constructed physically, e.g. a circular geoboard. Each object or 'manipulative' is designed with a limited number of uses, and they ensure that students are able to interact with the manipulative rather than just watch an animation. Their goal is to allow students to control events and to discover relationships – a similar philosophy to that behind *Logo* programming (discussed later). They report some

> unexpected responses or capabilities that an electronic manipulative possesses in contrast to the physical model that inspired the computer implementation.
> [. . .]
> Figures [8.2 and 8.3] show two screen shots of a virtual manipulative on the Platonic solids. To help develop spatial visualization, we wanted students to be able to see all sides of a solid object. What neither figure can show is that by moving the mouse the student can rotate the given object freely in space. In future variations of this applet,[9] we will paste

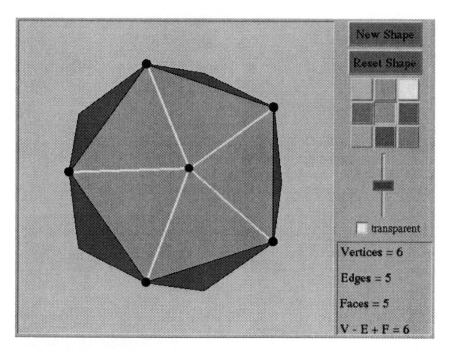

Figure 8.2 An icosahedron

different images onto the sides of a cube and ask questions about, say, opposite faces. But as we worked with this applet, we realized that there was an opportunity to let students discover Euler's relationship among vertices, faces, edges (V − F + E = 2). As the user rotates the solid in space, a Shift–Click changes the color of a face, an edge, or a vertex. In Figure [8.2], we have changed the color of five faces with their surrounding edges and corners. The color changes make it easy to determine when you have counted everything. In the implementation shown, there is a running tally of the numbers, which the teacher can either choose to show or not.

One of our most exciting experiences with this applet took place during a visit to several inner-city schools in Cleveland. . . . We took a projector and a laptop computer into the classroom and let the children (first, second, fourth and fifth graders) take turns with the mouse, rotating objects, selecting and changing colors while the entire class kept a (collective verbal) running count. The sense of ownership – and excitement – felt by the children as they controlled the magic of rotating the image and changing colors was palpable. . . . In the original

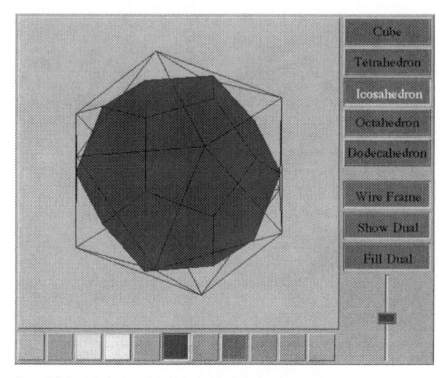

Cube
Tetrahedron
Icosahedron
Octahedron
Dodecahedron

Wire Frame
Show Dual
Fill Dual

Figure 8.3 An icosahedron in which the dual can be shown

discussions we had not thought of illustrating the idea of a dual of a solid (taking as vertices the mid-points of each face), but after seeing the solids in space, we serendipitously realized that we had another teaching opportunity. And, as may be seen from Figure [8.3], the electronic setting (using some fairly sophisticated mathematics) allowed us to show something that would probably never be constructed physically.

(Cannon *et al.* 2000: 1085)

Campbell (2000: 104), however, expresses concern that developments in enabling visualisation in mathematics through ICT can lead to an over-emphasis on the visual, and 'carries a risk of neglecting the more deductive, idealised, and symbolic aspects of mathematics'. His concern stems from the fact that the association–abstraction 'provides little insight into what learners actually experience and what they actually do when exposed to visual and symbolic aspects of mathematics'. He suggests that more work is needed to provide a theoretical framework that is 'comprehensive and detailed enough to do justice to the intrinsic complexities of synthesising visual and symbolic aspects of mathematical cognition' (*ibid.*).

Multiple representation software

According to O'Reilly *et al.* (1997: 88) 'connections and links between representations lies at the heart of much mathematics. . . . The concept of function, like all powerful mathematical ideas, contains many interconnected ideas. Multiple representation software (MERs) demonstrates these links explicitly. In such software, changes in one representation trigger automatic changes in another.' *COPPERS* is a program that uses multiple representations and 'aims to provide children with some understanding that there can be multiple correct solutions to single problems' (Ainsworth *et al.* 1997). Users are posed problems such as 'What is $3 \times 20p + 4 \times 10p$?' Learners answer these questions by clicking on a 'coin calculator' whose buttons are representations of British coins. To answer the above problem, a user may select '20p + 20p + 10p + 50p' or '10p + 2p + 2p + 1p + 5p + 10p + 10p + 10p + 50p'. Either answer is equally acceptable, as there is no notion of 'best' answer in the system. Users do not progress to new problems until they have produced a number of different solutions.

> One use of MERs in *COPPERS* is to describe answers in complementary representations. After answering a question, users receive feedback on their solutions.
> [. . .]
> The two representations [row and column; summary table] supply different types of information and require different interpretations. The row and column representation is a familiar one to children, used consistently once they start working with any multi-digit sum. Users are likely to need less new knowledge in order to understand this representation. The operations of multiplication and addition needed to produce the total are made very explicit in the row and column notation, making the arithmetical operations one of the most salient aspects of the representation. In contrast, the summary table is less familiar to the children and the arithmetical operations are implicit. To understand and make use of the information, children must decide what processes are involved and perform them for themselves, hence practising their multiplication and addition skills. The table also displays previous answers to the question. This allows children to compare their answers with those already given and (hopefully) prompts pattern seeking and reflection.
> (Ainsworth *et al.*: 97)

The results of an evaluation study with *COPPERS* conducted with forty 6–7-year-olds indicated that appropriate combinations of representations led to increased learning outcomes, although teacher support was considered an essential component. Ainsworth *et al.* cite another example of MERs, *Blocks World* (Thompson 1992), which combines Diennes blocks with numerical information. 'Users act in one notation (such as the blocks) and see the results of their actions in another (numbers).' One of the benefits of the activities just described is to move children away from the notion that mathematics is about getting *the* right answer, and getting them to see that often there are several right answers.

Pianfetti and Pianfetti (2000) have developed a Java-based application which combines digital video, a graph and a numeric table to 'present students with multiple and situated representations of a single event'. They found the combination helped students to visualise abstract concepts, and the interconnectedness of the three components places more emphasis on interpreting what is visually represented. Spreadsheets are especially useful in this respect, as they can be used for constructing number sequences and graphing the results, so making use of multiple representations. Much investigation work in mathematics involves looking at number patterns to find functional relationships. Development work can start with early uses of spreadsheets to investigate patterns in multiplication tables. Ainley (1996) describes a number of tasks in this area, some of which rely on the graphical representation of the times tables to help children relate the tables together. Strategies for developing numeracy through this technology include looking at relationships between tables, e.g. the six-times table is twice the three-times table, the

Worksheet2

	A	B	C	D	E	F	G	H	I	J
	1 times	2 times	3 times	4 times	5 times	6 times	7 times	8 times	9 times	10 times
1	1	2	3	4	5	6	7	8	9	10
2	2	4	6	8	10	12	14	16	18	20
3	3	6	9	12	15	18	21	24	27	30
4	4	8	12	16	20	24	28	32	36	40
5	5	10	15	20	25	30	35	40	45	50
6	6	12	18	24	30	36	42	48	54	60
7	7	14	21	28	35	42	49	56	63	70
8	8	16	24	32	40	48	56	64	72	80
9	9	18	27	36	45	54	63	72	81	90
10	10	20	30	40	50	60	70	80	90	100
11	11	22	33	44	55	66	77	88	99	110
12	12	24	36	48	60	72	84	96	108	120
13	13	26	39	52	65	78	91	104	117	130
14	14	28	42	56	70	84	98	112	126	140
15	15	30	45	60	75	90	105	120	135	150
16	16	32	48	64	80	96	112	128	144	160
17	17	34	51	68	85	102	119	136	153	170
18	18	36	54	72	90	108	126	144	162	180
19	19	38	57	76	95	114	133	152	171	190
20	20	40	60	80	100	120	140	160	180	200
21										
22										

Figure 8.4 Spreadsheet of times tables

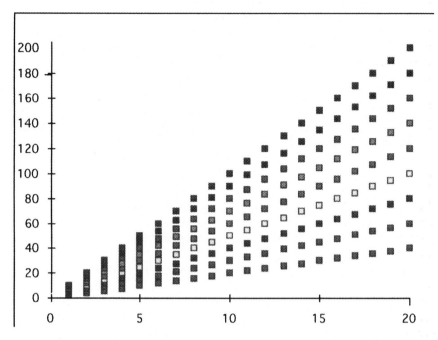

Figure 8.5 Graph of times tables

product of the digits in the nine-times table add to nine, and can all be seen by adding a further column in the spreadsheet. The act of producing the tables in itself stresses the relationships inherent in the tables, and children can be asked to find a number of ways to produce the six-times table and the eight-times table, for example (Figure 8.4). Once a table has been set up, the graphing ability of the spreadsheet provides a checking mechanism, and another way of seeing the relationship between the tables (Figure 8.5).

If a child generates a table by inputting the values directly, rather than using the spreadsheet functionality to do this, he or she can use the graph to check the calculation. If values are miscalculated, then a straight line will not result when they use the graphing function to plot the points.

Mathematics through programming: the case for Logo

There has been much written about computer programming and its relationship to learning in mathematics (see Noss 1985 for a review of the literature). Hoyles and Noss (1987: 207) suggested, in relation to Logo, that 'in order for positive learning effects to take place, an accessible programming language should be integrated into the mathematics curriculum, and that systematic and explicit links should be developed throughout the school experience between programming and "pencil and paper" activities'. Papert (1972) believed that Logo would provide students with an easy way into learning algebra and geometry; a claim validated to some extent by Noss (1986). The Hoyles and Noss believed that Logo programming provides students with an opportunity to engage in mathematical activity, rather than using Logo 'as a vehicle for either learning mathematical content on the one hand or "acquiring" some heuristics on the other' (1987: 207). Programming in Logo allows the user to design and test algorithms, generate hypotheses, pose problems, and investigate possible solutions. Students can do this in a non-threatening environment and the results can be quickly seen, allowing speedy feedback and therefore opportunities to try more cases than they might using pencil and paper methods. Papert (1980) has argued that the child needs to be exposed to a culture that helps to make abstract mathematical concepts simple and concrete, so that the child can relate them to existing knowledge. Papert envisaged Logo as being equivalent to an object to think with, something that helps to make the formal concrete. The notion is that through using the turtle in Logo children can explore mathematical shapes and ideas.

Logo can also help children resolve problems in their previous mathematical understanding. When researchers started to observe children programming in Logo (see Noss 1985), all of a sudden it seemed that many of the apparent difficulties which children had struggled with using traditional technologies (pencil and paper) began to disappear. For example, there has been a challenge to the received wisdom about the necessity of children struggling to understand the notion of the variable that arose from their being offered turtle geometry Logo environments on a computer. This is also true in the development of the use of spreadsheets. Pattern is an important part of mathematics and children are very comfortable with patterns; they see patterns in art, they form tessellations. The sense of order is also an important feature. Patterns can provide visual clues to number and help children develop that sense of order. Many of a child's early practical experiences are in sorting and ordering and a sense of pattern is developed early on in their experiences.

Logo software is now available in many formats aimed at beginners (*Roamer, FirstLogo*), at intermediate and at more expert users (Logo, *Microworlds Project Builder, StarLogo, SuperLogo*). Logo is the programming language for much of the control technology experience in both primary and secondary schools, and although there are critics of the language, there are many more who find it a useful and valuable tool in teaching and learning mathematics. A primary teacher told me how she used various types of Logo software:

'*Roamer* is used for estimation and measure. With *FirstLogo* I ask the children to direct a spider around a web. I find that the children soon start to develop mathematical language using the words "more", "less", "turn". I also noticed that the children were prepared to take risks because, if the spider came off its web, it was seen as acceptable as it was "only on the computer". Next I use *Crystal Rainforest*[10] in order to pull together the activities undertaken so far, and as an evaluation and assessment tool. I use *Space City*[11] with children in Years 2 and 3 for recognising right-angles, and I use Logo with children in Years 5 and 6 to construct polygons. I think this is a useful exercise in looking graphically at the effects of division.'

Building on this with ICT using pictorial representations of number can not only enhance numeracy, but can develop other aspects of mathematical thinking, and support the notion of mathematics as a whole rather than as comprising separate parts.

Logo can be used early on to help children understand the concept of magnitude represented by numbers. This can help a child move from the process of learning to count to seeing the link between the names of numbers (or to see numbers as labels), to seeing numbers as measures (see Pimm 1992). Children use programmable toys and make them move forward and back, and turn right and left. They then progress to a Logo screen turtle where movements are replicated but the magnitude might change; a move forward of ten might need to be replaced by a move of one. (This development can also be used in early work on non-standard units of measurement.) What children quickly learn is that the further along the number line the number input is, the further the screen turtle or toy moves. Vaughn's research findings confirm this view with his use of a space journey scenario using a Logo procedure. The task involved children typing in a single-digit number at a 'forward' prompt to aim for a 'star' from their 'spaceship'. The children soon started to name one, two and three as 'slow' numbers, whereas other numbers were called 'fast' numbers (Vaughn 1997).

Recasting Logo for developing numeracy instead of developing only shape and space can be beneficial. Logo procedures can then be written for arithmetic rules; to explore number patterns; and to encourage mental mathematics by asking children to guess what an answer would be before they pressed the Enter key. At the simplest level is the *print* function. Children can type *print 4 + 5* and the computer will give the answer. They can make up their own sums and guess before they press. The benefit over a calculator (except perhaps a graphic calculator) is that they can see what they have keyed in. They can also start to experiment with several numbers and operations, e.g. *print 7 + 6 − 4 + 24*, or more ambitiously *print 42/6 + 3 * (4 + 5)*. The commutative and distributive laws of arithmetic can be explored with comparisons like *print 3 + 6* and *print 6 + 3*, and *print (3 + 6) * 2* and *print 3 + (6 * 2)*. Procedures can also be written to replicate function machines, for example the procedure below will multiply a number by 3 and subtract 2.

```
to guess :number
print 3 * :number – 2
end
```

Pupils try different numbers by entering *guess x* into the computer, where *x* can be any number. Pressing the return key will run the procedure and then children have to guess the rule, test it out by running more entries and thus make conjectures as to what the procedure is doing to their original number. They are testing and hypothesising, and are therefore engaged in mathematical thinking.

Procedures in mathematics are routines that develop algebraic thinking, in that they encourage students to generalise from the particular. The use of procedures allows algebra to be introduced earlier in the curriculum as children can see the visual impact of their actions. For example, drawing a simple square in which they use a variable for the length of the sides will demonstrate that there is a general rule for generating squares of any size, using the procedure:

```
to square :length
repeat 4 [fd :length rt :90]
end
```

Later on in the curriculum this procedure can be generalised for any polygon, allowing students to develop a link between all polygons instead of viewing each one as a separate entity:

```
to polygon :side :angle
repeat :side [fd :length rt :side/360]
end
```

The link between number and shape can also be used the other way round. For example, generating the Fibonacci sequence can help in the construction of pentagons and their diagonals or in the construction of pentagonal stars. Consecutive numbers in the sequence give the length of the sides and diagonals respectively. The use of pictorial or graphical representations of number can help children to understand concepts like the difference between addition and multiplication. A procedure like 'spiraladd' (see Figure 8.6) will produce an 'addition' spiral; whereas changing the procedure to 'spiralmult' will produce a 'multiplication' spiral that grows far more quickly:

Addition spiral	*Multiplication spiral*
to spiraladd :number	to spiralmult :number
if :number > 300 [stop]	if :number > 300 [stop]
fd :number rt 90	fd :number rt 90
spiraladd (:number + 2)	spiralmult (:number * 2)
end	end

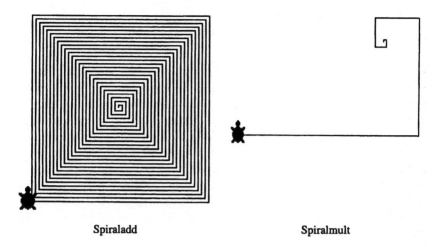

Spiraladd   Spiralmult

Figure 8.6 Addition and multiplication spirals

In addition, in spiralmult by changing the value by which the number is multiplied the effects of multiplying by a fractional number can be demonstrated, dispelling the myth that 'multiplication always makes bigger'. Working together with shape and number presents a holistic picture of mathematics.

THE ROLE OF THE TEACHER

So far I have looked at the use of ICT by students without due consideration of the role of the teacher, particularly in relation to mediation between student and machine, and how vital the teacher's role is in ensuring that students come to understand or 'know' mathematics. Elsewhere, a colleague and I wrote:

> Technology can be a vital medium for validating students' naive attempts to express their mathematical ideas. When a student expresses an idea on a graphic calculator, the feedback from the screen will usually indicate whether the mathematical idea expressed was that intended. However the student also needs to be sure that the representation they see on the screen is what *was* intended. Mediation between student, teacher and screen can now take place, but the representation has come as a result of interaction between the student and the screen and not between the student and the teacher. The

> negotiation of meaning and interpretation becomes more equal between
> student and teacher, and the novice/expert divide is reduced.
> (Alexander 1992: 39 cited in Selinger and Pratt 1998: 39)

When students are working on computers or with calculators, teachers
will need to make informal assessments of their progress – intervening
with questions to ascertain individual levels of comprehension and checking
the appropriateness of the task; making decisions about whether the pupil
needs to move on to a new task or, indeed, deciding whether ICT is
the best way of developing the aspect of mathematics being learnt. In
learning about multiple representations (discussed above), teacher support
is required to help students reconcile the connections between and the
meanings of the different mathematical forms. Students will need support
in developing strategies to make the connections, and to articu-late what
those connections are. Teachers also need to make decisions about whether
the tasks they engage students in would be better tackled collaboratively or whether it is the type of task that might be better completed
alone.

ILS has probably been the most researched numeracy and literacy
software in the UK. Both phase two and phase three of the ILS studies
(Wood 1998) indicated that there were significant and lasting gains in
basic mathematical skills, and the extent of the gains were due to the way
it was used in school. The particular ILS system used was also a factor
in the success, and it was reported that not all were universally successful. The findings from the three pilot projects are inconclusive about
the learning gains in general, but they do stress the essential role of the
teacher and the right teaching environment if ILS is to be effective
and to produce improvements in mathematical learning. Where ILS is
used effectively, teachers make use of the feedback from the ILS system
to plan more appropriate work for their students, or use the time
when one group of students is working on ILS to develop an aspect of
mathematics with another group of students. The very act of working with
a small group in which more focused attention can be given to individuals could be a contributing factor to learning gains.

Passey (1998), in reviewing a new ILS for primary mathematics, found
substantial gains in children's performance in number and shape and space.
In this system 'material was presented in a form which paper based resources
cannot match, including animation, three-dimensional and tactile interaction'. Nevertheless, he too encouraged the right environment and suggested
that the learning gains would not result from children using the software
on their own. He states that children will need 'support, encouragement
and opportunities to learn through social interaction. . . . [The ILS soft-
ware] should not be a substitute for the environment which teachers create

and use. It should be used to reinforce previous learnt skills and concepts, and it can offer new concepts to enhance attainment' (Passey 1998: 37).

There have been substantial gains in numeracy across all levels of attainment, but one wonders to what extent the computer has really helped children to formulate mathematical concepts in a different way. ILS systems are basically teaching mathematics in old ways using new technology, and the idea that mathematics is all about arriving at the correct answers and the 'right' ways of performing certain mathematical procedures is reinforced by ILS. It is the role of the teacher to move students beyond this notion and to counteract it by means of other examples where the answers can be reached via a number of routes, as illustrated earlier in this chapter. Too often mathematical concepts are taught in isolation from each other, and connections which would help students to develop their understanding and their ability to reconstruct methods for solving problems are not being made. ICT can help the teacher to develop and reinforce these connections, and it need not be the other way round.

The Calculator Aware Number Curriculum (CAN) project led by the Primary Initiatives in Mathematics team (PrIME) in the 1980s (see Shuard *et al.* 1991) indicated some promising mathematical developments for pupils, but they were premissed on teachers' own professional development in making use of the calculator in the classroom for developing pupils' mental mathematics rather than to make the latter redundant. With well-prepared teachers, calculators have a place in all classrooms. To be used effectively, however, pupils need to have a basic number sense, which is essential to assure them that they are using the correct number operation, and to judge whether the answer on the calculator is sensible or not. Calculator games can help to develop number sense. This all presupposes that teachers' own mathematical understanding is robust. Unless they have a firm grasp of the subject, then many of the big mathematical ideas underlying these games can be lost, and students exposed to instrumental learning of a different kind.

HOW ICT CAN MASK THE NATURE OF STUDENTS' LEARNING

The old chestnut 'Maxbox' can illustrate how vital the teacher is in the mediation process between student and machine, and how important a teacher's own subject knowledge is. The problem is often presented to the class by starting with a sheet of A4 paper from which pupils have to find the dimensions of a box that has maximum volume when four equal squares of side x are removed from the corners of the paper (so as to enable a box to be formed by folding up the sides – see Figure 8.7). The underlying mathematics here can be used to introduce ideas of maximum

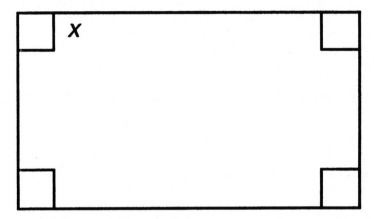

Figure 8.7 The 'Maxbox' problem

and minimum values, to introduce parabolas, or to illustrate a practical use of quadratics.

Students are encouraged to enter their information onto a spreadsheet and to use the spreadsheet's calculating facility to compute the volume. After one or two trials, the students usually stop making boxes as they begin to understand what happens as they change the value of x and start to enter successive increments of x on the spreadsheet. Next they use the graphing function of the spreadsheet to draw a graph of the results, usually with the teacher's support. The spreadsheet package will usually be one that has been designed for business and will 'know' that the quadratic form generated from these data will have a maximum value, so that even if the students have not found the maximum point the application will still draw the graph, as in Figure 8.8. If the students had plotted the graph themselves, and were unsure about the shape and meaning of a quadratic function, then it may be that they have drawn the graph by hand in a way similar to Figure 8.9. By using the spreadsheet graphing function, awareness of potential misunderstanding may be lost. The teacher would not know that the student did not understand about maximum or minimum points or the shape of quadratic functions.[12] However, in such cases, the teacher has to be aware of these potential pitfalls. This example also highlights a concern about the use of business applications for educational purposes. The software has been designed for functionality in the workplace, and therefore does not need to highlight errors in mathematical understanding. While teachers are stressing the higher-order concepts they are teaching and using the applications to automate some of the lower-order processes, there is a danger that they are ignoring students'

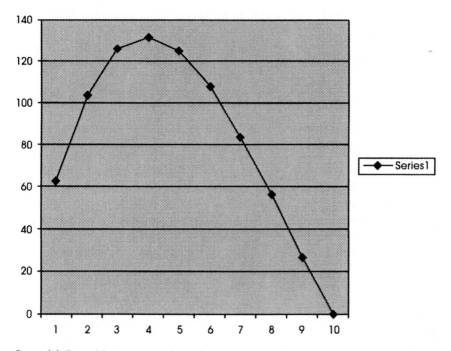

Figure 8.8 Spreadsheet-generated graph

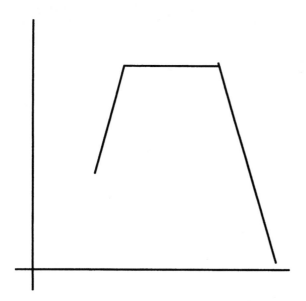

Figure 8.9 Learner-generated graph

understanding of some of the more fundamental concepts. It requires teachers to consider what needs to be taught first before the ICT application is used. Connell and Harnisch (2000) note that 'this would be analogous to letting your writing be totally edited by wizards in your word processor', and allowing the results to be accepted.

What to leave in and what to take out?

Given any technological apparatus, then, a fundamental question is what can it usefully release pupils from, and what does it displace? Love (1993) believes that 'learning how to carry out techniques, rather than using them, is, substantially, the school mathematics curriculum'. The ACOT report (Sandholz *et al.* 1996) states that 'math teachers reported they could reduce class time spent on practising arithmetic skills by relying on computer homework; this freed class time for developing problem-solving skills'. Perhaps this is one of the greatest benefits of computer technology. It frees pupils from the drudgery of 'carrying out techniques', and allows them to reinforce the uses to which mathematics can be put in solving a whole range of problems. Gray and Tall (1994: 137) report that they 'have evidence that the use of the computer to carry out the *process*, thus enabling the learner to concentrate on the *product*, significantly improves the learning experience'.

In the 'Maxbox' case considered above the techniques of calculating the volume are rendered trivial: as long as the students know how to enter the correct formula to calculate the volume, the spreadsheet will perform the calculations, and their focus can be on developing an understanding of quadratic functions through the construction of a box. This also gives a concrete example of how a quadratic function has a real-life application, and introduces students to the properties of quadratic functions (e.g. two values of x for each value of y, maximum and minimum values, and characteristics of the graph). In such situations questions need to be asked about the curriculum in place today. What is it that needs to be taught, and when? It seems that with ICT attention needs to be given to reconsidering the order in which concepts are taught, how ICT supports areas of mathematics to become more interrelated, and how subject software can support the development of mathematical understanding.

SUMMARY

Roy Pea (1987), in an imaginative and far-sighted paper published at a time when the pocket calculator was just getting going, drew on the analogy of pencil and paper to suggest that technology seems to enable people to externalise the previously ephemeral or mental, and make it available to inspection. Conversely, it can enable images and experiences with symbols to support new mental images.

The presence of such technology in schools raises some important questions in the construction of tasks, as well as the ways in which classrooms operate. Technology (including its absence) is claimed to have an influence on teaching styles and methods. For example, one claim is that many teachers introduce computer software in what might be termed a 'traditional' way, showing children what to do with it rather than letting them explore and discover, and this might be in spite of teachers' own learning methods, perhaps playing with it at the weekend to 'see what it will do'. As yet, the diversity of conceived environments on computers is only beginning to be explored. It must not be forgotten that educational electronic technology in school settings has really been available for less than twenty years, and schools as institutions are slow to appropriate new technologies – slow to embrace them in the first place, and slow thereafter to use them in new ways (see Cuban 1993).

But the key issue to be considered is twofold: on the one hand, there is the positive potential of such devices to free pupils from irrelevant activity so that they can engage in mathematics, and, be stimulated to think mathematically; and on the other hand, there is the negative effect of displacing or discounting the activity of these new mathematical tools. There is also the perennial concern about losing old, traditional ways of doing things and replacing them by the new, and the consequent loss of hard-won fluent skills. Certain algorithms, such as those for long division or finding square roots, could become mathematical art objects, still worth considering – but not as a functional means of computation, but rather for developing mathematical investigation and appreciation.

Given any technological apparatus, then, a fundamental question is what can it usefully release pupils from, and what does it displace? Using apparatus of any form does not in itself guarantee learning, or better learning; yet there are deeply held feelings that it should, and hence the need for careful consideration of the interaction between the contribution of ICT, the subject knowledge and the role of the teacher.

NOTES

1 Daniel didn't progress in mathematics in the way one might have expected and did not follow the subject to A level.
2 The seminar was part of an ESRC funded series, focusing on ICT and pedagogy, held over the period 1999–2000.
3 The four-colour theorem is the proof that describes how many colours are needed to distinguish between regions.
4 Small software is generally subject-specific and is aimed at teaching one or two concepts; e.g. *Factor* and *Angle 90* from the *SMILE* suite of software produced by ICT staff at the Inner London Education Authority in the 1980s.

5 *Traffic* is included in *Teaching with a Micro: Maths 2* and was produced around 1985 by the Shell Centre for Mathematical Education, University of Nottingham, UK.
6 *Cabri-Geometry* by the University Joseph Fourier of Grenoble (details available at http://www.ti.com/calc/docs/cabri.htm).
7 *The Geometer's Sketchpad*, by Key Curriculum Press, USA (details available at http://www.keypress.com/product_info/sketchpad3.html).
8 See for example:
http://www nrich.maths.org
http://www.exploratorium.edu/learning_studio/1001/mathematics.html
http://www.maths.usu.edu/matti
9 An applet is a tool used for programming dynamic images on the internet.
10 *Crystal Rainforest* is a Logo-based adventure game for the Acorn Archimedes computer.
11 *Space City* is a Logo-based adventure game for the Acorn Archimedes computer.
12 My thanks go to Stephen Baldwin, who alerted me to this potential problem and provided a fruitful discussion between ourselves and a combined group of trainee secondary mathematics and ICT teachers.

REFERENCES

Ainley, J. (1996) *Enriching Primary Mathematics with IT*, London: Hodder & Stoughton.
Ainsworth, S., Bibby, P. A. and Wood, D. J. (1997) 'Information technology and multiple representations: new opportunities – new problems', *Journal of Information Technology for Teacher Education* 6(1).
Alexander, P. A. (1992) 'Domain knowledge: evolving themes and emerging concerns', *Educational Psychologist* 27(1): 33–51.
ATM (1999) *Developing Number Software*, Derby: Association of Teachers of Mathematics.
Campbell, S. R. (2000) 'Computer-assisted synthesis of visual and symbolic meaning in mathematics education', in R. Robson (ed.), *Proceedings of M/SET 2000*, San Diego, CA, 5–8 February.
Cannon, L. O., Heal, E. R. and Wellman, R. (2000) 'Serendipity in interactive mathematics: virtual (electronic) manipulatives for learning elementary mathematics', in D. A. Willis, J. D. Price and J. Willis (eds), *Proceedings of SITE 2000*, San Diego, CA, 8–12 February.
Connell, M. L. (2000) 'Symbolic computers and mathematical objects', in D. A. Willis, J. D. Price and J. Willis (eds), *Proceedings of SITE 2000*, San Diego, CA, 8–12 February.
—— and Harnisch, D. L. (2000) 'A case for strong conceptualization in technology enhanced mathematics instruction', in D. A. Willis, J. D. Price and J. Willis (eds), *Proceedings of SITE 2000*, San Diego, CA, 8–12 February.
Cuban, L. (1993) 'Computers meet classroom: classroom wins', *Teachers College Record* 95(2): 185–210.
DfEE (1997) *Excellence in Schools*, London: Stationery Office.
—— (1998) *The Implementation of the National Numeracy Strategy: The Final Report of the Numeracy Task Force*, London: DfEE.
Fuglestad, A. B. (1997) 'Spreadsheets as support for understanding decimal numbers', *Micromath* 13(1): 6–9.

Gray, E. and Tall, D. (1994) 'Duality, ambiguity, and flexibility: a perceptual view of simple arithmetic', *Journal for Research in Mathematics Education*, 24: 116–40.

Hewitt, D. and Brown, E. (1998) 'On teaching early number through language', in A. Olivier and K. Newstead (eds), *Proceedings of the 22nd Conference of the International Group for the Psychology of Mathematics Education*, University of Stellenbosch, South Africa, vol. 3: 41–8.

Hoyles, C. and Noss, R. (1987) 'Synthesising mathematical conceptions and their formalization through the construction of a Logo-based school mathematics curriculum', *International Journal of Mathematics Education Science and Technology* 18(4): 581–95.

Kurta, J. (1997) 'Number crunching', *InteracTive* 15: 14–15.

Love, E. (1993) 'Software for mathematics education', in B. Jaworksi (ed.), *Technology and Mathematics Teaching TMT 93: A Bridge Between Teaching and Learning. Conference Proceedings*, Birmingham.

McIntosh, A., Reys, B. J. and Reys, R. E. (1992) 'A proposed framework for examining basic number sense', *For the Learning of Mathematics* 12(3): 2–8.

NCET (1997) *Primary Mathematics with IT*, Coventry: NCET.

Noss, R. (1985) *Creating a Mathematical Environment Through Programming: A Study of Young Children Learning Logo*, University of London: Institute of Education.

—— (1986) 'Constructing a conceptual framework for elementary algebra through LOGO programming', *Educational Studies in Mathematics* 17(4): 335–57.

Oldknow, A. (1993) 'Mathematics and computing – a continuing symbiosis', in B. Jaworksi (ed.), *Technology and Mathematics Teaching TMT 93: A Bridge Between Teaching and Learning. Conference Proceedings*, Birmingham.

O'Reilly, D., Pratt, D. and Winbourne, P. (1997) 'Constructive and instructive representation', *Journal of Information Technology for Teacher Education* 6(1).

Papert, S. (1972) 'Teaching children mathematics versus teaching children about mathematics', *International Journal of Mathematics Education Science and Technology* 3: 249–62.

—— (1980) *Mindstorms*, Brighton, Sussex: Harvester Press.

Passey, D. (1998) 'Integrated support for maths', *InteracTive* 18: 36–7.

Pea, R. (1987) 'Cognitive technologies for mathematics education', in A. Schoenfeld (ed.), *Cognitive Science and Mathematics Education*, Hillsdale, NJ: Lawrence Erlbaum.

Pianfetti, E. S. and Pianfetti, B. M. (2000) 'From the abstract to the practical: how motion media grapher helps students understand and interpret abstract mathematical concepts', in D. A. Willis, J. D. Price and J. Willis (eds), *Proceedings of SITE 2000*, San Diego, CA, 8–12 February.

Pimm, D. (1992) *Mathematics: Symbols and Meanings*, Milton Keynes: Open University Press.

Sandholtz, J. H., Ringstaff, C. and Dwyer, C. D. (1996) *Teaching With Technology: Creating Student-Centred Classrooms*, New York: Teachers' College Press.

Selinger, M. and Pratt, D. (1997) 'Mediation of mathematical meaning through the graphic calculator', *Journal of IT in Teacher Education* 6(1): 37–48.

Shuard, H., Walsh, A., Goodwin, J. and Worcester, V. (1991) *Calculators, Children and Mathematics*, London: Simon & Schuster (for NCC).

Skemp, R. (1976) 'Relational and instrumental understanding', *Mathematics Teaching* 77: 20–6.

Thompson, P. W. (1992) 'Notations, conventions and constraints: contributions to effective uses of concrete materials in elementary mathematics', *Journal for Research in Mathematics Education* 23(2): 123–47.

Vaughn, G. (1997) 'Number education for very young children: can IT change the nature of early years' mathematics education?', in B. Somekh and N. Davis (eds), *Using Information Technology Effectively in Teaching and Learning: Students in Pre-Service and In-Service Teacher Education*, London: Routledge.

Wadebridge, J. (1996) 'You can count on it', *InteracTive* 4: 6–9.

Wood, D. (1998) *The UK ILS Evaluations: Final Report*, Coventry: BECTA.

Chapter 9

ICT and science education

New spaces for gender

Katrina Miller

This chapter addresses issues of science and ICT in schools and in science teacher education. It does so specifically in the context of primary teacher education, where issues of gender are foregrounded. I want to argue that the model of science taught in schools and in teacher training is an outmoded one that is neither matched with science as it is practised today nor with the changing social conditions, values and ideologies of the twenty-first century. With ICT influencing science curricula and pedagogies, it is timely to explore the potential that new technologies might offer for developing a science curriculum better matched to shifts in social conditions. The questions I wish to raise concern women teachers, themselves gendered by modern science, who are doing science work in formal education. I particularly want to explore the potential that new technologies might have for changing teachers' gendered identities and practices in doing this science work and for making its underpinning values and ideologies more explicit. The chapter focuses particularly on the training and education of primary teachers of science rather than on science education in schools, although necessarily the two are closely related. The issues raised in this chapter are relevant to secondary or high-school age-phases, even though the culture there is different both in terms of curricular and pedagogical practices. Although secondary or high-school teachers of science still tend in the main to be male, they too are gendered by modernist science. They are doing modernist science work, engaging with ICT in this science work and could therefore interrogate their own practices and the values and ideologies underpinning them from a similar perspective.

No curriculum subject is taught in a vacuum and it is important to describe the social conditions in which we are presently working in order to set the context for the chapter. This also helps position my argument as I begin to critique science, recognising the social and ideological in scientific practices, challenging the discourses of these social practices and taking a feminist perspective in interrogating the impact of ICT in science education.

To contextualise the argument, the chapter begins with a presentation of the social conditions in which science and ICT education are taking place and a description of the science being promoted in formal education. This is followed by a section exploring science's role in the construction of gender, focusing on how science has constructed women. There follow three images of ICT in science education to illuminate some of the issues concerning science and women teachers of science. I then consider the impact of ICT on formal and informal science education, discussing the access to scientific ideas and debates made possible through new technologies. The chapter concludes with some ideas for a new science curriculum involving changing subject boundaries, teacher identities and pedagogical practices.

SOCIAL CONTEXT

The theoretical models I wish to draw on to contextualise this discussion about how ICT might change the subject of science in school and in teacher education are those of Anthony Giddens and Ulrich Beck. These describe the social conditions of the late-modern Age of Information or 'high modernity' (Giddens 1991; Beck 1992) which is described elsewhere as 'fast, compressed, complex and unstable' (Hargreaves 1994). It is the new technologies that are compressing time and 'quickening . . . the rhythms of industrial, social and cultural life' (Scott 1995: 114). For the German sociologist Ulrich Beck, one consequence of modern science, as it comes out of the laboratory, so to speak, surfacing in all aspects of our modern lives, is the 'risk society' that emerges when 'the gain in power from techno-economic "progress" is being increasingly overshadowed by the production of risks' (Beck in Scott 1995).

'Risk society' is an important concept in describing the context for science education because it has deep implications for the public's perception of science. While this perception is constructed largely through formal schooling, it is increasingly influenced by informal educational opportunities through access to mass media and to 'edutainment' in science. The impact of these changes in the context of schooling will be explored below. The environmental damage and climatic changes that have resulted from so-called scientific and technological progress are good exemplars of the risk society. Beck also talks about the way science is used to validate public policy decisions. This process occurs more visibly in a public arena made increasingly accessible to all through TV and new media technologies.

For Giddens (1991), one of the paradoxes of modern science and technology is the wide-ranging personal and social benefits that accrue from that very science and technology which simultaneously create hazard. We, the public, hold ambivalent views about science and technology, sometimes fear and outrage, sometimes gratitude and amazement. It is as if, naïvely and immaturely, we want our science and technology to be secure and risk-free, not wanting to be confronted with dilemmas that arise with the risks and hazard that come with a scientific society. The scientific age of information, then, has two features of importance when contextualising formal science education. First, we citizens (of the one-third world) undoubtedly are the beneficiaries of science and technology in many aspects of our high-tech lives. And, second, we have an increasing understanding of risk and hazard as products of that same science and technology. This analysis surfaces in Hilary Rose's contention that, as we move away from being able to believe in science's capability to produce 'Truth', we need rather to develop a relationship of trust with science – and this because 'Society increasingly feels that although no-one knows exactly which is the greatest risk, there is something wrong and that it is science and technology which is somehow causing the trouble' (Rose in Maynard 1997: 18)

Finally in terms of social context, we need to note how the mainstream modernist relationship between science and technology has been compressed so that we increasingly see references in the literature to 'technosciences' (Rose in Maynard 1997). 'Technoscience' perhaps more accurately conceptualises not only the nature and practices of present-day scientific research but also the fact that in many scientific fields, the separation of science from technology is no longer realistic. It is to this new hybrid subject 'technoscience' that policy makers appeal for legitimation in decision making. Examples of these new hybrid subjects are biochemistry and biotechnology and even, across disciplinary boundaries, bioethics. The concept of hybridity may itself be a useful tool in attempting to construct new identities for the teacher of these emerging technosciences, especially in the context of new technologies, as we shall see.

Formal science education is taking place, then, in a fragmenting and hazardous social context where science's traditional authority is being publicly challenged, where we, the public, hold contradictory views of science and where the boundaries between disciplines are collapsing to form new ways of looking at the world. Before setting up images of ICT as it is used in science, I want to describe the model of science that I see currently taught and learned in formal schooling.

MECHANISTIC SCIENCE IN TWENTY-FIRST-CENTURY SCIENCE EDUCATION

Science is traditionally practised within a paradigm that orders nature through reason in order to understand and control the phenomena and processes of the biological, chemical and physical worlds. The logico-mathematical tradition, empirical methodologies and an interwoven relationship with mathematics remain the hegemonic or dominant ways of knowing, prioritised and legitimated over all others (Marks 1983; Harding 1991). This is the modern scientific worldview with which we are familiar. It has produced a canon of globally powerful ideas and concepts, classically categorised within biology, chemistry and physics. The discourses and social practices of the science laboratory that have produced this canon are found universally. It is the model that frames school curricula and science teacher education. For example, it can be argued that the science in science education, blind to the changing social context in which we now find ourselves, remains firmly embedded within a modernist mindset with all the models of knowledge or epistemologies and ways of teaching – the pedagogical conventions – which that mindset implies (DfEE 1995 and 2000; Wenham 1995; Sherrington 1998; QCA 1999). In the current school science curriculum in England, all the programmes to introduce and develop basic scientific concepts are prefixed – 'Pupils should be taught that . . .' – and the ideas are presented in a list which, between the three traditional school sciences, amounts to 150 separate conceptual statements. In terms of doing science, there is one programme of study consisting of skills in a similarly reductionist vein, the prefix changing with the substitution of 'taught to' for 'taught that' (DfEE 1995 and 2000).

The construction of the teacher is clearly as a repository of the procedural and conceptual knowledge of classical science which she then has to transmit to her pupils. It is a misleading picture of science and the processes and practices with which it has generated powerful understandings of the world through a highly specific worldview. It expresses nothing of the way late-twentieth-century science shifted away from this classical scientific worldview or the social consequences of science's way of knowing. I am not suggesting that there is no justification for introducing some of science's fundamental principles or meta-concepts. What I am proposing is a science curriculum, enabled by the powerful opportunities offered by ICT, that could present science as the messy and contentious social practice which it now is, with a history of dissent and powerful consequences that reflect, and are reflected by, social circumstances and conditions.

As one would perhaps expect, the present initial teacher training National Curriculum for science in England is consistent with the model described for schools. It is presented as a list of competences for science teaching comprising some seventy-six 'facts' embodying the science knowledge that a student teacher must acquire in order to achieve Qualified Teacher Status (DfEE 1998). Interestingly, these are made up of 16 for biology, 14 for chemistry and 46 for physics, numbers which have caused some disturbance among the respective scientific institutions. As for ICT, the pattern is similar: student teachers have to demonstrate competence in, and understanding of, ICT as described in a total of sixty-two requirements (*ibid.*). In the current climate of public accountability and managerialism, it is the assessment framework that largely dictates practice. Today, it is this statutory instrument that binds UK university teacher education departments: 'If non-compliance with . . . [the statute] . . . is found in any aspect of provision . . . it will be drawn to the attention of the provider . . . so that the provider can instigate remedial action immediately and the . . . [authority] . . . can consider whether to start withdrawal of accreditation procedures' (OfSTED–TTA 1998: 4).

I am arguing, then, that the epistemological model of science in formal science education continues to resemble a mechanistic backward-looking science. In my analysis, there appears to be a growing gap between the nineteenth-century science of the school curriculum and science as it is practised in the twenty-first century and as it is perceived by the public. Arguments between scientists about specific research results, as well as about science's way of knowing the world, are increasingly conducted in the public domain, made possible through new communications technologies. This is a reflection of the changing social conditions I have described. 'Scientific literacy' as a concept has been widely debated in recent times as a requirement for active citizenship in post-industrial democracies (Michael 1996; Millar and Osborne 1998; DfEE 2000). This is perhaps due partly to the scientific community's response to the demand for greater public accountability of their practices. All of these issues are yet to be reflected in formal science curricula and assessment frameworks. The picture is similar for ICT. In formal schooling, ICT can be presented as a set of mechanistic skills to be acquired for practice across school disciplines where it serves to replicate traditional ways of learning, the same models of knowledge and through familiar pedagogies (Somekh and Davis 1997; DfEE 1998). There are parallels between the gap that exists between science in school and science in the modern world and how ICT is being developed for use in school and the way it is developing in the world outside. One important issue which impacts on the ICT and science work of women teachers in formal education is the relationship between women and science. I need to consider this before setting up three images of ICT use in formal science education as a focus for exploring this issue.

HOW SCIENCE HAS CONSTRUCTED WOMEN

The history of modern science and the consequences of its dualisms and reductionisms have been strongly argued in feminist literature critical of modern science (Keller 1985; Lykke and Braidotti 1996). Londa Schiebinger (1993), for example, describes how modern science's culture, values, ways of knowing and focuses of study have 'served to hold women at a distance'.

Carolyn Merchant (1980) has thoroughly described science's conception of nature as female. For Evelyn Fox Keller (1992), this female nature–male science pairing has been a foundational metaphor in science's body of knowledge. The biological sciences have legitimated two genders as socio-cultural categories so that the (heterosexual) male gender is aligned and associated with reason, with mastery and with power, science and technology (Walkerdine 1988; Bleier 1991; Harding 1991), while (heterosexual) women are 'othered' as irrational, 'natural', intuitive and unstable – outside of science. The male is constructed as the universal norm from which women deviate. This dualism means that there is an oppositional character to the relationship between nature and science–technology, body and mind, non-human and human, between men and women, around which classical science constructed clear boundaries. In the feminist literature critical of science and technology, three metaphors have been used to critique the construction and position of women: goddess, monster and, more recently, cyborg. The *goddess* metaphor refers to a matriarchal figure of human prehistory whose values could be used to re-orient science and technologies away from their inherent sexism towards a more socially democratic and ecologically benign construction. For some this is an overly roman-ticised and backward-looking metaphor which still positions women passively outside of science and technology (Haraway 1991).

On the other hand, the *monster* metaphor represents a more powerfully active hybrid figure which/who challenges science's attempts at neat classification and characterisation. The classic example of this figure is Frankenstein's monster, the inhuman product of the scientific laboratory, disturbing precisely because it is a hybrid of the human and non-human (see 'Feminist confrontations with science' by Lykke in Lykke and Braidotti 1996) and because it defies science's attempts to neatly classify – and to control. Women likewise, as constructed by science, exist in this border-zone of hybridity, a mixture of human and also non-human because of their affinity with nature and the natural. Where Frankenstein's monster is a mechanical product of the science laboratory with human character-istics, 'woman' is of the human species but is 'other', different from the male norm, because of her characteristics of irrationality and her affinity with the natural. Like the Frankenstein monster, in her hybridity woman disturbs science's attempts at neat classification and control.

The third metaphor, the *cyborg*, is a modern extension of the monster figure, one of those '. . . grotesque post-industrial boundary figures, ques-tioning the boundaries between human, organism and machine, celebrated cornerstones of the modern scientific world-view' (Lykke and Braidotti 1996: 5).

Unlike the goddess metaphor, which for Donna Haraway (1991) is 'technophobic', the cyborg is positioned within modern 'technoscience', a hybrid like the monster yet with an active and powerful identity, a product of technoscience and a user of it, too. The culture, values and discourses of science as it is practised are gendered as (heterosexual) male; women are traditionally positioned as outsiders, described in metaphors as goddess, monster or cyborg. These theorisations make the way science and ICT are constructed and learned in schools an issue for women in science education. The cyborg metaphor, positioned inside and yet still outside science, may be a powerful one when considering how women teachers might develop different identities as they do science and ICT work. To be 'cyborgian' is to take control of technology and science for *our* purposes rather than to be subjected to it, like the monster, or to remain in opposition to it, like the natural goddess figure.

The three images of ICT in science teaching and learning that follow are written to illustrate some of these issues concerning the relationship between women teachers, ICT and science. I want to contrast the present model of the teacher as passive, as nurturer or mother (Acker 1994), which is closer to the goddess metaphor, with the new and more positive cyborg metaphor described above. I will also explore the possibilities provided by new technologies for developing this new identity in science education, using the three images described. Some ideas for a different science curriculum are developed in the light of this argument.

THREE IMAGES OF SCIENCE

Image one

When television news needs an image of science, it broadcasts one of white-coated technicians in laboratories handling multiple pipettes in the process of biochemical experimentation. The image is one of precise quantification using complex computing technologies conducted in a clean, high-tech environment. There is no talking in the image, apparatus is controlled by an expert operator working alone. The image seems designed to promote security in the scientific understandings that emerge from these objective practices.

In the primary-school setting, children visit a local pond to collect measurements of temperature, light, pH-levels or humidity using sensors connected to laptops with data-capture packages. Back in the classroom, data-handling software is used to make graphical representations or tables. The children are 'being scientists' and, using sophisticated gadgetry to collect 'science data', are learning important lessons about the nature of traditional science.

This image of what looks like a positivist science is presented by a legitimating media with all the old messages about objective science. This is probably a consequence of the kind of science education that programme makers and teachers remember from their own schooling. We, the viewers, the public, are positioned as the non-expert excluded from the expertise of the laboratory as we receive the given knowledge. The children's activities replicate the image's representation of the ordered, stable science practices of the laboratory. Knowledge claims are validated by specific and expert scientific practices – quantifiable data give the impression of legitimating objectivity. In reality, of course, data are very likely to be messy and incoherent. How far this is acknowledged and used to explore the nature of science depends on the teacher and her perception of science's practices, a point I will develop later.

Image two

In response to a teacher training curriculum requirement, a woman student teacher uses a CD-ROM to research photosynthesis. She is required to demonstrate a secure understanding of this process so that this underpinning knowledge will facilitate her teaching of science in the primary school. She uses an interactive CD-ROM to read text and look at images which teach her about photosynthesis; she then completes the self-assessment exercises. Working with a group of fellow students, she may use her knowledge with a multimedia package to make a presentation.

Similarly, in the primary classroom children are accessing scientific ideas and explanations using CD-ROMs and multimedia packages. Investigatory work is carried out using digital cameras, photocopiers, computer-generated questionnaires, sensors for data capture, measurement, representation of data, audio equipment to record interviews with experts, scanners for children's own drawings, software to produce interactive databases.

While there are acknowledged advantages to using new technologies in science in this way, the image is one in which science is again represented as an incontestable body of knowledge to be transmitted to children and student teachers. It is constructed as value-free 'official knowledge' to be acquired by the non-knowers, be they student teachers or school pupils. The concepts of science are presented as incontestable and de-contextualised. While electronic technology replaces the print textbook in ways which may be more attractive and motivating, cheaper and much speedier, it is still classical school science that is being presented. There is no space for consideration of the process of the generation of scientific understanding through imagination and supposition, argument and contestation, which is the way that science works. Scientific understanding is 'received' through traditionally constructed images and standard practices. The student regards herself as a non-knower, deficient in 'proper science' understanding and placed outside of the community which holds the knowledge. She has no idea, yet, of the concept of 'situated knowledge' or of how that theoretical position might impact on her relationship with science. It is likely also that she is unaware of science's construction of her gender or of the gendered nature of science.

Image three

Our student teacher of science watches a documentary on the 'hot' science issue of the week. She finds the website of a non-governmental organisation where she is presented with conflicting scientific interpretations, scientists arguing as conflicting agendas are thrashed out in the public domain. Resisting pressure groups provide their own scientific evidence to counter government policy or the positions adopted by more powerful pressure groups, for example, in agribusiness or giant pharmaceutical industries. She is aware of the use of science and technology in the making of public policy in many aspects of her and her family's lives. She sees how modern science gives us both a powerful model of the world and a technology which comes complete with its own hazards too; she sees that science is about modelling and that science's predictions involve risk.

It is important to notice that, unlike the other two images described, there is no classroom equivalent to image three; children no longer have space or time in a school day, driven by increasingly assessed and inspected syllabuses and curricula, for meaningful debate as scientists do with their peers. Hard-pressed teachers manage their 'coverage' of the assessed National Curriculum study programmes rather than exploring science's work, procedures and explanations in a reflective and critical way.

The point about this third image is to foreground the ever-widening gap between school science and the science that impacts on our lives, which is one consequence of the increasing popularity of ICT use. School science aims to develop in pupils 'the basics' in terms of knowledge and understanding in biology, chemistry and physics. School science also aims to develop an understanding of a single scientific method. However, as it is the former which is largely the focus of assessment in England, from age 5 onwards, children's acquisition of 'official' scientific knowledge is prioritised increasingly in school syllabuses and schemes of work (QCA 1999). Whatever the local interpretative efforts of creative teachers on the ground, the discourses, values and practices of the primary science classroom, and the secondary science laboratory look like a transmission model of pedagogy – one that ensures a grounding in basic science as standard epistemology. It also seems to be the case that, so far, the use of ICT in science is replicating the transmission of 'official' scientific knowledge and a single empirical method. The model of science in initial teacher training in England mirrors that in school so that not only is a student teacher's own understanding of science regarded as essential for effective teaching, but there is so much of this to be secured that it occupies most of the students' energy during the university training programme. In the UK it has become a dominant and restrictive part of the work required to gain Qualified Teacher Status, excluding the kind of critical thinking associated with university education which would facilitate a teacher's more interrogative approach to science studies. ICT in science replicates the very values that underpin modern science, as I have described them above.

These images encapsulate some of the paradoxes in science education for women teachers in the Information Age. In terms of shifting epistemology, pedagogy and gender identity, the teacher is the key player. Her awareness of ideas challenging and contesting her positioning by modern science as monstrous 'other' will make a difference to her developing teaching role. A more 'cyborgian' identity, as active insider who engages with new technologies, will impact deeply on her classroom practices and relationship to science. How she will use the opportunities that arise with ICT in her science teaching to present science in a more relevant, perhaps even gender-neutral, way is crucial. Through ICT, the internet and television, the powerful impact of science and technologies, and the benefits and the hazards they generate, are being brought into our everyday lives. Sociological debates about science and technology are challenging the model of science learned in school, the way it is taught and learned, its underpinning values, the role of the teacher in science learning and in the relationships between science, teacher, pupil and ICT. These debates are contextualised in the rapid-change poststructural conditions of modern times.

My first concern is that the current UK school science and ICT curricula, as well as the science and ICT teacher training curricula, provide hardly any space and time for exploring the meaning of the scientific worldview and its underpinning values, let alone the implications for changing sociocultural conditions with ICT. My second concern relates to the difficult confrontations faced by women student teachers struggling with their self-identity as teachers, as teachers of science and as users of ICT. I am suggesting that rather than making student teachers 'know enough science' and giving them a mechanistic skills-focused perception of ICT in science work, we need to think about how we can help student teachers negotiate their developing identities and relationships with science and ICT and expose the values underpinning ICT as well as science. My argument is that women teachers of science are restricted from developing models of knowledge and pedagogies more appropriate to our changing times. They are still being constructed as passive consumers of new technologies which reproduce the same mechanistic science, a science itself increasingly divorced from developments outside the formal educational institutions and increasingly irrelevant to the social conditions of the Information Age. I am also suggesting that as teaching, especially primary teaching, is still largely a gendered profession, we cannot ignore the questions that are being raised in social theory and in feminist science studies about the conceptualisation of gender as a social category. Feminist confrontations with technology and science need to be brought into science education to confront the gendered nature of science and the gendered nature of teaching. This is particularly apposite as ICT impacts on both science and teaching and this is a time when we perhaps have a real opportunity to change the subject; and the subject is not only science and ICT but 'women' as subjects of science and the new technologies too.

NEW TECHNOLOGIES IN SCIENCE EDUCATION

ICT use in science classrooms is set to become more and more part of science education practices because of a massive national investment programme and also because ICT is a burgeoning part of our daily lives. As I have suggested, there is a danger that traditional representations of science are being replicated in software packages, CD-ROMs and through internet websites. Any impact in terms of changing pedagogy looks more like surface polishing of current models than a radical realignment in the social relations of the science classroom. Teacher training models in England are so constrained now that effectiveness in the classroom is measured by a model of the teacher as deliverer of a traditional curriculum where practices are determined by curricular coverage and assessment.

   The three images are presented to illustrate ICT and science education issues confronting women, both in their teacher training experience and in school practices. I have argued that science and ICT as used in science education are neither value-free nor gender-neutral, and this means trouble for women doing science and ICT work. In returning to the three images of science education I hope to see where the potential lies for a new 'cyborgian' teacher identity, and for a realignment in the relationship between ICT, science and women teachers. I then suggest a curriculum that makes its underpinning values more explicit and more relevant to changing social conditions.

Image one

School science and teacher training experiences include direct environmental explorations using sensors, data capture and graphing packages (Barton 1997). These experiences re-present a traditional hypothetico-deductive scientific method capturing empirical data, quantifiable through standard mathematical procedures. The representation is of a dualistic separation of 'human' from 'nature' in data implicitly produced for human ends. Implicit are the values of the traditional gendered scientific model of control and dominance of the natural world. However, if our teacher recognises and can articulate the values underpinning these methods and pedagogies, then ICT use can free up time for exposing these values, developing understanding not only of ecological principles but of the limitations as well as the advantages of scientific method. More importantly, if she understands that ICT is not a value- or a gender-free zone either, then this will inform and enrich her understanding of the significance of her teaching, not least the identity that she adopts for herself and projects to her pupils. With ICT use our teacher can manage debate about quality and relevance of different types of data, human sensory data for example, and explore difference in representation both in debate and, perhaps more importantly, in a range of images and writing genres. She can use the messiness of collected data to explore the values underpinning scientific modelling. Scientific writing can be compared with more reflexive forms to explore how science constructs itself as powerful knowledge through exclusive methodological and discourse practices. Women's ways of knowing can be incorporated into science and ICT work. A 'cyborgian' teacher can use her own images and models in addition to the mathematical ones to show how science is part of messy and unresolved ecological dilemmas. She can show how what is omitted from traditional representations of data is revealing of underpinning values and ideological positions.

Image two

Science CD-ROMs and multimedia packages are used increasingly in science education, providing highly motivating access to information and ways to communicate that information (Frost 1999). As I have argued, colourful graphics, moving images and accessible hyperlinks are all very well, but if scientific concepts are still presented as 'true', objective knowledge to be learned and recalled for test, then the traditional, partial and gendered construction of science is replicated. The learning remains on the level of information and the values and underpinning ideology remain implicit and unexposed, embedded in a male science, as I have described above. What is important for our student teacher is to learn how to critique the images used in new communications media, raising questions about the social practices and values that have produced our present scientific explanations of phenomena and processes as products of a history of specific discourses and practices. This critical and exposing lens can be introduced to pupils as they use multimedia packages to produce their own reports and presentations of their scientific learning; pupils can be encouraged to think critically about the images they capture with digital cameras, audio- and video-tape recordings and scanners, which represent their construction of 'scientists', of 'medical experts' or 'environmentalists'. This more interrogative approach can focus on the values underpinning both the science and the ICT, especially their gendered nature. Such critical thinking skills transfer into the informal sector and are of relevance to pupils and student teachers alike.

Scientific explanations presented as 'true' knowledge on CD-ROMs, such as *The Ultimate Human Body 2* (Dorling Kindersley 1996), ignore the 'alternative frameworks' (Driver *et al*. 1985) that pupils, and for that matter student teachers, bring to their science work. The implication again is that pupils and student teachers are 'in deficit' in terms of 'official knowledge'. This is another manifestation of the power and privileged position of science which ICT, rather than ascribing more authority, could expose. There is a danger that technological hardware and the discourses emerging in ICT are being constructed with similar power and positioning. At the same time, ICT is making new ways of communicating ideas which a critical teacher can exploit to value pupils' own ideas and explanations. These they can discuss not only with each other but with researching scientists, for example, through e-mail and online discussion groups, even contributing data to specific research projects such as the Pupil Research Initiative at Sheffield Hallam University.

Image three

It is both our student teacher and the community of school pupils who are exposed to informal science education through television and global communications networks, enriching the ideas and understandings that both bring to the science classroom and laboratory. Global communication systems provide opportunities for learning about the universality and power of modern sciences as well as about the contingent risks and hazards and the economic and ethical conflicts that surround science. Yet they also provide opportunities for direct learning about local and specific uses of science and technologies. This can provide enriched learning experiences about the nature of science through the possibility of comparing how local knowledge (as differentiated from official science) and local technology (as differentiated from high technology) are constructed in lived experiences. A good example of this is Edgar Jenkins's research of an elderly community's understanding of energy conservation (Jenkins in Baker *et al*. 1996). Comparisons of different models and metaphors explaining natural phenomena and processes in distinct communities show how those communities construct and use knowledge and how their values frame their models and metaphors. ICT provides new and quick access to forms of communication between communities previously disallowed in the culture and practices of science education, for example, accessing NASA. ICT can provide the means to develop connections between different explanations for phenomena and processes, the comparisons facilitating meaning-making, suggesting further ideas to test. Relevance to everyday lives becomes much more explicit, and teachers and pupils alike realise that 'official' scientific knowledge is one of many explanatory models, albeit an extremely powerful and hegemonic one.

Enrichment of science learning is also made possible through informal ICT-based 'edutainment'. There is an enormous and increasing number of science-based websites, from national museums to scientific research institutions and specific pressure groups. Science-based TV programmes are a regular and popular feature of broadcasting schedules, and further learning is encouraged by visits to TV channels' websites. These ICT-based and informal 'edutainment' opportunities make the understandings that pupils and becoming-teachers bring to their formal science education much more sophisticated. What becomes important in the noise of fast-changing social conditions is for our student teacher to develop a critical understanding of the ideological significance of her gendered identity and gendered position in this age of information and modern science in order to develop practices that expose ICT and science for the value-laden endeavours that they are. I am suggesting that an identity more 'cyborgian' than goddess-like would be potentially more emancipatory.

In the final section of this chapter, I suggest three ways to reform science in formal education, taking into consideration the arguments I have put forward about science itself, about ICT impacting on science education and about developing a more appropriate and more relevant metaphor for teacher identity. These three ideas are: hybridity and connectedness as characteristics of a new ICT–science curriculum in teacher training and in school; the removal of science teaching–learning from the laboratory; and the development of technoscience studies as cultural studies rather than science as it is currently constructed – a curriculum full of 'basic' concepts and single-model methodological procedures, as I have described.

A POST-MILLENNIAL TECHNOSCIENCE CURRICULUM

In presenting the social context of ICT and science education at the start of this chapter, I argued for Hilary Rose's concept 'technoscience' to be adopted in formal schooling curricula as being a better reflection of the nature of modern science. 'Technoscience' is also a concept Donna Haraway uses in her seminal 'cyborg manifesto' (1991) and is a more positive construction in which to develop a 'techno-friendly' (or teacher-as-cyborg) identity for the woman teacher of science. Hybridity and connectedness are concepts suggested to underpin a reformed curriculum. For the first time, ICT is providing us with the opportunity, through e-mail, the internet and CD-ROM, to get rid of the science laboratory as a powerful site for teaching and learning science, and I wish to argue that this could significantly alter the experience of science for women in positive ways.

Removing science teaching and learning from this specific site, and taking account of the opportunities afforded by ICT, I can finally suggest a model of technoscience studies more relevant to changing social conditions.

Hybridity and connectedness

Having described the contestations and challenges currently besetting modern science and the growing public awareness of the value-laden and ideological biases underpinning science, it seems clear that we need a science curriculum designed to develop trust and not one focused on 'Truth' (after Rose 1997). A flexible hybrid curriculum will have ICT at its core developing an awareness of the nature of science as discourse, as culture and as social practice. Explicit interrogation of the ideological distortions of any technoscience's curriculum would be at the core, as well as developing articulation through a multiplicity of voices, of underpinning values. Justification for a curriculum to represent science in this frame not only promotes the idea of science as culture but might motivate students to engage in further scientific study. Objectives in the new UK National Curriculum for science could be read as cultural rather than merely operational; for example:

> pupils make connections between different areas of science ... and understand a range of familiar applications of science. They think about the positive and negative effects of scientific and technological developments on the environment and in other contexts. They take account of others' views and understand why opinions may differ.
>
> (DfEE 2000: 28)

This at least acknowledges limitations to the modern scientistic project. ICT, as I have argued, is making possible ways of reconstructing science as a curriculum subject as well as reconstructing pedagogies as never before. Connectedness, it seems to me, needs to be a feature of an emerging ICT–technoscience curriculum: connectedness between the sciences as well as between science, RE, English and, of course, design technology. A 'cyborgian' teacher connects between the natural, the human and the machine through her manipulation and active control of ICT in her own learning and teaching.

No more labs

In a technoscience's curriculum, the emphasis would no longer be on doing science as it has traditionally been practised in the laboratory. The science laboratory is a space of enormous significance as a cultural construct and the site of specific social practices as well as powerful knowledge, as we have seen. Its contribution and influence need to be interrogated. Laboratory work is about the artificial control of conditions not possible in the everyday world, designed to remove the noise and interference of that ordinary world. In schools, laboratory work is used to demonstrate the known and accepted principles of normal science and has become sedimented in a false account of science. It is a naïve representation that denies the interpretative internalised biases and subjectivities of the scientist in the laboratory. Laboratory practices and social relations have had a key role, I would argue, in sustaining the 'othering' of girls and women by modernist science. They also have impacted on the general pathologising of the science teacher, expected to be a repository of all scientific knowledge presented as the 'right answers'. In a technoscience's curriculum, we need to ask: why sustain teaching–learning through practical activities in a laboratory? What are the skills and understandings to be developed through these stylised and sedimented practical activities? And how is science being understood through this experience?

The answers might include a certain logic, an intellectual tradition which appeals to empirical and quantifiable evidence for validation, close observation of evidence, ideas of reliability, validity, replication, the universality of 'good scientific explanation' and communication through an appropriate scientific discourse, both spoken and written. I have argued that these are the outmoded practices and culture of gendered traditional science. This model of school science 'experimentation' now seems increasingly irrelevant, and not least when it is inadequately replicated in the primary classroom. In our technoscience's curriculum, direct experiences of/with real-world technology can be integrated with, and interrogated by, virtual laboratory experiences. Controlled experiment, demonstration of principle or a historical replication of the original experimentation that uncovered the principle would all be 'virtually' possible. The emphasis for learning shifts to thinking, conjecture and talk about scientific method, about the reasons, limitations and benefits of carrying out controlled experimentation, and about qualitative interpretation of evidence. Facility to manipulate variables according to teachers' and pupils' immediate conjecture and argument would allow for a much enriched understanding at many different levels. The potential for data banks and secondary sources of multimedia information in the virtual lab is enormous. Our curriculum, then, would focus on argument and imagination; virtual 'science laboratory work' would become the minor part of the technoscience lesson, in which pupils–student teachers develop understandings not only about scientific concepts and principles but about the nature of the technoscientific endeavour itself. In other words, ICT would make possible a curriculum for science-as-culture rather than an outmoded model of science-as-practice (see Solomon 1999).

Technoscience studies

A new 'technoscience studies' curriculum in teacher education and in schools would be conditional on changes to the epistemology and pedagogy of current models. We would fuse sciences with technology and embed this new incarnation firmly in the social or some new hybrid subject, as it were, such as anthropological studies of technoscience. ICT would not only facilitate but actually necessitate the mergings of mainstream disciplines, so developing new epistemological alliances. Technoscience studies may then acquire features of historical, anthropological, philosophical and linguistic studies. Studies of and about science, while not wholly excluding practice in science, would look more like critical studies. For example, in emphasising the relationship between science education and its social context – the 'meanings to be attached to the learning of science' – Joan Solomon (1999: 14) has recently presented a case for a science education which concentrates on

> cultural arguments rather than on technical know-how. Its task is the making and passing on of a new cultural scientific heritage, the development of contemporary ways of thinking in science which need not be abstracted from context, and a preparation which will enable our young people to evaluate scientific issues from a personal and cultural point of view.

Although not going so far as to 'hybridise' science, or 'cyborgify' teachers and pupils, Solomon argues for a curriculum which reflects the popularisation of science – in other words, a curriculum about science-as-culture.

So what is the contribution of ICT here? As I have argued, ICT provides use of sophisticated data capture and representation, speedy and inexpensive communication among a vast range of different communities, and access to explanations and models of phenomena and processes in all the sciences. Science teachers and pupils across the globe can share critical views, talking to research institutions, acting as sources of data, dealing critically with web-based commercial sites, adding a critical edge to website design, sharing understandings, beliefs and sentiments. The disembodied nature of ICT-based communications offers curious opportunities for socially unrestricted identities to engage with technoscience studies in potentially emancipatory ways (Spender 1995; Doheny-Farina 1996). As I have suggested, the hybrid-laden world of new technologies changes balances of power in the social relations of school and university classrooms. I have argued that our technoscience teacher must be aware of her pedagogical practices as a manifestation of her own values and beliefs. Her practices will also reflect her own gender identity in relation to new technosciences. While exposure to an increasingly wide range of values and beliefs becomes the norm, so the role of teacher changes into that of mentor and cyberguide rather than of mother and heroine.

ENDNOTE

In discussing modern science's positioning of women outside of science, I drew on feminists' theorisation of the cyborg image as a monstrous, boundary, hybrid figure which, while 'othered' by modern science, unlike the goddess figure is positioned inside technoscience and therefore is in a powerful position to manipulate and influence, if not actually control. The concept is useful in supplying an alternative metaphor for gendered teacher identities in changing social conditions. I have used this meaning in the teacher-as-cyborg concept in order to interrogate current constructions or 'inscribings' of teacher identity, which so far seem to be blind to emerging human–machine evolution. What I have termed 'technoscience studies' has a crucial role to play in the process of developing strong, self-aware, 'cyborgian' identities for teachers of a re-framed science curriculum. Cultural productions such as this are inscribed in 'science work'. Teachers need to feel comfortable with fragmented identities when doing ICT and technoscience work, both in their training and education and in their own ICT–science work in school. ICT is providing the time and space, as well as a need, to reconstruct science teaching and learning in schools and in teacher education. Newly conceived science education that does not address the consequences of modern science or the tyranny of scientific ways of knowing continues to present only a partial narrative, keeping underpinning values and ideological biases hidden. This is an increasingly untenable position in the social context of fast-changing, complex, unstable and hazardous modern times. The role to be played by women teachers with 'cyborgian' identities in technoscience education will be crucial.

REFERENCES

Acker, S. (1994) *Gendered Education – Sociological Reflections on Women, Teaching and Feminism*, Buckingham: Open University Press.

Barton, R. (1997) 'Does data logging change the nature of children's thinking in experimental work in science?', in B. Somekh and N. Davis (eds), *Using Information Technology Effectively in Teaching and Learning*, London: Routledge.

Beck, U. (1992) *Risk Society: Towards a New Modernity*, London: Sage Publications.

—— (1995) *Ecological Politics in an Age of Risk*, London: Sage Publications.

Bleier, R. (ed.) (1991) *Feminist Approaches to Science*, New York: Teachers' College Press.

DfEE (1995) *The National Curriculum for Schools: Science*, London: Stationery Office.

—— (1998) *Teaching: High Status, High Standards*, London: Stationery Office.

—— (2000) *Science in the National Curriculum*, London: Stationery Office.

Doheny-Farina, S. (1996) *The Wired Neighbourhood*, New Haven, CT, and London: Yale University Press.

Dorling Kindersley (1996) *The Ultimate Human Body 2*, CD-ROM for Macintosh.

Driver, R., Guesne, E. and Tiberghien, A. (eds) (1985) *Children's Ideas in Science*, Milton Keynes: Open University Press.

Frost, R. (1999) *IT in Primary Science*, London: IT in Science.

Giddens, A. (1991) *Modernity and Self-Identity*, Cambridge: Polity Press.

Haraway, D. (1991) *Simians, Cyborgs and Women: The Reinvention of Nature*, London: Free Association Books.

Harding, S. (1991) *Whose Science? Whose Knowledge? Thinking from Women's Lives*, Milton Keynes: Open University Press.

Hargreaves, A. (1994) *Changing Teachers, Changing Times*, London: Cassell.

How Stuff Works; online (available: http://www.howstuffworks.com).

Jenkins, E. (1996) 'Scientific literacy: a functional construct', in D. Baker, J. Clay and C. Fox (eds), *Challenging Ways of Knowing in English, Maths and Science*, London: Falmer Press.

Keller, E. Fox (1985) *Reflections on Gender and Science*, New Haven, CT: Yale University Press.

—— (1992) *Secrets of Life, Secrets of Death: Essays on Language, Gender and Science*, New York: Routledge.

Lykke, N. and Braidotti, R. (eds) (1996) *Between Monsters, Goddesses and Cyborgs: Feminist Confrontations with Science, Medicine and Cyberspace*, London and New Jersey: Zed Books.

Marks, J. (1983) *Science and the Making of the Modern World*, London: Heinemann Educational.

Maynard, M. (ed.) (1997) *Science and the Construction of Women*, London: UCL Press.

Merchant, C. (1980) *Death of Nature: Women, Ecology and the Scientific Revolution*, San Francisco, CA: Harper & Row.

Michael, M. (1996) *Constructing Identities*, London: Sage Publications.

Millar, R. and Osborne, J. (eds) (1998) *Beyond 2000: Science Education for the Future. A Report with 10 Recommendations*, London: King's College.

Natural History Museum; online (available: http://www.nhm.ac.uk).

OfSTED–TTA (1998) *Framework for the Assessment of Quality and Standards in Initial Teacher Training*, London: OfSTED–TTA.

Pupil Research Initiative; online (available: http://www.shu.ac.uk/schools/sci/pri).

QCA (1999) *Primary Science: A Scheme of Work*, London: QCA.

Rose, H. (1997) 'Goodbye truth, hello trust: prospects for feminist science and technology studies at the millennium', in M. Maynard (ed.), *Science and the Construction of Women*, London: UCL Press.

Schiebinger, L. (1993) *Nature's Body: Sexual Politics and the Making of Modern Science*, London: Pandora.

Scott, P. (1995) *The Meanings of Mass Higher Education*, Buckingham: Open University Press.

Sherrington, R. (ed.) (1998) *The ASE Primary Science Teachers' Handbook*, Hatfield: ASE.

Solomon, J. (1999) 'Meta-scientific criticisms, curriculum innovation and the propagation of scientific culture', *Journal of Curriculum Studies* 31(1).

Somekh, B. and Davis, N. (eds) (1997) *Using Information Technology Effectively in Teaching and Learning*, London: Routledge.

Spender, D. (1995) *Nattering on the Net: Women, Power and Cyberspace*, Melbourne: Spinifex Press.

Walkerdine, V. (1988) *The Mastery of Reason: Cognitive Development and the Production of the Rational*, London: Routledge.

Wenham, M. (1995) *Understanding Primary Science: Ideas, Concepts and Explanations*, London: Paul Chapman Publishing.

Chapter 10

What effect will digital technologies have on visual education in schools?

Steve Long

In terms of what is important in developing children's visual awareness in the broadest sense, a simple answer to this question is 'None at all'. Such a sweeping claim will be qualified by the end of this chapter but it is not a question only of what digital technologies can do for art but of what art, via digital technologies, can do for learning and for the rest of the curriculum. Thanks in large measure to the microchip, visual literacy is now as basic a requirement as print literacy and the same technology could be the means by which the communicative power of images is applied in a way which transgresses perceived curriculum boundaries. Implicit in this statement is that art educators will play a central role in preparing a population which is able to communicate visually. There is a distinct sense of irony here in that art, considered a peripheral subject by many, will offer understandings which are a basic requirement for children.

There are two key themes which this chapter seeks to develop: the first is that 'the visual' is for everyone since we are operating at a time when computer-mediated forms of visual communication have become fast enough and cheap enough to be playing a major role in society. With the visual display screen being the principal communication between user and computer it is axiomatic that imagery has assumed a pivotal role within the communication that takes place. As such, the potential of 'the visual' may have simply become more visible! In this context the image, as a means of communication, is felt by many to have gained ascendancy over verbal text in terms of its persuasive power. Whether it is to entertain, inform or sell, digitally manipulated imagery constitutes a large proportion of the information to which all of us, adults and children, are exposed via television, the internet or other multimedia material.

The chapter will explore the idea that, by using digital technologies, children could develop the capability to express themselves visually in a wide range of situations through the learning that takes place within the art curriculum. The role for art education is changing as children need to be prepared to respond to – but also to shape – contemporary visual society. Therefore the second theme in this chapter is to develop a view as to what visual educators can do with digital technology. Opportunities may well be provided for art education in allowing children to make links with their experiences of consuming popular visual forms via digital technologies and to develop personal and contemporary ideas as a result. Similarly the assimilation of current fine art practice, which increasingly involves computer technology, into the curriculum would add much-needed contemporary reference for pupils. For both of these areas a framework will need to be developed within which children can place their learning in order to operate as informed consumers and educated producers of these forms. This chapter describes the nature of these changes and develops the idea that digital technologies are a new challenge for art educators but not a new language. Fresh directions for art education will be provided by referring back to what we, collectively and individually, think we know and also by looking forward to new possibilities (in essence, however, the task remains the same: to develop children's powers of visual expression and communication within a contemporary view of society).

GENERATING HEAT RATHER THAN LIGHT

Immense political pressure to integrate digital technology into education regardless of where or what is being taught has tended to produce more of a sense that something should be happening rather than a clear understanding of what that 'something' should be. In the UK, for example, Prime Minister Tony Blair, in his Foreword to the *National Grid for Learning*'s website, refers to a so-called 'information age' and says that computers 'have the potential to improve achievement in our schools and colleges', which, indeed, is a view shared by many. However, there is a feeling that, by simply putting learners and computers together with information, progress in learning will be made, and moreover, that there is a blanket approach which will work everywhere in the curriculum. Of course, commentators have been quick to point out the problems here and Stephen Heppell makes the case for creative and appropriate use of computers rather than for them being used as 'learning productivity tools' (Heppell 1999). Some teachers might not be familiar with Stephen Heppell's work, but feel, nevertheless, that computers are now so pervasive that they should be getting on with using them and that their classrooms should reflect life a little more closely.

From my perspective as an art educator with considerable experience of working with classroom practitioners, I can see no clear picture within the profession of what digital technology has to offer in the art classroom. The rapid expansion of digital technologies in our lives has, understandably, prompted many of us to consider the need to adapt the way we educate the next generation. However, the context within which the art curriculum currently operates is complex, and while much debate has focused on visual issues and hence is of considerable interest to art teachers, putting things into practical action in the classroom is not so easy. Access to facilities is difficult for many teachers of art, particularly in the secondary sector where ICT has tended to be associated with business education or specialist IT studies. In the same way art-related software is only now starting to appear in schools alongside the so-called 'basic tools' such as the word processor and spreadsheet/database packages. Similarly there is a conceptual confusion which manifests itself in looking backwards at what might be lost rather than forwards at what might be gained. While it is essential not to lose what is the core of the art curriculum there is a sense in which the oft-repeated statement, that we are 'judging a new technology by old understandings', seems to be very accurate at present. There is a possibility that a great opportunity will be missed if too much emphasis is placed on preserving particular processes or materials, as if they were the most important aspect of the learning, rather than considering the more fundamental elements of making art, such as personal communication and expression. Using digital technology creatively in the art curriculum needs to centre on exploring and developing ideas through a dialogue with processes. The appropriate use of the digital within such a framework could provide a valid basis for study, supporting children in developing a critical understanding of the strengths and weaknesses of making images with a computer and allowing them to reflect on this in relation to other media. Doing this effectively requires a delicate balance between curriculum planning, resources, teacher knowledge and pupil needs.

DESIGNING FUTURES

A key question for art teachers is clearly: 'In relation to my subject what do children need to understand and be able to do in order to operate successfully in contemporary society?' For an art teacher to answer this it is necessary to look at the societal and technological context in which we exist and particularly at the role of 'the visual' within both popular art forms and fine art.

There seems to be little doubt that digitally created or digitally manipulated methods of communication are playing an ever more central role in our society. Indeed it is difficult to find a book or article which in any way examines information and communications technology from a sociological standpoint that doesn't start with a description of how broad the penetration of the microchip is into our lives (although this could be because most such books are written by people with an interest in the technology who have perhaps become too close to the subject to remain critically aware). As an example: 'The message is simple: we have the technology to inform, entertain and educate. Miss it and you, your family and your school will be left behind' (Collins *et al.* 1997: 3).

The implication is that society in general, and children in particular as especially receptive elements of that society, are being confronted with increasing amounts of advertising, information and entertainment via digital media. In tandem with this, however, the mass of the population can be seen not only as consumers of this product but actually as producers. Gunther Kress, in his contribution to Snyder's *Page to Screen* (1998), makes the point that even when we are simply writing onto a computer screen the visual element of what we are doing, and our ability to explore it, are very much more evident than when we are working on paper. Using even relatively simple desktop computers, we have the option to change the size, colour, font or orientation of the script, or to add illustration in a wide range of forms, and produce relatively sophisticated outcomes. Add to this the multimedia authoring capability to produce image, video and sound pieces in an interactive format, and there seems little doubt that communicating in this way, via the internet, may be an increasingly attractive option. None of the concepts involved is an entirely new phenomenon; but, Kress reasons, the speed and ease with which such concepts *can* be enacted increases the chances that they *will* be. As such it could be argued that we now need to be aware of not only how to interpret digitally transmitted and constructed material but how to communicate our own information via the same digital media which will then be subject to interpretation by others. Indeed writers on visual culture such as Sean Cubitt (1998) raise the issue of our growing reliance on such methods of communication, with implications for a contemporary definition of 'literacy'.

Digital technology has the capacity to transmit bright, moving and persuasive material that we need to be prepared to use rather than be used by. This situation represents a real opportunity to anyone who is 'visually literate'. As Sefton-Green and Reiss point out, fine artists are being employed in the design industry in producing computer interfaces which use images to communicate as effectively as possible (Sefton-Green and Reiss 1999). This highlights two issues – that, not surprisingly, artists can manage the visual element of a computer screen and that it ought not to be only people described as artists who can do this.

IS THE ART CURRICULUM FOR ALL OR JUST FOR THE ARTISTS?

Where previously the idea of being visually literate had been felt by many involved in education to be important for the few pupils who would go on to be artists or designers, and frankly nice but irrelevant for the rest, there is now a feeling that in a wide range of vocations a sense of visual awareness

within a multimedia literacy is important. Using a digital format to dissem-
inate information or accessing knowledge from a digital source might well
include being able to decode or encode combinations of visuals and text
which could be placed there with relative ease. Universal understandings of
colour, scale, placing and proportion can be exploited often much more
effectively than where text is being used to carry out an equivalent task.

Is it the role of the art teacher to prepare children to decode or encode
the contents of a website or to realise that an image has been produced
in a certain way? Does the importance attributed to the visual within the
broader definition of 'multimedia literacies' now impact on the work of
teachers of art? Educators working in this field have seen it as their role
to develop in their pupils both the ability to 'read' the visual in the world
as they experience it and to respond visually in turn. The phenomena to
which we make our responses may include the experiences of other people,
and objects or places, whether real or imaginary. They may also include
the work of other artists, craftspeople and designers made in response to
the world as they experienced it and intended specifically as means by
which to share those experiences. Within the school art curriculum it has
traditionally been recognised that developing visual literacy in children
would be arrived at by achieving a balance between two strands. The first
strand is that all children need to develop as artists and designers through
engagement with making work in various forms – an action-learning
approach to gaining practical understanding. The second is that they would
need to understand the work of other artists in order to learn how images
can be made to function, enriching their own work but also enabling
them to decipher visual information in a much wider range of situations.
The intention, integral to all of this, is to support a fundamental human
need: to communicate visually. The advent of computers has not changed
what is essential in these activities: visual literacy is a concept that tran-
scends the use of a particular visual form or medium. What it has perhaps
changed is the balance between making one's own images and reading
those of other people. For very simple reasons, children are exposed to a
great deal of visually mediated information: it is fast; it can be interactive;
it can communicate a great deal; and, moreover, it can be very persuasive and engaging. However, the purpose of the art curriculum is not
simply to develop a vocational 'read only' visual literacy for children which
allows them to access information: it is also, crucially, to support them all
as expressive artists.

CONNECTING WITH POPULAR FORMS

Framed by the debate concerning the context for visual literacy is the
possible redefinition of the content and structure of the art curriculum.

The arrival of digital technology represents a great opportunity to address a number of issues, certainly in UK art education, which have been a source of considerable unease in recent years. Making links with popular image forms is a potential contribution that digital technology may be able to make to a possible new direction for the art curriculum. The view that art in schools fails to refer to children's contemporary experiences of visual culture is held by many and exemplified by Allen who makes a strong case for the fact that we can no longer claim that art practices like painting impact on children's daily lives in the way that the products of the mass media do. We can no longer say that we are giving children a full and relevant experience without exposing them to contemporary art and design practice and to the workings of contemporary mass media (Allen 1994).

Indeed in this respect the nature of what children perceive to be art needs to be reconsidered. Many teachers have spent years explaining to pupils, in response to their attempts to use some of the techniques they have seen in comic strips and picture novels, that drawing cartoon-like images is not 'proper' art as compared with the products of fine art or design. Many teachers felt these images to lack the necessary reference to first-hand sources and to rely too heavily on the use of a narrow range of the visual elements. While this was always a position that was difficult to defend, the pervasive popular visual forms of the digital age, such as computer-generated animations or website graphics, have all the sophistication of line, tone, pattern and colour. As children appropriate the ideas of other image makers, a question now might be: 'Is there still a need for them to distinguish between the "approved" fine art or design references and "unapproved" forms such as those mentioned above?'

It could be argued that the time has come for the art curriculum to make connections between the nature of popular and more traditional fine art imagery, and digital technology presents an opportunity to make these links. By engaging in the making of digital images which incorporate the full range of visual elements, children will develop a much more universal and inclusive set of visual understandings. There is little doubt that computer-generated image forms have looked mechanistic and 'clunky', and that contemporary games' environments have a smooth metallic aesthetic. This has tended to set them apart as kinds of 'outsider art'. However, it is important for children to realise that the visual building-blocks with which these images are constructed are common to all image making, and the way that these images operate through critical references needs to be acknowledged in teaching and learning. In this way, visual education will be able to make powerful links to cultural forms which surround children and enable them to bring in those references.

DIGITAL CONTRIBUTIONS: THE HALF-PEPPER PHENOMENON

Just as society is changing, in part due to technological developments, so also are the works produced by fine artists. However, it has been argued that the work of contemporary practitioners has been ignored within children's formal visual education (Meecham 1999). Of particular concern is that much of this work is 'issues based' and revolves around personal themes and ideas, while the reverse is reflected in what many children are doing in art at school, where there is a distinct lack of a sense of the personal and the subject matter is often irrelevant to pupils. Anyone who has taught the subject in recent years will probably recognise this in the repeated use of certain subjects. For example, red peppers sliced in half have for some time been a favourite as a starting-point for projects, and, although they may be an excellent vehicle for teaching certain concepts, they might not be closely related to imagery that the pupils themselves would be interested in. Several reasons have been cited for this so-called orthodoxy in approach, but one of the main ones is the need felt by teachers to give pupils secure understandings of the formal elements like line, tone and colour. The result has been an evident improvement in skills at the expense of content and meaning. The blame for this can, in part, be laid at the door of an assessment culture that has affected all areas of the curriculum by encouraging a 'safe' approach to teaching based on a set of proven methods of constructing educational experiences which score well in assessment or test situations. Familiar sets of materials and predetermined outcomes for projects have begun to be criticised recently, with calls for more autonomy for both learners and teachers (Steers and Swift 1999).

A spin-off of this 'formalist' approach has been the need to show children examples of the formal elements in action. This has tended to centre on a sanitised version of modernist French painting, often de-contextualised and depersonalised in the way it is employed, rather than by making reference to the work of more recent artists. Modernist French painting has often been chosen because of its accessibility through the copious reproductions and the clarity of the use of particular elements, such as the handling of material or colour. This seems unfortunate particularly at a time when the work of young British artists has been in the vanguard of developments in the international art scene through recent high profile exhibitions in the UK such as Freeze (held in 1989), the annual Turner Prize at the Tate gallery and as a part of Sensation (held at the Royal Academy in 1997) which showcased the collection of Charles Saatchi. Of the latter, Norman Rosenthal wrote in the introduction to the catalogue:

> A visitor to this exhibition with an open mind and well-developed antennae for life and art will perceive an uncommonly clear mirror

of contemporary obsessions from a perspective of youth. Presented with both seriousness and humour (often black), and in an extraordinary diversity of materials and approaches, both traditional and unexpected. These works serve as memorable metaphors of many aspects of our times.

(Rosenthal 1997: 10)

We could probably not say the same of what is happening in art classrooms. Is there scope for digital technology to move the curriculum forward in this respect? It could be argued that there is, especially given that there are quite a number of artists included in the new wave whose work employs digital media. However, accessing this kind of work is not without its problems, and using it in the classroom is, therefore, in its infancy.

By contrast with the situation in popular visual forms where digital technology is hard to avoid, finding fine artists using computers as part of their work takes some persistence. Indeed the technical issues involved can tend to mitigate against being able to save or retrieve such work, and making it visible to pupils in classes in appropriate ways can also be problematic if there is lack of access to large screen monitors or data projectors. In some senses the teaching of art follows the path of least resistance when it comes to finding critical reference material, and multimedia work particularly is unlikely to appear in classrooms until the problems of access and communications are solved. Nevertheless none of these points affect the potential or the concepts involved, but they do dictate the practicalities. Without improvements in this respect, the gap between current practice and what pupils are seeing will remain, and it is only through seeing processes such as multimedia being used in a fine art context that children might discover new creative outlets for their ideas.

AN INDIVIDUAL CURRICULUM: 'I WANT TO DRAW A WINDSURFER!'

There is growing evidence that digital methods can allow pupils to develop personal themes within their work. By connecting with a range of popular, design and fine art sources through software such as *Photoshop* pupils can import and manipulate images which otherwise might be beyond them. Similarly they can incorporate personal imagery to which more traditional approaches, particularly the use of observational drawing as an unavoidable starting-point, can sometimes act as a barrier. I have vivid recollections of pupils who wanted to make images that were technically beyond their capacity to draw, and who were unimpressed by the possibilities of collage and mixed media. A particular example was a boy of 15 who wanted to draw himself on a windsurf board flying over a wave, in my view an overly ambitious undertaking for the individual in question. However, the advent of digital image manipulation software and equipment like scanners has removed some of these barriers, particularly for less-able students, and allows a more open definition of the purpose of drawing. This might move beyond hand-rendering a likeness of an object and be modelled more on the 'sampling' in music production where already recorded music or sounds are mixed in new combinations and new meanings are constructed.

SOME DIGITAL SOLUTIONS

In the examples of artwork shown here, the pupils involved were able in the first instance to incorporate a series of images which had been gathered in different ways. The choice of method was dictated by the task that the image had to perform and the nature of the subject matter; they included images that were hand-drawn, scanned or taken from a digital camera. These imports were then manipulated to produce an outcome

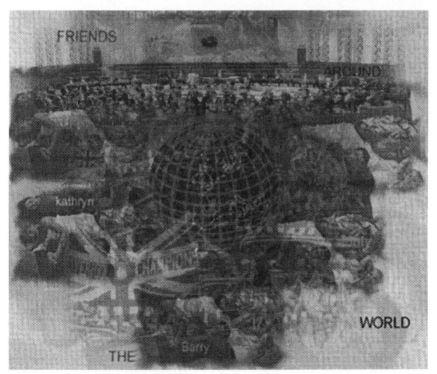

Figure 10.1 Work, using *Photoshop*, by a sixth-form student at the Judd School, Tonbridge, Kent

Figure 10.2 Still from a multimedia work by Year 10 students at Beacon Community
College

only possible in a digital environment. In evaluating the work with the
teacher responsible, there were felt to be distinct contributions made by
the use of digital technology. First, the software used had allowed for the
incorporation of images in an assemblage which could then be subtly
adjusted. Ideas had then been moved forward using processes within particular software applications, such as the capacity to repeat and juxtapose in
limitless combinations. Second, the 'issues' were very much at the centre
of the projects rather than the demonstration of formal skills. Students
involved had felt that they were operating as artists with something unique
and personal to communicate. There were, however, also aspects of the
work that were anything but new. Considerations such as composition
and use of colour were universal elements that these students were able
to apply having learnt to use them in much more traditional media. Re-
scaling, moving and multi-layering were all exploited within the digital

manipulation (see Figure 10.1); but, again, although these processes are in some ways easier to carry out, they do not constitute a new way of thinking.

The second set of examples shown here (see Figure 10.2) are from a multimedia project, and are included as a means of introducing possibly the most radical developments in the art curriculum.

In these pieces many of the individual images were produced in a similar way to those of the first project, at Judd School; however, what was then apparent, as the multimedia sequences were constructed, was that areas such as sound, sequence, time and interactivity became important. Within contemporary forms such as gaming, the internet or interactive CD-ROMs, these concepts are an established element. For art teachers, however, they do represent a new departure. The average computer can run moving and sequenced images; it can play sound or video, and it can be interactive. If all of these things are possible, then, in a creative context, it is quite natural that they will start to be explored. An assimilation of the possibilities offered by multimedia 'authoring' into what is currently considered to be a visual education is probably essential in order that children learn how to apply universal image-making understandings through such technology. Students taking part in the project began, from an early stage, to liken the work to something they would encounter in drama or English. When investigated in more depth, the substance of this feeling was the sequential and narrative nature of the pieces they were making and the fact that the relationship between the potential audience and the work itself was an integral element from the outset.

TRANSFERABLE SKILLS: NO MORE STICK MEN

If there is scope to widen references within the art curriculum to include the broader visual culture, there is also an issue over the application by children of their visual understanding throughout the general curriculum. Learning which has taken place within the art area could have a considerable impact in other curriculum subjects, specifically through digital technology. Sinker (2000: 211) identifies this as a central conclusion in her exploration of the use of multimedia in education: 'multimedia technologies cry out for a joint approach to teaching and learning by art and media education, which threads through all the subjects'.

The potential power of the visual now is that it can be deployed through the available technology. However, one of the dangers is that, if a balance is not maintained, art will lose itself philosophically into other subject areas. Because there are such strong vocational and curriculum roles for the visual, art educators might find themselves equipping children with low-level understandings of digital image software to be used as required. This tendency might then spread across the curriculum in a variety of ways, none of which have the core art values of personal communication and expression as integral elements. There needs to be space in the curriculum for the development of those core values in a context of creativity and for the visual literacy, which develops as a result, to then be genuinely applied across the curriculum. This is not a new phenomenon: it is a long-running 'sore point' for art teachers, who have often been aware of children employing images for a whole range of other purposes outside of art lessons. One of the most striking features of such activities, for example as illustrations for project work, is the amnesia from which the children appear to be suffering in terms of the visual language being used and the lack of reference to what has been learnt in art. Stick men abound in drawings done by the same pupils who have sat for hours in art lessons drawing the figure from life. Inconsistencies like this are often the result of the context in which the work takes place, where the materials might be different from those of the specialist art room and the general support for making images might be at a much lower level.

The evidence from pre-computer work is that a lot of the formal aspects of the learning are lost and other means are found in order to communicate ideas. All too often the emphasis in such situations is on free-hand drawing as the quickest way of putting an image with some text; however, the situation might be very different if, with digital technology available, pupils have access to the same imaging software as they have worked with in the art area and there is a definable element of familiarity and continuity. Images scanned in, or downloaded from the internet or from a digital camera, could be manipulated and placed with text in a word-processed, DTP or multimedia format to include more reference to what had been learnt about visual communication in the art curriculum.

TEACHERS AND COMPUTERS

Societal and curriculum concerns, while being important as a backdrop, are not the only place to look in an investigation of the effects of digital technologies on visual education in schools. A central feature must also be the attitude and approach of art teachers to the use of computers in the curriculum. There are a number of problem areas in giving children a critical understanding of what computers can do in art. Indeed, this chapter is in part an attempt to address one of those concerns: that art educators are having problems developing a relationship with new technologies. Interestingly there has not been enough work done yet in classrooms to say that the pupils also will have problems with it. At the moment we are at the stage where the issue is with teachers' preparedness to teach and exploit new technologies, and it is only through teachers' attitudes and approaches in this area that steps forward are going to be made. There are two main issues here in relation to art teachers in the classroom – the nature of their experiences as 'makers' of art themselves and the relationship between any art 'maker' and the tools with which he or she is working. These concerns may be unique to art teaching, where the practitioner element of the role and identity is both sensitive and particularly important. The introduction of digital technology into the equation has proved problematic and has upset delicate balances for many in the profession.

I think that most teachers of art would say that their enjoyment of, or involvement in, art practice was what led to their involvement in teaching, and that this is the unique strength in what art educators do. Leaving aside George Bernard Shaw's 'those who can't, teach' remark, it seems clear that whether art teachers are active practitioners, or have become inactive having not had the time to keep their practice going, their evaluations and reflections on their own work are formative in the way that they approach teaching. Therefore it is fair to say that an art teacher with experience of using a computer creatively in his or her own work would be well placed to integrate this experience with classroom teaching. However, in the light of my experience as a tutor on an art and design PGCE course, it is evident that the majority of art – as distinct from design – graduates entering the teaching profession via PGCE courses have had little if any experience of making art with a computer. In the majority of cases, it would be true to say that formal education does not constitute the entirety of these students' artistic experience, but could be said to account for a healthy proportion of it. As such, computers simply will not have been part of their means of making visual statements and, while many degree courses make claims about the incorporation of digital technology, the reality seen in student portfolios is somewhat different. This is understandable if one considers that the higher education lecturers teaching those courses are themselves in the same position as their students. It is much easier for them to build fine art experiences around defined processes such as painting or sculpture than it is to delve into new practices that might include the use of computers. As a result such work is often developed in a self-supported way by students, with consequent difficulties in assessing it due to a lack of tutor understanding and/or engagement with the process of making it.

Conversely graduates of design courses might well have experienced the integrated use of computers because those courses give computers a much more identifiable role to play. Lecturers planning programmes in, for example, 3D design must acknowledge the potential offered by a computer with a 3D modelling package or the fact that a large number of the interior designers currently working use software such as *Minicad* as a drawing tool. It would be out of step to prepare students without including this in some form. Students can then see the benefits and pitfalls, and make their own decisions about the appropriate use of the relevant software. There is, therefore, a divide between new teachers of art with fine art backgrounds and those who come from design courses, although with the currently buoyant state of the UK design sector fewer of the latter are entering the education sector, so that the former constitute the majority of teachers.

The second issue of concern for art teachers is the relationship between a maker of art and the computer. It can be argued that there is something fundamentally different about using a computer to make art as compared with any other process, in that the computer is a piece of equipment which most users only 'understand' to the extent of knowing which buttons to push or click on in order to make something happen. In other words, we see the consequences of actions taken, not the action taking place itself. When compared with other processes, such as drawing on paper with a pencil, painting, photography or video, the awareness of how marks/statements are being made informs the development of ideas; it is 'hands on'. In terms of working with computers there is a distinction between those who work with pre-written software and those who create their own programming as a part of the process of making art. An example of the latter would be Harold Cohen, working in the USA, who has used the language of computer programming itself in order to make images, so that the material is literally binary codes which produce, in his case, a visual output; a kind of digital 'hands on' experience (Cohen 1973).

In this sense there is an active engagement with the 'stuff' of computing, and a legitimate dialogue with the process develops as a result. However, for most makers of art with a computer the activity is directed towards the artist being the composer and the computer being the instrument by which his or her thoughts are translated into an image. But is there a sense in which the computer can become an 'autonomous composer' (Lansdown 1995) in such circumstances? The relationship between user and computer thus becomes complex and the computer can be much more than a simple tool – something which plays a formative part in the process of creation (*ibid.*: 31).

When working visually, the computer is effectively an interface which encodes and decodes binary sequences, giving no engagement with that process itself. The user simply deals with an input device and responds to a visual or multimedia output. For an art teacher, who might be unused to working on a computer, this constitutes one of the major barriers to gaining familiarity with what digital technology can achieve. What is required is that the user abandons the well-established 'action-learning' approach which was probably used with every other media and which involved getting 'inside' the process in order to fully exploit it. There has to be a suspension of disbelief around the requirement for a tangible physical object as an outcome. In addition, there has to be a conscious abandonment to the machine itself of parts of the process taking place. Working with postgraduate trainee teachers has proved illuminating in this respect, as they learn not so much to understand what is happening when, for example, working with a graphics package, but to accept which bits they don't understand and to focus on dealing with inputs and outputs. Is the machine making the marks, then, anything more than just another tool, or is it, of its nature, playing a part in how the image looks?

Artists and designers have often used external mechanical or artificial means as a part of their work, and I am not suggesting that the computer can be likened to a surrealist investigation of random image formation by some means, but that part of the making of images does indeed 'belong' to the machine. The history of art is consistently supported by examples of the relationships between technological progress and the development of ideas. Based on a broad definition of any technology as a socially applied extension of some aspect of our own function, there is an implied understanding of that function – whether that be of a car as a faster means of transport or of a camera as a means of recording an image. Technological advances have been consistently applied in many fields and have often transferred from one area to another as a use for them becomes apparent. This is not the case with a computer, where the functional elements, physically and conceptually, are hidden. As a result, in the making of art, there is an immediate issue over where control of the process lies and whether the authorship belongs to the machine or the maker. Illuminating this issue is probably not going to produce a clear-cut outcome, and experience from my teaching suggests that there is a growing pragmatism regarding the acceptance that one doesn't need to understand 'the ghost in the machine'. There is no certainty yet as to whether this acceptance will be fruitful or simply represents a loss of critical control. Seen in this light, there is not only an issue for teachers but a question to be addressed in their teaching: if a computer plays a role in creativity, how is it possible to assess the work that pupils produce using computers?

PROBLEMS AND SOLUTIONS

Art teachers are under pressure from several directions – criticised for not exposing pupils to contemporary art practice, not equipping them to deal with popular forms of visual communication. Any technology will, if used for communication or expression, affect the content and nature of the messages it carries. Marshall McLuhan, when he said 'The medium is the message', gave us both the problem and the solution by suggesting that society would organically adapt and shift its priorities in response to new methods of communication (McLuhan and Zingrone 1995). Implicit in such a belief is the idea that the technology itself becomes part of the subject of any message transmitted. For artists this represents a very normal relationship with any process; they have habitually explored the properties of new media, and expressive communication has resulted from those interactions. The predominant problem for many teachers of art is that they are not considering using the medium through choice but through a feeling that they should be, and the organic period of development has not taken place. Hence the technology itself seems to be occupying centre stage in a non-productive way.

The stimulus for making art has always been, and remains, the need to respond to the world around us and to communicate those responses both to ourselves and to others. Digital technologies can play a double role in this relationship, being both an increasingly important part of the visual world itself and possibly an increasingly important element in our visual responses to it. The current situation offers teachers of art a real opportunity in preparing children to play a full visual role in contemporary society. Computers may be the boost that is required to enable us to address the problem of critical studies' references, currently lost in a sea of late-nineteenth- and early-twentieth-century French painting and the resulting lack of individuality in pupils' outcomes. In the same sense there are also opportunities to make connections in the curriculum to the design industries, to graphics and to popular forms such as gaming and movies – all of which employ digital image manipulation. By such means, art educators can only improve their chances of eliciting more personal responses from children and allowing more useful learning to take place. Although digital fine art practice, as I have indicated, is more difficult to clearly identify and use in the art classroom, the situation will improve as more teachers realise the potential and begin to demand more access to computers, the related software and the internet.

The greatest danger is that the art curriculum will become merely an opportunity for media studies rather than an opportunity to develop expressive capability; but this will only happen if those involved fail to play a proactive role in integrating digital technologies creatively into visual education. If they do fail to play this role, the visual will be appropriated by the curriculum areas in which it is put to use, and children at school will find themselves limited to working without useful reference in, for example, a piece of work in a multimedia format. A more imaginative approach would be provided by applying universal design strategies, learned in a creative context, through the relevant technology. There is an opportunity for the art curriculum to give children understandings which are of tremendous value across the curriculum. What is vital is that art educators remain aware of the implications of technological change in the broader picture, while maintaining contact with the enduring core values of art practice.

REFERENCES

Allen, D. (1994) 'Teaching visual literacy – some reflections on the term', *Journal of Art and Design Education* 13(2): 133- 43.

Cohen, H. (1973) 'Parallel to perception: some notes on the problem of machine generated art', *Computer Studies* 4.

—— (1997) 'Representing representation: artificial intelligence in drawing', in S. Mealing (ed.), *Computers and Art*, Exeter: Intellect.

Collins, J., Hammond, M. and Wellington, J. (1997) *Teaching and Learning With Multimedia*, London: Routledge.

Cubitt, S. (1998) *Digital Aesthetics*, London: Sage.

Heppell, S. (1999) 'The ICT of creation', *The Times Educational Supplement* (Online supplement), 7 January: 12.

Kress, G. (1998) 'Visual and verbal modes of representation in electronically mediated communication: the new forms of text', in I. Snyder (ed.), *Page to Screen: Taking Literacy into the Electronic Era*, London: Routledge.

Lansdown, J. (1995) 'Artificial creativity: an algorithmic approach to art', Paper given at *Computers in Art and Design (CADE) Conference*, University of Brighton.

McLuhan, E. and Zingrone, F. (eds) (1995) *Essential McLuhan*, London: Routledge.

Meecham, P. (1999) 'Of webs and nets and lily pads', *Journal of Art and Design Education* 18(1): 77–83.

Rosenthal, N. (1997) 'The blood must continue to flow', *Sensation* (exhibition catalogue), London: Royal Academy.

Sefton-Green, J. and Reiss, V. (1999) 'Multimedia literacies: developing the creative uses of new technology with young people', in J. Sefton-Green (ed.), *Young People, Creativity and New Technologies: The Challenge of the Digital Arts*, London: Routledge.

Sinker, R. (2000) 'Making multimedia', in J. Sefton-Green (ed.), *Evaluating Creativity: Making and Learning by Young People*, London: Routledge.

Steers, J. and Swift, J. (1999) 'A manifesto for art in schools', *Journal of Art and Design Education* 18(1): 7–15.

Chapter 11

Music education in a new millennium[1]

Robert Mawuena Kwami

New technologies are currently being used to create new forms of music, and in the UK technology now plays a crucial role in linking music education at school and in the community. Compared with the past three decades or so, schools are generally better resourced and now provide a number of services beyond the teaching of children. Some schools make their facilities available for use after school hours. Others serve as community centres which unemployed youths, adults and pensioners frequent for social gatherings and events. Where children are concerned, the focus is on producing multi-skilled people. In the curriculum, the general emphasis is on numeracy and literacy.

In the secondary music curriculum, there is a practical orientation, with performing and composing activities and groupworking being the norm. In this work, electronic keyboards, mainly Casios and Yamahas, play an important part in giving greater credibility to students' work. Students are taught to improvise and experiment, and technological tools – recording machines, keyboards and computers – are crucial for storing drafts.

At the primary level, a more integrative and holistic approach is taken whereby music is sometimes combined with topic and project work. Pupils are taught to improvise, perhaps using criteria based on modes, scales or chord clusters. Graphical and other notational systems are introduced while more traditional teaching involves listening and the 'rudiments of music'. Even here, we find the availability of mini-keyboards with record, auto and single-finger chord facilities, and sound and memory banks. Keyboards which a few years ago might have been classed merely as toys now have MIDI inputs and are used with computers.

Since the 1990s, partly as a result of technological advancements, 'world' and 'pop' music have found a more secure footing in the content and repertoire of the curriculum, and since 1995 music technology has been offered as an 'A' level subject. In this chapter, it is argued that the future of curriculum music rests on the ability of new technologies to bridge the gap between 'community' and 'school' music. In the first of two main sections, it is suggested that technology can help to highlight the importance of a musical literacy which does not rely on the ability to 'read and write' music. In the second, it is argued that technology has a crucial role in re-invigorating and sustaining curriculum music. It is the new technology that can guarantee the continued survival of music as a curriculum subject. After a discussion considering the uses and applications of music technology in the National Curriculum in England, the chapter ends with a summary and conclusions section. To provide a context for the discussion it is helpful to review the past and assess the present. So, I now briefly consider some of the recent significant developments which have impacted on music education in the school curriculum.

BACKGROUND

Technological matters have constituted an essential and integral component of the British school music curriculum for much of the twentieth century. However, the development of music technology is a distinctive feature of the last few decades of the previous century. The association of music making with technology probably began when human beings first started using implements to order and organise sounds. In the West, one obvious close link is the development of the keyboard – from the unwieldy organs of the Middle Ages, to the spinets, virginals and harpsichords of the Renaissance and Baroque periods. Since its invention in 1709, the fortepiano developed, through the Classical era, into the pianoforte of the Romantic period and the twentieth century. And, currently, in the twenty-first century, there are various kinds of electronic equipment – computers, keyboards and other musical instruments – capable of producing synthesised, digital and 'virtual' music.[2]

Starting from the early part of the twentieth century, the musical compositions of 'the great masters' of Western classical music were made available to a wider mass of people due to the availability of the phonogram (see Simpson 1976). The 'appreciation' lessons of the period did not give pupils the opportunity to engage in music making, and may have contributed to the widening of the artificial gap between the 'musical' and 'unmusical'. Also, the use of staff notation has probably alienated many pupils; and, in spite of the apparent utility of solfa notation within the 'payment by results' system (cf. Taylor 1979), its potential for the musical empowerment of the masses has not been realised.

The introduction of Orff instruments, developed from African and Indonesian prototypes, was superseded by the progressive era of the 'creativity' movement. The 1960s and 1970s, the period when the movement, championed by the likes of John Paynter (cf. Paynter and Aston 1970; Paynter 1982) and George Self (1967), flourished, was also a time when justifications were made about using pop music in the curriculum (cf. Swanwick 1968). Towards the end of the century, pop music, 'world music' (cf. Vulliamy and Lee 1982; Kwami 1998a) and information and communications technology (ICT) made significant inroads in curriculum music (cf. NCET 1997; BECTA 1998, 1999). In particular, the technical and vocational initiative (TVEI) of the 1980s and 1990s catapulted technological issues into the forefront by creating new opportunities and possibilities (cf. Green 1992).

MUSICAL LITERACY, CREATIVITY AND TECHNOLOGY

Over the centuries, the notation of music has involved the application of new technologies. The neumes of the Middle Ages were developed into staff notation with its C, G and F clefs. Also, Guido d'Arrezo's 'Ut, Re, Me' system, the precursor of tonic solfa, was developed from the lines of a Latin text. With the advent of printing, the system, originally a mnemonic device, has undergone further development to become a notational system in its own right. And it now, perhaps, functions as a downmarket version of the conventional staff notation system in many parts of the world.

Advancements in technology have become fashionable and influence the nature of the music education transaction in classrooms. In composition, for example, multitrack recording and MIDI sequencing make the process a more practical endeavour – all the more so when one considers the prospect of the relegation of the notation to the background as a result of the increasing availability of score-writing facilities on such sequencing software packages as *Cubase* and *Micrologic*. The fact is that the prices of dedicated score-writing packages like *Sibelius* and *Finale* are coming down, and their availability across computer platforms is also a boon. Judging by the fast pace of technological change and its influence, it seems reasonable to suggest that unless a broader, more holistic and technological, approach is adopted, the future of music as a curriculum subject, dependent on the written symbol – notation – may be doomed (Kwami 1993, 1998a).

Currently, the application of new technologies involves such things as keying in characters on a computer keyboard, mobile phone, or through touch pointing, using voice-recognition software and such like. These technological developments suggest that multimedia, multi-disciplinarity and oracy (cf. Lanham 1993) will become more prevalent. If holistic multi-skilling applications and interactions become more valued, it is possible that the act of writing music will in future become a backup system to the new technology.

The combining of audio-visual technological developments such as digital camcorders and cameras, MIDI sequencing, multimedia and hyperstudio applications opens up other possibilities for 'transforming conventional literacy practices' (see Sefton-Green and Buckingham 1996: 50). In musical contexts, the audio-visual dimension can enable children to do things creatively, to manipulate sounds in ways that they may not be able to execute in 'real' time. They can, on their own, create complex performances and compositions in multi-timbral mode, involving the sampled sounds of many instruments.

Musical literacy does not mean only the ability to operate according to the canons of the Western classical tradition which, during the seventeenth and eighteenth centuries, at least laid some premium on the ability to improvise. Rightly, the term needs to be demystified and expanded to involve creative music making without recourse to written notation. From a musical perspective, it is possible to identify at least three types of literacies. First, there are written notation-based systems such as staff and graphical notation. Second, the recording of music using technological aids such as cassettes and disks constitutes another form of musical notation or literacy. Finally, there are aural–oral systems of notation,[3] which rely primarily on human memory and the ability to recall music. In addition, it is possible to talk about different states of musical reality, such as the physical, the imagined and the virtual.

Among the musical literacies, it seems that it is only aural–oral notational systems that may not be threatened, fully accommodated within, or made redundant by, ICT. This is significant in the sense that it is an area where a kind of musical creativity common to many musical cultures and to jazz can be demonstrated. African-American music traditions and styles have probably been the most influential musics of the twentieth century (cf. Small 1983, 1987), and it is possible that jazz, a music originally with a strong African base, will become the dominant music, the 'classical' music of the present century (Kwami 1998b). This has implications for the definition of musical literacy and the expression of musical creativity in a general sense. For musical literacy also implies a knowledge and ability to operate in a number of significant 'world musics', and this puts teachers in a situation where appropriate subject knowledge may be an issue.

A redefinition of musical literacy also now entails the ability to manipulate and navigate technological tools and equipment – primarily keyboards, computers and recording and playback equipment. The use of technology can help in a more general definition of musical literacy, emphasising creativity through improvisation and practical work. ICT intensifies the relationship between literacies of the curriculum and those of the community, and makes more explicit the differences between learning in the wider community and in educational institutions. It seems that the potency of the enculturation (or growing up) process, which takes place in the wider community, would support an argument for a new paradigm for music education, one that includes the validity of virtual technological musical worlds (cf. Lanham 1993).

If it is the technological developments that are driving the nature of music making in curricular contexts and dictating the music education transaction in formal and informal contexts, what does all of this portend for the future? We might want to consider the misplaced notion of democratic enfranchisement (cf. Lanham 1993: 200) resulting from the 'explosion of digital instruments for musical and artistic composition and performance'. For example, recent surveys of ICT music in initial teacher education have revealed a wide disparity in provision for secondary students. While some music departments offer students lessons in MIDI sequencing, some do not even have a computer. The survey data do not support the interpretation that students in poorer and disadvantaged schools are worse off. However, the wide disparity in provision regarding computers and other musical equipment has repercussions in maintaining, if not widening, the gap between those who have and those who don't.[4]

It may be difficult to achieve equality opportunity and an even playing field (cf. Apple 1992) so far as technological resources and musical instruments in schools are concerned. In disadvantaged schools, the technological aspects might be more of an issue. There are also negative implications for music making as a social activity, particularly the danger that girls may generally find it more difficult to participate and engage fully (cf. Brown 1992; Green 1993). It is also worth noting that it is possible to depend too much on 'hard' technology instead of on its application for educational ends. In music education, there would need to be a balance between human-made acoustic sounds and what is recorded or produced electronically, with the latter complementing rather than subsuming the former.

The new technology has an essential part to play as the core constituent of the future music curriculum and in bridging the gap between music in schools and the community. In doing so, it can empower the 'have nots' through the linking and legitimisation on the internet and in the curriculum of popular and hybridised musics, new music and bands.[5] This can be effected through giving a 'voice' to minorities, the disenfranchised in society, and those not in the mainstream of the Western classical music genre. Music technology, it can be argued, has provided a context for, on the one hand, intensifying, and, on the other hand, bridging the gap in terms of 'literacies' and concepts of musicality (cf. Blacking 1976) and musical creativity. ICT has played an important role in the production and reproduction of popular and fashionable musics. It can grant access and opportunity to those who have been marginalised in the past, allowing them to express and communicate their musical creativity.

I have argued that technology has contributed in expanding the definitions and applications of literacy and that it is the aural–oral that is the most important in terms of musicality, something which should be a prime aim of formal music education. Aural–oral musical literacy can legitimise and can lend more credence to musical forms which do not depend on the ability to read and write music. Although technological aids such as keyboards, and sequencing and score-writing programs, are particularly suited to the Western classical system, they also enable and enhance musical outputs and capabilities so far as aural–oral musics are concerned. The technological also shifts the emphasis away from that which is written and theoretical to the practical, and this is something which favours pop and world musics. Used properly, the technological supports the 'sound before symbol' principle in music teaching. The valuing of aural–oral literacy can also empower disadvantaged groups in society by allowing them to express their musicality in practical ways. Such musicality, based on popular rather than high-art culture, can be given a 'voice' not only through the media but in 'virtual' technological worlds.

THE MUSIC CURRICULUM OF THE FUTURE

In this section, I consider the teaching of ICT in music by referring to the revised music National Curriculum for England (DfEE–QCA 1999), giving some examples of the application of music technology.

Three specific uses of ICT are listed in the SEN 'inclusion' statement of the National Curriculum (DfEE–QCA 1999). First, teachers are to use 'ICT, other technological aids and taped materials' when 'helping [pupils] with communication, language and literacy'. Second, teachers are to use 'ICT, visual and other materials to increase pupils' knowledge of the wider world'. Finally, teachers are to provide 'support by using ICT or video materials, dictionaries and translators, readers and amanuenses'. In addition to the statement on 'additional information for music' where 'some pupils may require . . . access to adapted instruments or ICT to overcome difficulties with mobility or manipulative skills', other sections of the curriculum mentioning ICT include 'the use of ICT across the curriculum' and Key Stage statements.

At all three Key Stages, there are opportunities for applying ICT under the 'interrelated skills of performing, composing and appraising', under 'listening, and applying knowledge and understanding', and under 'breadth of study' headings. The first mention, at Key Stage 2, says pupils are to be taught musical 'knowledge, skills and understanding' in a variety of ways, including 'using ICT to capture, change and combine sounds'. The only other mention of ICT at Key Stage 2 is non-statutory and relates to the use of different resources in the production of music. At Key Stage 3, of the three instances where ICT is mentioned, two appear under 'listening and applying knowledge and understanding', while the third appears under 'breadth of study'. In the first instance, pupils are to be taught to 'identify the resources, conventions, processes and procedures, including use of ICT, staff notation and other relevant notations, used in selected musical genres, styles and traditions'. In the second, pupils are to be taught to 'identify the contextual influences that affect the way music is created, performed and heard (for example, intention, use, venue, occasion, development of resources, impact of ICT, the cultural environment and the contribution of individuals)'. Finally, building on the statement made at Key Stage 2, ICT is to be used 'to create, manipulate and refine sounds'.

From the above, it is clear that it is at the secondary level that ICT is to be fully exploited in the music curriculum. Even at Key Stage 1, where there is no explicit mention of ICT, pupils can use instruments such as keyboards, recording equipment and computer software programs, in particular, to perform ('control sounds'), compose ('create and develop their musical ideas') and get a better understanding of the elements of music. For example, the same melody can be played using different synthesised sounds on a computer; aural training programs and CD-ROMs can be used at this key stage.

Curriculum content in music relating to ICT includes conceptual knowledge, skills and understanding in all areas including the recording of music, together with its notation, and in theoretical and academic studies. In recording, storing or saving music, students can learn to use recording facilities, including cassette tape (two-track), multitrack (four-track) recorders and an external microphone; they can save music on a computer diskette, videotape, minidisk, DAT or CD. In manipulating sounds students can learn to use a mixing desk and, in MIDI sequencing, they can arrange, compose and use audio inputs. In using the internet, students can be taught to access and download music, including MIDI and MP3 files, and other relevant information. CD-ROMs provide yet another means of accessing information about music. Other applications include using keyboards, synthesisers, and reel-to-reel cassette recorders.

To summarise, applications of music technology by students include the following specific examples:

- using microphones, cassette recorders and multitrack recorders to record performances and compositions;
- performing with a backing track, arrangement or accompaniment played from a computer workstation to practise or perform music in groups;
- downloading MIDI files and other out-of-copyright music to make a backing track for a rap or other composition;
- word processing a written account on a performance or composition
- compiling a database or spreadsheet on music in the charts, on a survey of a class's musical preferences, the lives or works of a performer or composer;
- producing a concert programme via DTP;
- recording compositions onto disk (floppy, mini), tape (audio, digital), CD;

- sequencing music on keyboards and/or computers;
- using CD-ROMs to learn about or research a music topic;
- accessing internet sites to learn about an unfamiliar topic such as the tabla or other non-Western music.

Although most school music teachers are generalists, there is no reason why they cannot use ICT to introduce students to units of work on such topics as responsorial form, drones, ostinato, and colotomic structures and devices. In this, technological tools can be used to set the context as well as in manipulating elements and in producing music. Units of work on such topics as Indian, Japanese, Chinese, African, Arabic and folk musics can employ keyboards, computers and other instruments, with CD-ROMs and the internet being used to find information about the music being studied. Even if there is only one computer in a classroom, it is possible to use a looped, sequenced arrangement with parts muted as appropriate to teach a performing or a listening lesson to students.

In some secondary schools, Key Stage 3 students are able to take the floppy disks that they use between home and school. The disks store work in MIDI format and are used interchangeably on keyboards and computers. Also, for a fee of less than £2, some pupils are given copies of their performances and compositions on a CD, to play to their parents, other relatives and friends. Sequencing can be positively used in creating loops, cycles and other repetitive patterns and structures that can be used as a base for improvisation and creative performance. For example, a melody can be improvised above a drum loop or chord sequence.

Creative links between technology and music can be explored in sampling sounds, tracks and loops, in creating new sounds, and in the development of new applications (cf. Hunt and Kirk 1997). Also, projects such as 'sound technologies' (Ellis 1997), whereby pupils make sounds by moving part of the body across beams of light, create opportunities for severely disabled pupils to participate in creative work in music. Also, children with visual impairment or limited movement can use large font or touch-screen facilities, respectively. Those with limited movement can input data step by step and hence be able to create and perform music that they might otherwise be incapable of doing.

The new technology has an important role in ensuring that the foremost focus in music education is on *music making*, involving the acquisition of musical knowledge and understanding, skills and attitudes through practice. This is possible through the use of digital processing of sounds via sequencers, sound cards on computers and sampled sounds on keyboards, opening up possibilities for children to produce performances and compositions which can sound close to those produced by professional musicians at a fraction of the cost. Also, the replacement of Orff-type instruments by keyboards and computers opens up an almost limitless bank of sound possibilities not available on such instruments as xylophones, metallophones and drums, which sometimes cost as much as four times the price of a keyboard.

DISCUSSION

Recent technological advances may seem to encourage a situation whereby many people are relegated to the position of musical recipients. However, the greater availability of inexpensive keyboards has given more access and opportunity, with keyboards becoming a basic feature in secondary-school music lessons. It can be argued that the situation whereby students work on their own at computers and keyboards is a negative application of technology. However, keyboard and computer labs can be organised so that there is student–student and student–teacher communication through headphone splitters and other controllers.

Sampled sounds, which are copies of 'real' sounds, are now commonplace in the music that most children listen to. In the classroom, it comes in the form of the ubiquitous electronic keyboard. Coupled with computers, their use signals a new revolution in music education in schools. The use of keyboards in the classroom calls for the acquisition of new skills, particularly in performance, as the new 'instruments' are quite different from the originals which they 'imitate'. Bowing, phrasing, fingering and sticking techniques may all have to be 'virtualised' within keyboard parameters, and such challenges may contribute to the emergence of new forms. Single instruments now have the capability to perform orchestral ensemble and band music, all at the push of a button by an individual.

There are clearly positive as well as negative implications in the use of ICT in the music classroom. When students improvise, compose and arrange music, they bring to the transaction their experiences including what they hear outside of schools. Much of this comprises elements of new and popular music genres and styles such as rap, hip-hop, house, garage, rave, acid, jungle, ethnic, and world musics – influenced by the new technology. Within the popular genres, Western classical music is sometimes used in remixes and other fusion music.[6] Whereas the dominant paradigm of curriculum music may seem to prefer 'authentic' acoustic instruments, new and popular musics have a propensity for using new technology – electronic keyboards, synthesisers and sampled sounds, and herein may lie a tension.

The internet, another medium emerging from developments in new technologies, can provide greater access and opportunity by bridging huge distances between people, and can allow students to play music in real-time with their counterparts on another continent. In addition to megastores, the internet provides another avenue for listening to a wide range of music that can be freely downloaded.[7] At some internet sites,[8] it is also possible for individuals to make their own compilations, after browsing, searching and sampling tracks from albums, using MP3 and other technologies. Apart from the convenience and flexibility that this provides, one can get information on particular artists, music pieces and so on.

Another advantage of the new technology pertains to the storage, transferability and transmission of musical data. In hardware, bigger memory capacities enable smaller storage space for data, and there is also more flexibility in the storage and transmission of music in various formats – as a 'hard' manuscript score, in digital form on a mini-disk or compact disk, or in analogue form as a tape (or vinyl). Music can also be preserved as downloadable digital audio and wave files in the 'virtual' world, and there is an increasing transferability of musical data between electrical keyboards and computers.

There is a tension between the dual purpose of technology assisting (access, opportunity, bridging) and hindering (i.e. technology 'for its own sake') the gaps in music education between schools and the community. Used in a negative way, the technological tools can create a barrier between the advantaged and the disadvantaged, between the 'haves' and 'have-nots', and between girls and boys (cf. Comber *et al.* 1993; Green 1993, 1997; Hodges 1996). There is also a danger of paying undue attention to mastering the technology; it might be seen as 'masculine', with the disadvantage that 'hard' mastery of the technology becomes the prime focus rather than 'soft' mastery – the effective use of technology to further musical learning (Armstrong 1999). With the increasing availability of digital technologies via the information superhighway, the lower costs and increasing capability of musical hardware and software, it is likely that music technology, currently available as an 'A' level option, will become an essential and core aspect at all phases of secondary schooling. But it is vital that technology is used to service music education rather than the reverse.

SUMMARY AND CONCLUSIONS

First, I presented a scenario of the increased use of new technologies in the production and transmission of music for the future. The scenario showed an increasing use of technology in intercultural and fractured communities, the new technology playing a crucial role in linking music education at school with music in the community, and helping to give a 'voice' to minorities, including through the invention of new musical forms. The scenario was contrasted with a picture of what happens currently in the music curriculum and the role technology plays in it. Then the technological developments and metamorphoses of the keyboard, perhaps the most influential musical instrument currently used in British schools, were briefly traced to indicate one way in which technology has serviced the development of music.

In the first main section, it was argued, first, that aural–oral musical abilities constitute an emergent literacy that have a particular relevance in the application of new technologies. Second, it was argued that the ICT developments in music technology, the 'digital' notation of music, sequencing, and the manipulation of keyboards represent a new form of musical literacy.

In the section on the music curriculum of the future, musical literacy and creativity were related to the use of technology in the classroom. There was a consideration of the positive aspects and problems of using ICT in the classroom and of some ways in which ICT can provide access and opportunity to a wider range of musical types, traditions and forms of knowledge.

To summarise, ICT is likely to exert a strong influence on the direction of music education in the twenty-first century. The stretching of musical boundaries in the wider community suggests that music education is likely to be a more hybrid phenomenon, demanding aural–oral and multimedia abilities and capabilities rather than literary skills, improvisation rather than the ability to read from notation. The technological developments require a redefinition of the nature and role of 'musics' in schools. For their part, music teachers need to continue to encourage the use of new technologies, and explore ways in which they can be used to further musical learning as a social transaction rather than merely as tools in their own right.

Finally, in music education, the new technologies pose new challenges that may further mar distinctions between composer and performer and between musical process and product. The widespread availability of different musics in the media, and in the real and 'virtual' worlds, portends a future in which issues of ownership and copyright may need to be re-examined and redefined in a complex, changing, intercultural and technological world.

NOTES

1 Some of the points raised in this chapter were made in a paper presented at a conference on Music Notation organised by the National Music Council and the Qualifications and Curriculum Authority held at the Royal Albert Hall, London, in November 1998.
2 Other examples of the development of musical instruments are given by Hunt and Kirk (1997: 152) who also discuss how technology has 'serviced' music.
3 For example, the *sargam* and *bol* systems in Indian music, drum mnemonics in African music, and the solfa system.
4 Michael Apple (1992: 105ff.) argues that beyond the technological changes, including that of resource provision, we need to interrogate the dominating and persistent 'cultural and economic inequalities' in society.

5   See, for example, the MP3.com, Real.com, and 2look4.com internet sites.
6   A recent example is Sweetbox's *Everything's Gonna Be Alright* hit, featuring
    Pachelbel's Canon.
7   E.g. *RealPlayer, RealJukebox* and *Take5.*
8   E.g. mp3.com, napster.com, and real.com

REFERENCES

Apple, M. (1992) 'Is the new technology part of the solution or part of the problem
    in education?', in J. Beynon and H. Mackay (eds), *Technological Literacy and the
    Curriculum.* London: Falmer Press.
Armstrong, V. (1999) 'Gender, composition and music technology styles of mastery',
    unpublished MA dissertation, University of London Institute of Education.
BECTA (1998) *Music Technology in Action: Teachers' Support Materials*, Coventry:
    BECTA.
—— (1999) *The Music IT Support Project*; online (available: http://www.becta.org.uk),
    26 April 2000.
Blacking, J. (1976) *How Musical Is Man?*, London: Faber & Faber.
Brown, C. A. (1992) 'Girls, boys and technology', in R. McCormick *et al.* (eds),
    Teaching and Learning Technology, Wokingham: Addison-Wesley Publishing
    Company and the Open University.
Comber, C., Hargreaves, D. J. and Colley, A. (1993) 'Girls and boys and tech-
    nology in music education', *British Journal of Music Education* 10: 123–34.
DfEE–QCA (1999) *Music: The National Curriculum for England Key Stages 1–3*, London:
    Stationery Office.
Ellis, P. (1997) 'The music of sound: a new approach for children with severe and
    profound and multiple learning difficulties', *British Journal of Music Education* 14(2):
    173–86.
Green, L. (1992) 'The position of music in the Technical and Vocational Initiative
    (TVEI): a critical appraisal', *British Journal of Music Education* 9(2): 152–62.
—— (1993) 'Music, gender and education: a report on some exploratory research',
    British Journal of Music Education 10: 219–53.
—— (1997) *Music, Gender and Education*, Cambridge: Cambridge University Press.
Hodges, R. (1996) 'The new technology', in C. Plummeridge (ed.), *Music Education:
    Trends and Issues*, London: Institute of Education, University of London.
Hunt, A. and Kirk, R. (1997) 'Technology and music: incompatible subjects?', *British
    Journal of Music Education* 14(2): 151–61.
Kwami, R. M. (1993) 'Music education in Britain and the school curriculum: a
    point of view', *International Journal of Music Education* 19(2): 25–39.
—— (1998a) 'Non-Western musics in education: problems and possibilities', *British
    Journal of Music Education* 14(2): 161–70.
—— (1998b) 'Music education practice in primary and secondary schools in Britain:
    inclusion of the black contribution to classical music', a research report for the
    Standing Conference on Studies in Education, London: Institute of Education,
    University of London.
Lanham, R. (1993) *The Electronic Word: Democracy, Technology and the Arts*, Chicago:
    Chicago University Press.

NCET (1997) *A Guide to CD-ROMs for Music Education*, London: NCET.

Paynter, J. (1982) *Music in the Secondary School Curriculum*, Cambridge: Cambridge University Press.

—— and Aston, P. (1970) *Sound and Silence*, Cambridge: Cambridge University Press.

Sefton-Green, J. and Buckingham, D. (1996) 'Digital visions: children's "creative" uses of multimedia technologies', *Convergence* 2(2): 47–79.

Self, G. (1967) *New Sounds in Class*, London: Universal Edition.

Simpson, K. (1976) *Some Great Music Educators*, Dover, Kent: Novello.

Small, C. (1983) 'The vernacular in music', *Educational Analysis* 5(2): 65–75.

—— (1987) *Music of the Common Tongue: Survival and Celebration in Afro-American Music*, London: John Calder.

Swanwick, K. (1968) *Popular Music in Schools*, London: Routledge.

Taylor, D. (1979) *Music Now*, Milton Keynes: Open University Press.

Vulliamy, G. and Lee, E. (1982) *Pop, Rock and Ethnic Music in School*, Cambridge: Cambridge University Press.

Index